Something Warm from the Oven

Something Warm from the Oven

⟶•❯ Baking Memories, Making Memories ❮•⟵

Eileen Goudge

𝓌𝓂

WILLIAM MORROW

An Imprint of HarperCollinsPublishers

To my mother,
who taught me that the most
important ingredient of all
is love.

Contents

Acknowledgments

THIS BOOK CAME ABOUT IN A FUNNY WAY, as do most serendipitous things in life: I was at a party chatting with a delightful cookbook editor named Harriet Bell. We were talking about our shared passion for baking and I happened to mention that I'd put together a booklet of recipes for my fans. She asked to see a copy, and the rest is history. So, Harriet, I anoint you the guardian angel of my kitchen and I thank you for opening this exciting new chapter in my life. I can honestly say it wouldn't have happened without you.

Thanks, too, to my agent and friend, Susan Ginsburg. This wouldn't have happened without her either, as the party at which I met Harriet was in celebration of Susan's birthday. Susan is also a fine cook and baker, one of the many reasons I count her as a kindred spirit.

Without my husband, Sandy Kenyon, and all his coworkers in the WINS newsroom acting as my unofficial tasters, I wouldn't have known what to do with the baked goods pouring out of my test kitchen. They provided helpful comments and, most of all, unflagging appetites and encouragement. Sandy knows that I couldn't be married to a man without a sweet tooth.

Last, but not least, I'd like to thank all those—friends, family, and fans—who contributed their own recipes to this collection, many of them steeped in fond memories. My favorite recipes of all didn't come out of cookbooks; they were copied by hand off stained, dog-eared recipe cards.

Yet the concept behind Tea & Sympathy was so simple that when people called it a stroke of genius, Kitty had to bite her lip to keep from laughing. The idea had come to her in the most mundane way possible—while eating lunch in the staff room at Miramonte Elementary. Nibbling on a stale Fig Newton, she'd idly mused about how much she missed her grandmother's icebox cookies. Where had they gone, she'd wondered, all those remembered treats from childhood. Baked goods as heartwarming as they were toothsome, that you didn't need a culinary degree and half a day to prepare. What insidious plot had succeeded in abolishing them from cupboards and cookie jars where they'd once reigned supreme?

—From *One Last Dance*

Introduction

M<small>Y EARLIEST AND FONDEST MEMORIES</small> are of food. I grew up in northern California, one of six children. We lived miles from the nearest grocery store, which for my mother meant that shopping expeditions had to be planned carefully; most of our food was either bought in bulk or made from scratch. She baked all our bread; at any given time the deep freezer in the garage contained at least four or five different varieties. Cheese came in wheels. Flour and sugar were stored in barrels in the garage next to the one with the diatomaceous earth for the swimming pool filter, which led to a memorable occasion in which my sister Karen, mistaking the powdery substance for flour, baked cookies that were literally hard as rocks (no reflection on her baking ability; she's since become a gourmet cook).

Tucked in beside the deep freezer was the white fifties refrigerator from my parents' first house. My mother kept it stocked with whatever fruit was in season: apples from Mr. Jellich's orchard in the fall; oranges and grapefruit in winter; flats of strawberries in early summer, and peaches, apricots, and grapes in late July and August. (Blackberries we picked from the woods behind our house.) And since fruit was the only snack we were allowed between meals, the old refrigerator provided more than extra storage—it was a lifesaver. Arriving home from school each day after the long trek from the bus stop, most of it up a steep hill, I was always starving. I'd come in through the garage, grabbing a handful of fruit from the fridge along the way. In those days, it wasn't unusual for me to devour five or six apples in a sitting. In fact, I ate so many growing up that if the old saying is true, about an apple a day keeping the doctor away, I should live to be one hundred.

Stepping through the back door into the kitchen, I was often met by the sight of my mother elbow deep in bread dough at the counter. (I don't think she ever made a single recipe of anything in those days; everything was doubled, tripled, or quadrupled.) If I hung around to watch, she'd pinch off a handful for me to knead. I loved everything about it: the squishy feel of the dough between my fingers, the little popping sounds it made as the air bubbles were squeezed out, the dense yeasty smell mingled with the nutty aroma of oatmeal, rye, or cracked wheat.

When the dough was pounded into submission, it went into a huge brown ceramic bowl, which was covered with a dishtowel and placed in a warm spot to rise, out of reach of small hands. By the time the loaves emerged from the oven, crusty and brown, the smell had wafted into every corner of the house, and the call to supper would unleash a small stampede. Breakfast the following morning would bring wondrous toast. If heaven is a place where you can eat anything you want without gaining an ounce, I would start each day with a slab of my mother's oatmeal bread, toasted and buttered, spread with my grandmother Mimi's marmalade.

Mom also made what are to this day still my favorite desserts. The only time we ever ate store-bought cookies was on our annual camping trip to Pinecrest Lake, when my dad would "treat" us to Mallomars and Oreos from the general store. Birthday cakes from mixes were for children less fortunate than us. And the only thing a commercial pie was good for, as far as I knew, was on shows like *The Three Stooges,* when it was thrown in someone's face.

My mother wasn't a fancy cook, but everything that came out of her kitchen was the essence of comfort food. For Sunday dinners she'd make apple crisp—the only night of the week my sisters and I would vie to clear the table, all the better to "even up" the edges of whatever was left in the pan. Her lemon chiffon pie was the product of lemons from the tree in our front yard. (Even then, I knew the difference between Meyer lemons and the inferior kind sold in supermarkets.). Gelatin molds were made from scratch, with real fruit. And if you've never tasted warm persimmon pudding with lemon sauce, you don't know what you're missing.

On birthdays, she made your favorite cake. Mine was, and still is, banana cake. My father's was either German chocolate cake or maple chiffon, depending on his mood. My sisters' and brother's taste ran from the prosaic, like yellow cake with chocolate frosting, to the more exotic baked Alaska. The tradition has carried over into the next generation, with the grandchildren putting in requests for their favorite birthday cakes.

Valentine's Day and wedding anniversaries brought heart-shaped cakes ringed with miniature pink Cecile Brunner roses from the garden. For Easter, there was a chocolate cake decorated with marshmallow bunnies, their smiley faces painted on with a toothpick dipped in red food coloring. For kids' parties there was a cake in the shape of an elephant or a giraffe. And for one memorable Fourth of July, which happens to be my birthday, someone had the bright idea of putting sparklers on the cake instead of candles—which I don't recommend unless you like your frosting covered in a gritty gray film.

With all this bounty came bowls and beaters to lick. We'd fight over who got the last smear of batter or frosting. We became experts at snitching cookie dough when my mother's back was turned. Once, when my mother was called out of the kitchen, my sister Patty seized the opportunity to scoop up a handful of cookie dough, which she crammed into a baggie and stuffed down the front of her pedal pushers. Unfortunately, the baggie broke just as my mother walked back in, sending a stream of batter down Patty's leg. Talk about busted!

My own love affair with baking began with a copy of *Betty Crocker's Cookbook for Boys and Girls,* given to me one Christmas by my Aunt Betty (no relation to Ms. Crocker). Inspired, I donned my mother's apron—I had to wrap the ties twice around my middle, I was so small, and went to work mastering such delicacies as pigs in a blanket and three men in a boat. Before long, I was on to blondies and brownies, velvet crumb cake, and molasses crinkles. I learned to make a heart-shaped cake using a square layer and a round one, cut in half. And who knew there were so many uses for Bisquick? I still have that book. Torn and dog-eared, it's one of my most prized possessions.

Every so often my sisters and I would play what we called "bakery day." We'd each choose a recipe, usually something easy like cookies, and with Mom's blessing (her only rule was that we had to clean up afterward), we'd spend the day making them. By the time the last tray came out of the oven, the kitchen would be a mess and we'd be so sick of it all—literally, given the amount of cookie dough we'd consumed—we wondered what we could have been thinking: This was as much fun as a trip to the dentist. Amazingly, it did nothing to dampen our enthusiasm the next time one of us piped, "Let's play bakery day!"

Now I think of the days when I'm free to putter about my kitchen as my own private bakery days. No sooner are the breakfast dishes cleared away than I'm measuring flour and sugar, creaming butter I'd taken out earlier to soften. Throughout my roller coaster of a life and career, baking has been the one constant. When I was a young bride living with my first husband in British Columbia, cut off from family and friends, it was the one thing that connected me to my past. At the time, I had only one cookbook in my possession, a battered paperback of international recipes I'd picked up at a garage sale. I must have made every recipe in that book, which was a bit of a challenge considering that I didn't have an oven and the kitchen was about the size of a smallish walk-in closet; I baked everything in small batches in my toaster oven. Which brought home an important lesson: Where there's a will, there's a way. Baking isn't about loads of equipment and reams of recipe books; its about the desire to create something from scratch. There's something deeply satisfying to me about kneading dough or frosting a cake, or watching slimy egg whites transform magically into snowy peaks.

Those of you familiar with my novels know that some element of food and baking always seems to figure in. In *Such Devoted Sisters,* Annie becomes a chocolatier. In *One Last Dance,* Kitty Seagrave owns a tearoom called Tea & Sympathy, where her famous cinnamon sticky buns are gobbled up as fast as they come out of the oven. Kitty and her tearoom make an encore appearance in *Taste of Honey,* the second book in my Carson Springs trilogy. The baked goods so lovingly described therein inspired a number of readers to write to me requesting the recipes. In response, I posted them on my Web site, www.eileengoudge.com. Later, I compiled them in a small book as a promotional giveaway. As a result, I've received mail from all over the country and more than a few from abroad. One woman wrote that she'd worn her copy of *Something Warm from the Oven* to tatters, and could I spare another? Another reported that my Kahlúa brownies were such a hit at her company picnic, several of her coworkers had asked for the recipe. A woman who'd made my Mocha Buttercrunch Pie for a French friend (with predictably high standards) who was staying with her at the time reported that he'd been wowed. A number of fans have even shared recipes of their own, several of which are included here.

I get letters from such far-flung places as Malaysia, South Africa, and New Zealand, where a woman wrote asking if she could substitute Golden Syrup for Sucanat in the apple pie (the answer is no). What seems to have struck a chord is the idea of baked goods that are more homey than fancy, and often reminiscent of childhood. (The two most popular are the banana bread and the Kahlúa brownies, with the chocolate cake and apple pie close runners-up.)

I've since expanded my repertoire, and with so many new recipes to share, I thought it was time for an updated version of my earlier homegrown effort, one that would be available both to fans of my novels and those yet unfamiliar with my work. The following recipes aren't fussy or complicated for the most part; even novice bakers shouldn't feel intimidated. The few exceptions are such standouts that they're worth the little bit of extra time or effort involved.

Because I'm partial to certain foods and flavors, you'll see recurring themes. I love almost anything made with maple or coconut. Same goes for bananas, cranberries, apples, and citrus. Because my husband adores marzipan, you'll find a number of recipes with almond paste. I have my dislikes, too (though only a few). If you don't see raisins in the recipes, it's because I harbor what I'm sure is an entirely unfair prejudice against them, as a result of being teased by my sisters when I was young: They put raisins in my bed, and being terribly nearsighted, I mistook them at first glance for bugs. My absolute, if-you-could-only-have-one-on-a-desert-island favorites are generally the homiest and easiest to prepare, like cranberry cornbread, the culinary equivalent of curling up in front of the fire; my mother's apple crisp; and banana bread so steeped in banana flavor you can almost hear Carmen Miranda singing.

All of my recipes come wrapped in memories, of those times, as a child, when we all sat around the dinner table, my father telling stories; of the rhubarb that grew wild in the back-yard of my house in Burnaby, British Columbia; of my desk in the kitchen when I was a struggling writer and the delicious smells wafting from the oven that accompanied my early literary efforts. Along with the scrumptious pies, cakes, cookies, and breads coming out of your oven, I hope you'll be making memories of your own.

Tools

If equipping a kitchen from scratch, start with a trip to a well-stocked cooking supply store, such as Williams-Sonoma or Sur La Table (see Sources), for basic tools like bowls, pans, measuring cups and spoons, and mixers. I've found the clerks in those stores generally very helpful, though it's best if you go at non-peak times (forget the holiday season rush!). If you don't see what you're looking for, ask; often they have it in stock or they can order it for you. Buy the heavier, good quality pans, if possible. Cheap aluminum ones will warp and don't distribute heat as well as the better-made ones.

➤ I recommend investing in a food processor if you don't have one. I use a **Cuisinart,** which is available in most cooking supply stores and on-line at Cuisinart.com and Cooking.com (see Sources).

➤ If you do a lot of baking, and have room for one on your kitchen counter, a standing mixer is a real time-saver. The one I use is the 9-cup **Tilt Head KitchenAid,** available in most cooking supply stores and on-line at KitchenAid.com and Cooking.com (see Sources).

➤ A kitchen scale comes in handy for weighing unmarked or bulk items, like nuts and chocolate. I use a spring-loaded scale, which has a stainless steel bowl deep enough to hold loose items that weigh up to eight pounds. **Salter** makes a sleek electronic scale with a nifty glass platform that gets a five-star consumer rating from Cooking.com. They are available at well-stocked cooking stores and on-line outlets.

➤ An immersion blender is one of the handiest tools you can own. I use mine for puree-ing cream soups and making blended sauces and smoothies. For baking, it's most useful for removing lumps from thin batters. Cheesecake batter, in particular, tends toward lumpiness and an immersion blender saves you the time and effort involved in transfer-ring it to a food processor or standing blender. I recommend the **KitchenAid Immer-**

Tips for Better Baking

Before starting a recipe, read it through carefully and make sure you have all the ingredients and proper equipment. Nothing is more frustrating than having to stop in the middle of making something to run to the store.

In recipes that call for **softened butter,** *that means room temperature.* Avoid the temptation to cream it too soon or to soften butter in the microwave (you'll end up with a half-melted stick). Using cold butter will result in a heavier, flatter cake. When a recipe calls for unsalted butter, don't substitute salted butter.

When making cakes, follow this rule of thumb: **The longer you beat the butter and sugar, the lighter the cake.** Beat well after adding the egg or eggs, too. When adding dry and liquid ingredients (generally you alternate), *the less you beat, the better.* Overbeating will result in a tougher cake. Beat only until each addition is incorporated, unless otherwise called for.

For cakes, **eggs should be at room temperature.** It's also important to use the size called for in the recipe. Large means U.S. Grade A large; use extra-large or small only when specified.

In unbaked pies and frostings that call for raw eggs, **I use eggs from cage-free hens raised on organic grain,** which have a reportedly low incidence of salmonella. This is a matter of personal preference. You can choose to take the tiny risk present even in organic eggs, as I do, or you can play it safe. Since I've never baked with powdered eggs or egg substitutes, I can't recommend using them in place of raw eggs. What I would suggest, if you don't wish to experiment, is that you choose another recipe, one that doesn't call for unbaked eggs or whites. For the elderly and very young, or those in poor health, I would strongly recommend against taking any risk, however small.

When buying eggs, always check to make sure none are cracked. If you find a cracked egg in an already purchased carton, discard it; it's not safe to eat.

In recipes that call for milk, **always use whole milk or 2 percent,** unless otherwise specified.

Use dry measuring cups for dry ingredients, such as flour and sugar, and liquid measuring cups for liquids, such as milk and oil. **When measuring dry ingredients,** spoon into the cup and scrape level with a spatula or the back of a knife. When measuring liquid ingredients, place the cup on a level surface and watch at eye level as you pour.

A sifter isn't necessary for sifting dry ingredients. I dump everything into a fine-mesh sieve, and simply shake it over the bowl.

Don't substitute all-purpose flour when cake flour is called for, or vice versa. Cake flour, which is lower in gluten than all-purpose flour, is milled from a soft red wheat, then bleached; thus, it results in a finer crumb and lighter cake. For most cakes, I find all-purpose flour suitable and, in some cases, preferable, but there are those exceptions where cake flour simply makes for a better cake. Don't confuse either with self-rising flour, which contains leavening; since I never use it, you won't need it for any of the following recipes.

Everyone knows what granulated sugar is, but **there can be some confusion about other types of sugar,** so I've provided a breakdown:

Superfine sugar is white sugar ground finer than standard granulated sugar. It's ideal for meringues and boiled frostings; also for lighter cakes such as chiffon and angel food.

Confectioners' sugar is powdered white sugar with a little cornstarch mixed in. It's most commonly used in frostings and for dusting; also for sweetening whipped cream.

Brown sugar, both light and dark, is granulated sugar with some molasses mixed in. Light generally can be substituted for dark in a pinch, or vice versa, but it's best to use what's called for in the recipe.

Turbinado sugar is unrefined granulated sugar, meaning it's less processed, thus healthier (if you can apply the word "healthy" to sugar!). It has a grainier texture than brown sugar and pours like white sugar, but it usually can be substituted for brown sugar in recipes.

Demerara sugar is basically the same as turbinado sugar, only coarser.

Sucanat is a brand name for minimally processed, dehydrated cane juice, with all the nutrients (scant though they might be) and molasses of cane juice. In my opinion, it's the richest in flavor; Also, the "healthiest" of all the sugars. The only disadvantage is that most supermarkets don't stock it. However, you can buy it at most health food stores. A similar product is sold under the brand name *Rapadura*.

Maple sugar is maple syrup in crystallized form. It can be hard to find and costly, but the results, when used in baking or for dusting, are well worth any extra effort and expense.

When nuts are called for, always buy the freshest available. **Remember that nuts contain oil,** and oil will quickly go rancid if not properly stored (I keep mine in the freezer). In my experience, the packaged kind sold in supermarkets are often stale. For that reason, I generally buy in bulk from gourmet markets or health food stores (the busier the store, the less chance the nuts have been sitting in bins for who knows how long). You can also purchase nuts by mail order or on-line (see Sources).

Same goes for fruits: Always buy the freshest, and try to stick with what's in season. Which is why I make fruit pies in the summer . . . and pumpkin, apple, and sweet potato pies in the fall. **If a particular fruit isn't in season, I'll choose frozen fruit,** picked at its peak, over last season's withered offerings or pallid, flavorless imports.

Spices should be fresh. Anything stored longer than a year (ideally six to eight months) should be tossed out and replaced. I buy spices from the supermarket only as a last resort. A better bet is gourmet markets and spice emporiums, such as Kalustyan's (see Sources). **Buy nutmeg whole, if you can find it;** freshly grated nutmeg is often the "secret" ingredient that livens up an apple pie or spice cake.

For recipes that call for lemon or lime juice, heat the whole fruit in the microwave for fifteen to twenty seconds before cutting it open and squeezing it. It will practically squeeze itself! **Leftover citrus juices can be frozen for later use.** Place in an ice cube tray in the freezer; when frozen, pop into a zip-top freezer bag.

In recipes that call for finely grated peel or zest, **grate just the colored part of the peel,** leaving the pithy white part.

For separating eggs, the best method I've found is to **drop a cracked egg into your cupped hand while holding it over a bowl.** If you handle it carefully the white will slip easily through your fingers without the yolk breaking.

For meringues: A soft peak is where the tip folds over. A medium peak is where the tip holds firm. A stiff peak is somewhat firmer. A *very* stiff peak (such as used in chiffon cakes) is where the whites stick in a clump to the beaters when they're pulled out of the bowl. For extra fluffy meringue, add ¼ teaspoon white vinegar or lemon juice for every three egg whites before beating.

To avoid overbaking, **always set the timer for the lowest recommended time,** as oven temperatures can vary. Check for doneness, and watch carefully if a few more minutes in the oven is needed.

While food processors are huge time-savers, they must be handled with care (and I don't mean just for safety reasons). It's all too easy to overprocess in just seconds or with a few too many pulses, so follow instructions and watch carefully. This is especially important with delicate pastry dough, which will become tough with overprocessing. **When making pastry dough, use a large food processor** (14-cup capacity), otherwise you risk having it clump together.

Use the size of pan called for in a recipe, as substitutions will create uneven results.

When using a **Pyrex pan for baking,** reduce the oven temperature by 25 degrees.

To keep crumbs from sticking when frosting a cake, **frost the whole cake with a thin layer of frosting,** starting with the sides and ending with top, then repeat using the remaining frosting. Any crumbs will stick only to the first layer.

A tube of uncooked **macaroni or ziti poked vertically (like a spout) into the center of an unbaked pie** will keep its filling from bubbling over around the edges as the pie is baking.

sion Blender, which is easy to use as well as to assemble and disassemble; it also comes with a whisk attachment for whipping cream and egg whites and a nifty blending beaker. It's Available on-line at Cooking.com and at KitchenAid.com (see Sources).

➤ I use a *Microplane* grater for grating lemon zest. They come in different sizes and grades, and make a formerly awkward and messy job a snap. They're more precise, too, so you get only the zest, and none of the bitter white pith. They are available at Cooking.com, Williams-Sonoma, and New York Cake & Baking Supplies (see Sources).

➤ *Wilton Bake-Even Cake Strips* prevent domes from forming on cakes while they're baking. You simply wet one of the nonflammable fabric strips and wrap it around the pan before it goes into the oven. The layers come out nice and flat, as well as evenly textured. They are available on-line at Wilton.com and New York Cake & Baking Supplies (see Sources).

➤ A very cool way to whip cream is the **Wilton Dessert Whipper Pro.** Just pour the cream and a little confectioners' sugar into the stainless steel canister, inject a nitrogen cartridge, shake a few times, and voilà, instant whipped cream. It keeps as long as it would in the carton, and these days, with most heavy creams ultra-pasteurized, that could be several weeks. And no more fussing with bowls and beaters before serving a dessert that calls for the last minute whipping of cream for garnish. Available at New York Cake & Baking Supplies, and on-line at Wilton.com. Cooking.com carries a different brand: the **ISI Brushed Aluminum Cream Whipper** (see Sources).

➤ For precise results when making candy or boiled frostings, use a digital thermometer, such as the **Maverick Candy & Oil Thermometer,** available at New York Cake & Baking Supplies and on-line at Cooking.com (see Sources).

➤ Use a pastry cloth when rolling out pie dough; it will keep it from sticking and you won't need as much flour, which results in a stiffer dough. They are available at hardware stores and supermarkets as well as specialty stores.

➤ In recipes that call for a pan or pans to be greased and floured, coat the bottom and sides of the pan or pans with vegetable shortening, oil, or *unsalted* butter (I use a paper towel to apply it), then sprinkle with flour and shake off the excess. A quicker and more efficient method, is to use either **Baker's Joy,** an oil spray that contains flour (available at New York Cake & Baking Supplies and in well-stocked supermarkets), or **Pam** (spray) for baking, which also contains flour (available in supermarkets).

➤ When recipes call for pans to be lined, I use precut parchment rounds, such as **Easy-Out Baking Liners,** available at New York Cake & Baking Supplies (see Sources).

➤ Invest in good spatulas that are heat-resistant, such as **KitchenAid Red Silicone Spatulas,** which can withstand temperatures of up to 500°F. They come in handy when stirring things on the stove, when you want to ensure that nothing sticks to the bottom of the pan.

➤ A quick and nifty way to peel apples for pies or applesauce is to use the **Back to Basics Cast Iron Apple Corer and Peeler.** It's sturdy and has a suction cup that affixes to a hard, flat surface, such as a kitchen counter. They are available at Cooking.com and Sur La Table (see Sources).

Coffee Cakes and Cupcakes

In a world that had slipped its axis, the pleasure her baking brought to others seemed the only sane thing left. Here, away from the rapacious press and lurid headlines, Kitty could find a small measure of serenity. When Gloria Concepción asked timidly if she could have the recipe for Kitty's lemon cake—just until Kitty was up to baking it herself—she was flattered. And when Gladys Honeick asked in a hushed voice if what she'd heard was true—that poor Lydia had been denied bail—Kitty didn't feel as if Gladys was prying, only that she had one more sturdy shoulder to lean on.

—From *One Last Dance*

Glazed Orange Cake

You can't go wrong with this cake. I was so confident about it, in fact, that I made it for my spot on the Food Network. The host took one bite and pronounced it, on air, "Delicious!" Saturated with orange syrup, it's moist through and through. And if you love the taste of oranges, as I do, the intense citrus flavor alone will have you reaching for the knife to even out that crooked edge. It also keeps well—my husband insists it's even better a day or two later—and is easily transportable for picnics and such.

Serves 12 to 14

For the cake

1 cup (2 sticks) unsalted butter

2½ cups sugar

1 teaspoon vanilla extract

6 large eggs, at room temperature

2 teaspoons orange zest

3 cups all-purpose flour

½ teaspoon baking soda

½ teaspoon salt

1 cup (8 ounces) sour cream

For the glaze

¾ cup sugar

1 cup fresh orange juice

1 tablespoon lemon juice

¼ cup (½ stick) unsalted butter

1. Preheat the oven to 350°F. Grease and flour a 9- or 10-cup Bundt pan.

2. *For the cake:* Cream the butter in a large bowl with an electric mixer. Add the sugar a scoop (about ¼ cup) at a time, beating until pale and fluffy (about 5 minutes total). Blend in the vanilla. Add the eggs one at a time, mixing well after each addition. Blend in the orange zest. Sift the flour, baking soda, and salt together. To the creamed mixture, add in the following order, beating on low speed after each addition, just until incorporated: a third of

the flour mixture; half of the sour cream; half of the remaining flour mixture; the remaining sour cream; then the remaining flour mixture. Be careful not to overmix! Spoon the batter into the pan, smoothing with the back of a spoon so it's a little higher around the sides of the pan, which will prevent a dome from forming while baking.

3. Bake in the oven for 60 to 70 minutes, until a toothpick inserted into the center comes out clean. Gently cover with aluminum foil during the last 10 or 15 minutes of baking, if the top is browning too quickly.

4. *Meanwhile, make the glaze:* Combine the sugar, orange and lemon juices, and butter in a small saucepan. Place over low heat and bring to a boil, stirring continuously. Simmer for 3 to 4 minutes, stirring occasionally, until slightly thickened. Keep warm while the cake is baking. Remove the cake from the oven, and while still in the pan, poke holes with a skewer every few inches or so over the entire surface, to a depth of 3 to 4 inches (see Note). Slowly drizzle the warm glaze over the top, allowing it to seep into the holes and around the sides of the pan. When cool, invert onto a serving plate.

Note: I use a turkey baster with a sharp metal tip that screws on the end to inject the warm glaze into the cake. Poke a hole in the top of the cake with the sharp tip of the baster, and inject some of the glaze, squeezing the bulb gently to prevent splattering; repeat, spacing holes 2 or 3 inches apart, until all the glaze is injected.

Chocolate Swirl Cake

This recipe was sent to me by a fan of mine and fellow baker, Harriet Schmidt. She reports that, at the bakery café she and her husband used to own, it was their best seller. Once you've tried it, you'll see why. I've made it many times, always with great success, though I've substituted the Hershey's chocolate-flavored syrup (see Note) in the original recipe for a more authentically chocolate homemade syrup. The cake has a lovely taste and texture, with a chocolate swirl that lends a dramatic touch. It also travels well. For years, I've sent one to each of my godsons, Jason and Ethan, on their birthdays. **Serves 12 to 14**

For the syrup (see Note)

1½ cups sugar

¾ cup cocoa (*not* Dutch-process)

Dash of salt

2 teaspoons vanilla extract

For the cake

¾ cup (1 stick plus 4 tablespoons) unsalted butter, softened

4 tablespoons vegetable shortening or lard

2 teaspoons vanilla extract

2 cups sugar

1¼ teaspoons baking soda

½ teaspoon salt

3 large eggs, at room temperature

2¾ cups all-purpose flour

1 cup buttermilk

1 cup chocolate syrup (see Note)

For the glaze

½ cup semisweet chocolate chips

3 tablespoons unsalted butter

1 tablespoon corn syrup

¼ teaspoon vanilla extract

1. Preheat the oven to 325°F. Grease and flour a 9- or 10-cup Bundt pan.

2. *For the syrup:* Combine the sugar, cocoa, and salt in a 3- to 4-quart saucepan. Slowly mix in 1 cup of hot water, stirring or whisking to keep lumps from forming. Bring to a boil over medium heat, stirring constantly. Let boil for 3 minutes, continuing to stir. Remove from the heat, and stir in the vanilla. Pour into a heatproof container and leave to cool. It makes approximately 1⅔ cups. (You can make this up to a week in advance. Refrigerate any leftover syrup; use it as a base for hot chocolate, or reheated, poured over ice cream.)

3. *For the cake:* Cream the butter and shortening in a large bowl with an electric mixer, adding the sugar a little at a time until the mixture is pale and fluffy. Blend in the vanilla, 1 teaspoon of the baking soda, and the salt. Add the eggs one at a time, mixing well after each addition. Sift the flour and add to the creamed mixture in three parts, alternating with the buttermilk, starting and ending with the flour. Mix each part just until incorporated. In a smaller bowl or measuring cup, stir the remaining ¼ teaspoon of baking soda into the cooled chocolate syrup. Spoon half the batter into the prepared pan. Mix the remaining half with the chocolate syrup, just until blended, then spoon over the batter in the pan, lightly smoothing with the back of a spoon. DO NOT MIX.

4. Bake for about 1 hour, until a toothpick inserted into the center comes out clean. (Cover lightly with a sheet of aluminum foil the last 10 or 15 minutes of baking, if it's browning too quickly.) Let cool in the pan for 15 minutes or more before inverting onto a wire rack.

5. *Meanwhile, make the glaze:* Combine the chocolate chips, butter, and corn syrup in a small saucepan. Cook over low heat, stirring constantly, until the chips are melted and the glaze is smooth and satiny. Stir in the vanilla. When the cake is completely cool, drizzle with the warm glaze.

Note: *You can substitute Hershey's syrup for homemade syrup, if you wish; chocolate-flavored isn't as good as the real thing, but kids and adults accustomed to the taste won't know the difference.*

Velvet Bundt Cake

T his gorgeous cake is courtesy of my sister-in-law, Sidney Kenyon, who grew up in Little Rock, Arkansas. It's very rich, so save it for special occasions, which, as far as my husband is concerned, could be every day of the week—it's that irresistible. Recently, I sent one to work with him—he's a reporter for WINS radio, in New York City—and it was gobbled up in no time. It's good with ice cream, whipped cream and berries, or just plain.   *Serves 12 to 14*

For the cake

1 cup (2 sticks) unsalted butter, softened

½ cup vegetable shortening or lard

3 cups sugar

5 large eggs, at room temperature

1¼ teaspoons vanilla extract

1¼ teaspoons lemon extract

1¼ teaspoons almond extract

3 cups sifted all-purpose flour

½ teaspoon baking powder

⅛ teaspoon salt

1 cup milk

For the glaze

1 cup sugar

1 teaspoon vanilla extract

1 teaspoon lemon extract

1 teaspoon almond extract

1. Preheat the oven to 325°F. Grease and flour a 10- to 12-cup Bundt pan.

2. *For the cake:* Cream the softened butter and shortening in a large bowl with an electric mixer at medium speed. Add the sugar a scoop (about ¼ cup) at a time, beating until pale and fluffy. Add the eggs one at a time, mixing well after each addition. Stir the extracts into the milk (don't be put off by the combination; it all works somehow). Sift the flour together with the baking powder and salt. To the creamed mixture, add in the following order, blending on low speed after each addition just until incorporated: a third of the flour mixture; half of the milk mixture; half of the remaining flour mixture; the remaining milk mixture; then the remaining flour mixture. Don't overmix at this point! The magic of this cake is its feather-lightness.

3. Spoon the batter into the pan. Bake in the oven for 1 hour and 15 minutes, until a toothpick inserted into the center comes out clean. (Lightly cover with aluminum foil the last 10 to 20 minutes of baking.)

4. *Meanwhile, make the glaze:* Combine ½ cup of water, the sugar, and the extracts in a small saucepan. Bring to a boil over low heat, stirring constantly. Simmer for 3 to 4 minutes, until thickened slightly. Remove from the heat. Immediately pour half of the glaze over the cake while it's still in the pan. Let it cool for 15 minutes, then invert it onto a wire rack and pour the rest of the glaze over the top.

Peaches and Cream Cake

*P*erfect for festive occasions. Baked in a decorative Bundt pan, it's almost too pretty to eat, though I have yet to find anyone who can resist it. You can substitute berries for the peaches, if you wish (see Note).

Serves 10 to 12

For the cake

¾ cup (1½ sticks) unsalted butter, softened

2¼ cups sugar

1 teaspoon almond extract

1 tablespoon Amaretto

5 large eggs, at room temperature

2¼ cups all-purpose flour, sifted

½ teaspoon baking soda

½ teaspoon salt

⅔ cup sour cream

1½ cups fresh or frozen peaches, peeled and roughly chopped
   (if using frozen, let thaw for 5 minutes or so for ease in chopping)

For the glaze

⅔ cup sugar

1 tablespoon Amaretto

Confectioners' sugar for dusting

1. Preheat the oven to 350°F. Grease and flour an 8- or 9-cup Bundt pan.

2. *For the cake:* Cream the softened butter in a large bowl with an electric mixer. Gradually add the sugar, and beat until pale and fluffy, about 5 minutes. Add the almond extract and Amaretto, and beat until blended. Add the eggs one at a time, beating well after each addition (about 1 minute per egg). Re-sift the flour together with the baking soda and salt; set aside 1½ tablespoons. Add a third of the flour mixture to the creamed mixture; then half the sour cream; half of the remaining flour mixture; the remaining sour cream; then the remaining flour mixture, beating on low speed after each addition just until incorporated.

3. Mix the chopped peaches with the reserved flour mixture, gently tossing with your fingers. Fold two-thirds of the peaches into the batter. Spoon half the batter into the pan. Sprinkle with the remaining peaches. Spoon in the remaining batter and smooth with the back of a spoon, pushing it higher around the sides of the pan (to keep a dome from forming while the cake is baking). Bake in the oven for 1 hour, until a toothpick inserted into the center comes out clean. Let the cake cool in the pan on a wire rack.

4. *Meanwhile, prepare the glaze:* Combine the confectioners' sugar and ⅓ cup of water in a small saucepan. Cook over medium heat, stirring occasionally until it reaches a boil and the sugar is dissolved. Simmer for 2 minutes more. Remove from the heat, and stir in the Amaretto.

5. Invert the warm cake onto a wire rack placed over a sheet of wax paper. Drizzle or brush with glaze. Let cool thoroughly, then dust with confectioners' sugar. Serve at room temperature.

Note: *If using berries, eliminate the almond extract and substitute Chambord for the Amaretto (in the glaze as well). Use a mixture of fresh or frozen unthawed berries, such as blueberries and raspberries, in place of the peaches.*

Banana Streusel Coffee Cake

A *pet peeve of mine is banana cake that tastes only vaguely of banana. On many occasions, I've turned up my nose for no other reason than that. I'm of the opinion that any fruit-flavored dessert should be easily identifiable without the aid of a menu. This cake is a perfect example: so rich in banana flavor, and so moist, you'd swear you were in the tropics. The streusel swirled throughout gives it a nice crunch. Perfect for Sunday brunch, or for dessert with a scoop of coconut ice cream.* *Serves 10 to 12*

For the streusel

½ cup chopped walnuts or pecans

½ teaspoon ground cinnamon

¾ cup light brown sugar

For the cake

½ cup (1 stick) unsalted butter, softened

1½ cups sugar

1 teaspoon banana extract (if unavailable, you can substitute vanilla)

3 large eggs, at room temperature

2 very ripe bananas, lightly mashed (peels should be generously freckled)

3 cups all-purpose flour

2 teaspoons baking powder

1 teaspoon baking soda

Pinch of salt

1 teaspoon ground cinnamon

1 cup (8 ounces) sour cream

1. Preheat the oven to 350°F. Grease and flour a 9- or 10-cup Bundt pan.

2. *For the streusel:* In a small bowl, combine the chopped nuts, cinnamon, and light brown sugar. Set aside.

3. *For the cake:* Cream the softened butter in a large bowl with an electric mixer at medium speed. Add the sugar a little at a time, beating for several minutes until pale and fluffy. Blend in the banana extract. Add the eggs one at a time, mixing well after each addition. Blend in the bananas. Sift the flour together with the baking powder, baking soda, salt, and cinnamon. To the creamed mixture, add in the following order, beating on low speed after each addition just until incorporated: a third of the flour mixture, half of the sour cream, half of the remaining flour mixture, the remaining sour cream, then the remaining flour mixture. Be careful not to overmix!

4. Sprinkle a third of the streusel mixture over the bottom of the prepared pan. In generous spoonfuls, drop half the batter into the pan, evenly distributing (gently!) so it covers the streusel mixture. Sprinkle half of the remaining streusel mixture over the batter in the pan. Spoon in the remaining batter, and sprinkle with the remaining streusel mixture.

5. Bake in the oven for 50 to 60 minutes, until a toothpick inserted into the center comes out clean. Cool in the pan on a wire rack, then invert onto a serving plate.

Sweet Potato Pound Cake

*T*his humble loaf is every bit as delicious as its fancier cousin, the decorative Bundt cake. Sweet potatoes provide its rich flavor and lovely orange-gold color, which distinguishes it from ordinary pound cakes. And what better use for sweet potatoes left over from Thanksgiving? I like it warm from the oven, or toasted, with butter and a smear of marmalade.

Serves 10 to 12

1¼ pounds sweet potatoes

¾ cup (1½ sticks) unsalted butter, softened

1¼ cup sugar

3 large eggs, at room temperature

1 tablespoon orange zest

1½ teaspoons vanilla extract

1¾ cups all-purpose flour

1½ teaspoons baking powder

¼ teaspoon ground mace

¼ teaspoon salt

1. Preheat the oven to 375°F. Grease an 8½ × 4½-inch loaf pan.

2. Prick the sweet potatoes with a fork or a knife, and place them in a roasting pan or on a cookie sheet. Bake in the oven until tender when pricked, about 40 minutes. Remove from the oven and lower the temperature to 350°F. When the sweet potatoes are cool enough to handle, cut in half and scoop out the insides, discarding the skins.

3. An alternate method is to peel and cube the raw potatoes, and boil them in a quart or so of water until tender.

4. Puree the cooked potatoes in a blender or food processor. If you end up with more than a cup, save the extra for another use.

5. Cream the softened butter and sugar in a large bowl with an electric mixer. Add the eggs one at a time, beating well after each addition. Add the sweet potato puree, zest, and

vanilla; blend well. In a separate bowl, combine the flour, baking powder, mace, and salt. Add to the batter, blending just until incorporated. Scrape into the pan. Bake for 1 hour and 10 minutes, until a toothpick inserted into the center comes out clean. (Cover lightly with aluminum foil during the last 10 to 12 minutes of baking, if browning too quickly.) Remove from the oven, and let cool in the pan for 15 minutes before inverting onto a wire rack. Serve warm or at room temperature.

Mocha Cake

This velvety, fine-crumbed cake should please java junkies and chocoholics alike. If you want the coffee flavor but not the caffeine, make it with decaf.　　　　**Serves 10 to 12**

4 ounces unsweetened chocolate

½ cup (1 stick) unsalted butter, softened

2 cups sugar

3 large eggs, at room temperature

1 tablespoon Kahlúa or other coffee-flavored liqueur

2 cups all-purpose flour

1 teaspoon baking soda

1 teaspoon baking powder

½ teaspoon salt

¼ teaspoon ground cinnamon

1 cup strong coffee (regular or decaf), cooled to room temperature

½ cup (6 ounces) plain yogurt

2 ounces semisweet chocolate

2 teaspoons vegetable shortening or lard

1. Preheat the oven to 350°F. Grease and flour an 8-cup Bundt pan or tube pan.

2. Place the unsweetened chocolate in a small microwave-safe bowl; heat in the microwave on high for 30 seconds at a time, stirring after each interval, until the chocolate is melted (a total of about 1½ minutes). Set aside to cool while you start the batter.

3. Cream the softened butter with the sugar in a large bowl with an electric mixer. Add the eggs one at a time, beating well after each addition. Blend in the cooled chocolate and Kahlúa. Sift together the flour, baking soda, baking powder, salt, and cinnamon. Add to the creamed mixture in the following order, beating on low speed after each addition just until incorporated: a third of the flour mixture; half of the coffee and half of the yogurt; half of the remaining flour mixture; the remaining coffee and yogurt; then the remaining flour mixture. Spoon into the pan, smoothing with the back of a spoon and pushing it up a little higher around the sides (to prevent a dome from forming while baking). Bake in the oven for about 50 minutes, until a toothpick inserted into the center comes out with only a few moist crumbs stuck to it. Let cool in the pan for 15 minutes before inverting onto a wire rack.

4. Meanwhile, in a small microwave-safe bowl, melt the semisweet chocolate with the shortening, following the same instructions as with the unsweetened chocolate (a total of about 1 minute). Drizzle over the cooled cake.

Cayou Cove Coffee Cake

*R*ecently my husband and I, in the course of our travels, stumbled upon a place so magical I hesitate to tell anyone about it, for fear that it will not remain so unspoiled (though its remote locale makes that unlikely). The Place at Cayou Cove, on Orcas Island in the Pacific Northwest, is a gracious arts and crafts inn, overlooking a serene harbor, with three separate cottages, each with its own unique character and water views. Best of all, in summer it comes with unlimited access to their organic vegetable garden and all the fruit you can pick—pears, apples, plums, blackberries, and figs so plump and sweet you have to harvest them early in the day before the bees start to swarm. As if such bounty weren't enough, every morning a basket of fresh-baked pastries is delivered to the door of your cottage. Charles Binford, who runs the inn with his wife, Valerie, was kind enough to share the recipe for his scrumptious coffee cake. It's easy to make; the only hard part is saying no to seconds. *Serves 10 to 12*

For the cake

2 cups all-purpose flour, sifted

½ cup sugar

1 teaspoon baking powder

½ teaspoon baking soda

½ teaspoon salt

½ cup (1 stick) unsalted butter, chilled

2 large eggs, slightly beaten, at room temperature

1 cup buttermilk

1 teaspoon lemon zest

For the topping

3 tablespoons all-purpose flour

4 tablespoons dark brown sugar

1 teaspoon ground cinnamon

Rounded ⅔ cup walnuts or pecans

3 tablespoons unsalted butter, cut into pieces

1. Preheat the oven to 375°F. Grease a 9 × 12-inch baking pan.

2. *For the cake:* Place the flour, sugar, baking powder, baking soda, and salt in a food processor, and pulse to blend. Add the butter and pulse until the mixture is crumbly and the butter is the size of lentils. Alternate method: Place the above ingredients in a bowl and crumble with your fingers or a pastry cutter.

3. In a large bowl, whisk the eggs. Add the buttermilk and zest, whisking until blended. Add the flour-butter mixture and stir just until blended. Spoon into the pan, smoothing the top with a spatula (this batter is quite thick).

4. *For the topping:* In a food processor, combine the flour, dark brown sugar, cinnamon, and nuts. Pulse until the nuts are roughly chopped. Add the butter and pulse until the mixture is the consistency of coarse meal.

5. Alternate method: Place the flour, dark brown sugar, and cinnamon in a small bowl. With a pastry cutter or your fingers, work in the butter until the mixture is the consistency of coarse meal. Chop the nuts and stir into the mixture.

6. Sprinkle the topping evenly over the batter in the pan. Bake in the oven for 20 to 25 minutes, covering lightly with aluminum foil during the last 10 minutes of baking, until a toothpick inserted into the center comes out clean. Cut into squares and serve warm.

Almond Cookie Cake

This buttery, almond-studded cake was adapted from a Pillsbury Bake-Off Grand Prize winner. Don't be fooled by the simplicity of the recipe; the results are so spectacular it looks like it came from a Viennese bakery. It's the perfect thing for a fancy tea, when you want to impress your guests, although they may find it hard to believe you made it yourself—it's that professional looking! Better yet, it tastes as good as it looks.   *Serves 10 to 12*

For the crust

> 1 large egg, at room temperature
> 1⅓ cups (2 sticks plus 5⅓ tablespoons) unsalted butter, softened
> 1⅓ cups sugar
> ½ teaspoon salt
> 1 teaspoon almond extract
> 2⅔ cups all-purpose flour

For the filling

> 1 large egg
> 1 cup finely ground almonds or almond flour (see Note)
> ½ cup sugar
> 1 teaspoon lemon zest
> 19 or 20 whole almonds
> Confectioners' sugar for dusting

1. Preheat the oven to 325°F. (Place a sheet of aluminum foil over the rack below to catch drips.) Grease a 9-inch springform pan.

2. **For the crust:** Whisk the egg slightly in a large bowl. Add the softened butter, sugar, salt, almond extract, and flour. Beat with an electric mixer on low speed until the flour is incorporated, then increase the speed to medium and beat until a dough forms (it should pull away from the sides of the bowl). Divide the dough in half and shape into two smooth balls. Wrap one ball in plastic wrap and chill while you roll out the remaining ball on a floured pastry cloth to fit the bottom of the pan (9 inches in diameter).

3. *For the filling:* Whisk the egg in a small bowl. Add the ground almonds, sugar, and zest. Stir or whisk until thoroughly blended. Spread the mixture evenly over the dough in the pan to within ½ inch of the edges.

4. Roll out the remaining dough on the floured pastry cloth to form a 9-inch round. Place the dough over the filling and lightly press with your fingertips around the edges to seal. Arrange the whole almonds in a circular pattern around the outer edges, placing them about 1 inch apart and pressing them lightly into the dough; reserve 4 almonds for the center of the cake, which you can arrange in a star pattern.

5. Bake in the oven for 55 to 60 minutes, until golden. If browning too quickly, cover lightly with aluminum foil for the last 5 to 10 minutes of baking. Let it cool in the pan, on a wire rack, for 15 minutes before removing the sides. Let it cool thoroughly before gently, with the aid of a thin knife or spatula, transferring onto a plate. Dust with confectioners' sugar.

Note: *When grinding almonds finely, it's best to use a food processor. To keep them from clumping together, add 1 tablespoon of the sugar for the dough. Finely ground almonds should be the consistency of coarse cornmeal.*

Pineapple Marzipan Cake

*T*his is an old family recipe, translated from German, that was sent to me by one of my readers. My husband, Sandy, is a huge marzipan fan (he wanted it for our wedding cake, which I nixed, reminding him that not everyone is as crazy about it as he is), so I was eager to try it out. The result is sure to satisfy hardcore marzipan lovers, and will even gain some new converts. It's rich yet light, with just the right blend of fruitiness and marzipan.

Serves 10 to 12

¾ cup (1½ sticks) unsalted butter, softened
7 ounces marzipan, cut into small chunks (see Note)
1 cup sugar
1 teaspoon vanilla extract
6 large eggs, at room temperature
2 cups all-purpose flour
2 teaspoons baking powder
Pinch of salt
1 teaspoon lemon zest
One 10.6 ounce can crushed pineapple, well-drained

1. Preheat the oven to 325°F. Grease and flour an 8-cup Bundt pan.

2. Cream the softened butter together with the marzipan in a large bowl with an electric mixer. Add the sugar a little at a time, beating until pale and fluffy. Add the vanilla, and mix at medium speed for several minutes more. Add the eggs one at a time, beating well after each addition. Sift the flour together with the baking powder and salt. Add to the creamed mixture, beating on low speed just until incorporated. Add the zest and pineapple, mixing gently just until blended. Spoon into the pan, smoothing the top with the back of the spoon and pushing the batter higher around the sides of pan (to keep a dome from forming while baking). Bake in the oven for 1 hour, until a toothpick inserted into the center comes out clean. Let cool in the pan before inverting onto a serving plate.

Note: *It's best if you soften the marzipan in the microwave before creaming it with the butter: Cut it into chunks and place in a small microwave-safe bowl; heat, covered, on high for 30 seconds.*

Carrot Cake

T here are two schools of thought when it comes to carrot cake: Those who prefer it in layers slathered with cream cheese frosting; and those, like me, who prefer it home-style, baked in a square or rectangular pan and dusted with confectioners' sugar. This is my mother's recipe. She made it often for her large brood, and there was seldom any left over.   *Serves 8 to 10*

2 large eggs, at room temperature
⅔ cup vegetable oil or coconut oil
1 cup firmly packed dark brown sugar
1⅓ cups all-purpose flour
1 teaspoon ground cinnamon
Dash of nutmeg
½ teaspoon salt
1¼ teaspoons baking soda
1 cup (about 1½ large) peeled and finely grated carrots
One 8-ounce can crushed pineapple, well-drained
¼ cup chopped walnuts or pecans
Confectioners' sugar for dusting

1. Preheat the oven to 350°F. Grease an 8-inch square pan.

2. Lightly beat the eggs in a large bowl, with an electric mixer. Add the oil and brown sugar, and beat at medium speed until well blended. Stir together the flour, cinnamon, nutmeg, salt, and baking soda. Add to the egg mixture and mix just until blended. Stir in the carrots, crushed pineapple, and nuts.

3. Pour into the pan, and smooth the top with a spatula or the back of a spoon. Bake in the oven for 30 to 35 minutes, until a toothpick inserted into the center comes out with only a few moist crumbs stuck to it. Let it cool in the pan for 5 to 10 minutes before cutting into squares. Dust with confectioners' sugar. Serve warm or at room temperature.

Oatmeal Cake

I f you love oatmeal cookies, then this cake is for you. It's similar in taste, only denser and moister, with a slightly chewy broiled coconut topping. I make it for potluck brunches and any occasion catering to "a cast of thousands"—a little goes a long way. It keeps well, too; it's even better the next day.

Serves 12 to 14

For the cake

 1 cup quick-cooking oats

 1 cup (2 sticks) unsalted butter, softened

 1 cup granulated sugar

 1 cup dark brown sugar

 1 teaspoon vanilla extract

 2 large eggs, at room temperature

 1⅓ cups all-purpose flour

 1 teaspoon baking powder

 1 teaspoon baking soda

 ½ teaspoon salt

 1 teaspoon ground cinnamon

For the topping

 1½ cups dark brown sugar

 6 tablespoons unsalted butter, softened

 1½ cups sweetened flaked coconut

 ¾ cup chopped walnuts or pecans

 ½ cup half-and-half

1. Preheat the oven to 325°F. Grease and lightly flour a 9 × 12-inch baking pan.

2. Place the oats in a medium bowl and pour 1⅓ cups of boiling water over them; stir to blend and let soak for 20 minutes while you prepare the batter.

3. Cream the softened butter with the sugars in a large bowl, with an electric mixer. Blend in the vanilla. Add the eggs one at a time, beating well after each addition. Blend the oats into the creamed mixture (the liquid will have absorbed). Sift the flour together with the baking powder, baking soda, salt, and cinnamon. Add to the creamed mixture, and blend for 1 minute.

4. Pour the batter into the pan and smooth the top with a spatula or the back of a spoon. Bake in the oven for 30 to 35 minutes, until a toothpick inserted into the center comes out clean.

5. *Meanwhile, prepare the topping:* In a small bowl, combine the brown sugar, softened butter, coconut, chopped nuts, and half-and-half. Stir vigorously, or mix on low speed with an electric mixer, to blend. If too thick, dribble in an additional tablespoon or more of half-and-half.

6. Immediately after removing the cake from the oven, preheat the broiler. Dot the cake with spoonfuls of topping, placing each dollop an inch or so apart. Broil 4 to 5 inches under the broiler until the topping bubbles and runs together to evenly cover the top of the cake, about 3 to 5 minutes (keep an eye on it, so it doesn't overcook!). Let it cool in the pan for several minutes before cutting it into squares. Serve warm or at room temperature.

Pineapple Upside-Down Cake

I think of this as a "company" cake, because I recall my mother making it mostly when we had people over for dinner, but over the years, I've made it for all sorts of occasions. For variety, substitute whole cranberries (fresh or unthawed frozen) for the maraschino cherries.   ***Serves 8 to 10***

⅓ cup plus 3 tablespoons unsalted butter

One 20-ounce can pineapple slices

14 to 18 walnut halves

12 to 15 maraschino cherries, cut in half (see Note)

⅔ cup firmly packed dark brown sugar

½ cup granulated sugar

1 large egg, at room temperature

1 teaspoon vanilla extract

1¼ cups all-purpose flour

1½ teaspoons baking powder

½ teaspoon salt

1. Preheat the oven to 350°F.

2. Place 3 tablespoons of the butter in a 9-inch round cake pan and bake in the oven just until the butter is melted. Remove from the oven and tilt the pan to evenly distribute the butter. Drain the pineapple slices, reserving ½ cup of the juice or syrup. Place a whole slice in the center of the pan. Cut the remaining slices in half, and arrange the halves in a pinwheel pattern around the sides. Fill in the spaces with walnut halves and maraschino cherry halves. Sprinkle the brown sugar evenly over the top.

3. Cream the remaining ⅓ cup butter and granulated sugar. Add the egg and vanilla, beating until light-colored and fluffy. Sift the flour together with the baking powder and salt. Add to the creamed mixture in two parts, alternating with the reserved juice or syrup; beat on low speed after each addition just until blended. Drop by generous spoonfuls over the pineapple-sugar mixture in the pan, gently smoothing the top with a spatula or the back of a spoon. Bake in the oven for 40 to 45 minutes, until a toothpick inserted into the center comes out clean. Cool in the pan before inverting onto a serving plate.

Note: If substituting cranberries, you'll need more than if using maraschino cherries.

Chocolate-Cherry Cake with Easy Fudge Frosting

*C*hocolate and cherries are like a good marriage: They complement each other without one dominating the other. This cake is moist and light, with nuts and cherries to give it a nice chewiness.

Serves 8 to 10

Two 1-ounce squares unsweetened chocolate
½ cup (1 stick) unsalted butter, softened
1 cup sugar
1 large egg, at room temperature
2 tablespoons maraschino-cherry syrup
1 cup milk
1½ cups sifted cake flour
1 teaspoon baking soda
¾ teaspoon salt
¼ cup chopped maraschino cherries
½ cup chopped walnuts
Easy Fudge Frosting (recipe follows)

1. Preheat the oven to 350°F. Grease and lightly flour an 8-inch square baking pan.

2. Place the chocolate in a microwave-safe bowl; heat on high for 30 seconds at a time, stirring after each interval (1 to 1½ minutes total). Alternate method: Bring a pan partially filled with water to a boil, then remove from the heat; place the chocolate, in a heat-resistant bowl, *over* (not in) the pan of hot water and stir every so often until melted. Set it aside to cool while you prepare the batter.

3. Cream the softened butter in a large bowl with an electric mixer. Gradually add the sugar, beating until pale and fluffy. Add the egg, blending for several minutes on medium speed. Blend in the cooled chocolate.

(continued)

4. Stir the maraschino cherry syrup into the milk. In a small bowl, combine the sifted flour, baking soda, and salt. To the creamed mixture add in the following order, beating on low speed after each addition just until incorporated: a third the flour mixture, half of the milk mixture, half of the remaining flour mixture, the remaining milk mixture, then the remaining flour mixture. Stir in the chopped cherries and nuts.

5. Pour the batter into the pan, and bake in the oven for 40 to 45 minutes, until a toothpick inserted into the center comes out with only a few moist crumbs attached. Let the cake cool thoroughly in the pan, on a wire rack, before frosting. Frost with Easy Fudge Frosting.

Easy Fudge Frosting

Makes enough to frost one 8-inch square cake

2 ounces unsweetened chocolate

1 cup sifted confectioners' sugar

3 tablespoons maraschino cherry syrup

1 large egg

1 teaspoon vanilla extract

3 tablespoons unsalted butter, softened

1. Place the chocolate in a microwave-safe bowl; heat on high for 30 seconds at a time, stirring after each interval (1 to 1½ minutes total). Alternate method: Place the chocolate in a bowl over (not in) a pan of boiling water removed from the heat. Stir occasionally until melted. Set aside to cool.

2. Meanwhile, in a medium bowl mix together the confectioners' sugar, maraschino cherry syrup, egg, and vanilla. Blend in the cooled chocolate with an electric mixer on low speed, until thoroughly incorporated. Add the softened butter a tablespoon at a time, beating well after each addition. Refrigerate the frosting for 10 to 15 minutes, until it starts to firm up, then beat until it's spreading consistency. If it's not thick enough, nest the bowl in a larger bowl partially filled with ice water and continue beating for another minute or so.

Note: *You might be uneasy about the raw egg in the frosting. I settle it by using eggs from free-range hens fed on organic grain, for which incidences of salmonella are reportedly quite low (though admittedly there is still a small risk). If you want to be one hundred percent safe, frost the cake by the following alternate method: Immediately after removing it from the oven, sprinkle an 8-ounce package of semisweet chocolate morsels over the top. Let stand until the morsels are soft, then spread smooth with a spatula. Let cool, then serve.*

Applesauce Cake with Maple–Cream Cheese Frosting

This is one of those classics that dates back to my grandmother's day. There's a reason it has stood the test of time: It's plain delicious, and even better a day or two later—a claim not many cakes can make. Spicy and studded with nuts and dried fruit, it's just the thing to go with a cup of tea or coffee on a snowy day after you've come in from shoveling the walk.

Serves 12 to 14

2½ cups all-purpose flour
¼ teaspoon baking powder
1½ teaspoons baking soda
1½ teaspoons salt
¾ teaspoon ground cinnamon
½ teaspoon ground cloves
½ teaspoon ground allspice
1 cup sugar
½ cup (1 stick) unsalted butter, softened
½ cup chopped walnuts or pecans
1 cup chopped dates or raisins
One 1-pound jar unsweetened applesauce
1 large egg, at room temperature
Confectioners' sugar for dusting or Maple–Cream Cheese Frosting (recipe follows)

1. Preheat the oven to 350°F. Grease and flour a 9 × 12-inch baking pan.

2. In a large bowl, sift the flour together with the baking powder, baking soda, salt, cinnamon, cloves, and allspice. Stir in the sugar. Add the softened butter, ½ cup of water, the nuts, and dates. Beat with an electric mixer at medium speed for 2 minutes, scraping the bowl with a spatula as you go along. Add the applesauce and egg, and beat for 2 minutes more. Pour the batter into the pan, smoothing with a spatula or the back of a spoon. Bake in

the oven for 40 to 45 minutes, until a toothpick inserted into the center comes out with only a few moist crumbs stuck to it. Let cool in the pan. Frost with Maple–Cream Cheese Frosting.

Maple–Cream Cheese Frosting

Makes enough to frost one 9 × 12-inch cake

¾ cup pure maple syrup (not imitation)
½ cup (1 stick) unsalted butter, softened
4 ounces cream cheese, softened
½ cup confectioners' sugar, sifted

Bring the maple syrup to boil in a small saucepan over medium-high heat. Turn the heat to the lowest setting and simmer, tilting the pan occasionally, until the syrup is reduced to ½ cup (about 10 minutes). Meanwhile, in a medium bowl, with an electric mixer, cream the softened butter and cream cheese together with the sifted confectioners' sugar. Pour the reduced syrup into a Pyrex measuring cup nested in a mixing bowl partially filled with ice water, submerging to the level of the syrup in the cup. Stir constantly until lukewarm (3 to 4 minutes). It will thicken and lose its gloss, turning a creamy caramel color. Working quickly, scrape the syrup into the butter–cream cheese mixture and beat until the frosting is spreading consistency.

Orange-Cranberry Cake

I adapted this cake from the 1950 (the year I was born) Pillsbury Bake-Off by substituting dried cranberries for the raisins called for in the original recipe. The whole orange is used—pulp, peel, and all—which gives the cake a powerful citrus punch. With a food processor, it's literally a whiz to make.

Serves 12 to 14

For the cake

1 medium navel orange

1 cup dried cranberries

⅓ cup walnuts or pecans

2 cups all-purpose flour

1 cup sugar

1 teaspoon baking soda

1 teaspoon salt

1 cup milk

½ cup (1 stick) unsalted butter, softened

2 large eggs, at room temperature

For the topping

½ cup walnuts or pecans

⅓ cup sugar

Ground cinnamon

⅓ cup reserved orange juice from the cake

1. Preheat the oven to 350°F. Grease and flour a 9 × 12-inch baking pan.

2. Squeeze the orange, reserving ⅓ cup of the juice. Toss the remaining pulp and rind (cut into quarters) into the food processor along with the dried cranberries and nuts. Whir for several seconds, then pulse, scraping down the inside of the bowl once or twice, until it forms a sticky mass (1 minute or less). Set aside.

3. Place the flour, sugar, baking soda, salt, milk, butter, and eggs in a large bowl. Beat with an electric mixer at medium speed for 3 minutes. Add the orange-cranberry mixture and mix until thoroughly blended. Scrape into the pan, smoothing the top with a spatula or the back of a spoon. Bake in the oven for 30 to 35 minutes, until a toothpick inserted into the center comes out clean.

4. *Meanwhile, make the topping:* Whir together the nuts, sugar, and cinnamon in a food processor until the nuts are finely ground. Set aside. Immediately after removing the cake from the oven, drizzle with the reserved orange juice and sprinkle with the topping. Serve warm or at room temperature.

Apple-Spice Cupcakes with Caramel Frosting

The flavor is reminiscent of apple pie, while the texture is that of a light nut bread. These aromatic cupcakes studded with bits of Calvados-infused apple can be served plain, with a dusting of confectioners' sugar, or frosted. Either way, they're the perfect thing to go with a cup of hot mulled cider. ***Makes 1 dozen cupcakes***

1 small, tart apple (such as Granny Smith), peeled, cored,
    and finely chopped to measure ½ cup
1 tablespoon Calvados or other apple brandy
¼ cup (½ stick) unsalted butter, softened
½ cup plus 2 tablespoons sugar
½ teaspoon vanilla extract
1 large egg, at room temperature
1 cup sifted cake flour
1 teaspoon baking powder
⅛ teaspoon baking soda
¼ teaspoon salt
1 teaspoon instant coffee granules
½ teaspoon ground cinnamon
¼ teaspoon ground nutmeg
¼ teaspoon ground allspice
6 tablespoons apple juice
¼ cup chopped walnuts or pecans
Caramel Frosting (recipe follows)

1. Preheat oven to 375°F. Line a muffin tin with baking cups.

2. Place the apple in a small bowl and toss with the Calvados. Set aside.

3. In a large bowl, cream the butter with the sugar until fluffy, occasionally stopping to scrape the sides of the bowl with a spatula. Blend in the vanilla. Add the egg and beat well.

Sift together the flour, baking powder, baking soda, salt, coffee granules, cinnamon, nutmeg, and allspice. Stir in the apples and lightly toss with a fork or your fingers. To the creamed mixture, add in the following order, beating after addition just until incorporated: half the flour mixture, all of the apple juice, the remaining flour mixture. Stir in the nuts. Drop the batter by spoonfuls into the lined cups, to about half full. Bake in the oven for 20 to 25 minutes, until a toothpick inserted into a cupcake comes out clean. Let cool thoroughly, then frost with Caramel Frosting.

Caramel Frosting

This recipe was shared by one of my readers, Elaine Gaines, who wrote, "Happy hours in your kitchen, but please keep writing also."   ***Makes enough to frost 1 dozen cupcakes***
(double the recipe to fill and frost two 9-inch layers)

6 tablespoons dark brown sugar
¼ cup dark corn syrup
2 medium egg whites
½ teaspoon vanilla extract

1. In a small saucepan, combine the sugar, corn syrup, and 1½ tablespoons of water. Bring to a boil over medium-high heat, stirring constantly and scraping the sides and bottom of the pan with a heat-resistant rubber spatula. Reduce the heat to medium-low and simmer without stirring until it reaches the thread stage (230°–234°F), 2 to 3 minutes.

2. Meanwhile, beat the egg whites in a large bowl with an electric mixer on high speed until stiff peaks form. Pour the hot syrup over the whites in a slow, steady stream as you continue beating, until the frosting is stiff and glossy. Blend in the vanilla.

Golden Cupcakes with Lemon Buttercream Frosting

N ew York City is in the grip of a cupcake craze, with home-style bakeries springing up in every neighborhood. It seems that for those addicted a cupcake covered in sprinkles, with its pleasant associations of a simpler time in our lives, back when our mothers packed our school lunches and the most excitement to be had at birthday parties was pin-the-tail-on-the-donkey, is more comforting than a backrub. This is a basic butter cake recipe, feather-light and frosted with Lemon Buttercream Frosting. Don't forget the sprinkles.   **Makes 1 dozen cupcakes**

6 tablespoons (¾ stick) unsalted butter, softened

¾ cup plus 2 tablespoons sugar

1 teaspoon vanilla extract

2 large eggs, at room temperature

1¼ cups cake flour, sifted

1¼ teaspoons baking powder

Rounded ¼ teaspoon salt

¾ cup buttermilk

Lemon Buttercream Frosting (recipe follows)

1. Preheat the oven to 350°F. Line a muffin tin with baking cups.

2. In a medium bowl, cream the softened butter with an electric mixer. Add the sugar a few tablespoons at a time, beating until pale and fluffy. Continue beating for 1 minute more. Blend in the vanilla. Add the eggs one at a time, beating well after each addition. Re-sift the flour together with the baking powder and salt. To the creamed mixture, add in the following order, beating on low speed after each addition just until incorporated, and scraping the bowl with a spatula as you go along: a third of the flour mixture, half of the buttermilk, half of the remaining flour mixture, the remaining buttermilk, then the remaining flour mixture. Spoon the batter into the baking cups to about three-quarters full.

Bake in the oven for 18 to 20 minutes, until a toothpick inserted into the center of a cupcake comes out clean. Cool thoroughly before frosting with Lemon Buttercream Frosting. Decorate with sprinkles.

Lemon Buttercream Frosting

Makes enough to generously frost 1 dozen cupcakes

3 tablespoons unsalted butter, very soft
2½ cups confectioners' sugar, sifted
2 teaspoons lemon zest
1 tablespoon lemon juice
1 large egg yolk
2 to 3 tablespoons heavy cream or half-and-half
Sprinkles for decorating

In a medium bowl, cream the softened butter with an electric mixer. Add 1½ cups of the confectioners' sugar, zest, lemon juice, and egg yolk; beat until well blended. Add the remaining 1 cup sugar and 1 tablespoon of the cream. Beat until blended, dribbling in more cream as you go along, until the frosting is spreading consistency. Frost the cupcakes immediately, or the frosting will become too hard. (If that happens, place the bowl in a larger bowl partially filled with warm water, and beat until spreading consistency.)

Note: *If using sprinkles, it's a good idea to decorate each cupcake as soon as you've frosted it; otherwise the frosting will set and the sprinkles won't stick.*

Mochaccino Cupcakes with Hazelnut-Coffee Frosting

I *can hardly remember a time when there wasn't a Starbucks on every other block. Where we New Yorkers once had to settle for coffee shop joe, there's now a variety of flavored coffees, lattes, mochaccino, frappuccino, and you name it, to choose from in addition to regular and decaf. Since I think of anything ending in "ino" as more of a dessert than a brew, I've created this dense, coffee-flavored chocolate cupcake, frosted with a hazelnut buttercream frosting. If they sold these at Starbucks, you could save on that mochaccino and still get your caffeine fix.*

Makes 1 dozen cupcakes

1 cup sugar

¾ cup plus 2 tablespoons all-purpose flour

6 tablespoons unsweetened cocoa (not Dutch-process)

¾ teaspoon baking powder

¾ teaspoon baking soda

Rounded ¼ teaspoon salt

1 large egg, at room temperature

½ cup milk or half-and-half

¼ cup vegetable oil or coconut oil

2 teaspoons Kahlúa or other coffee-flavored liqueur
    (you can substitute 1 teaspoon vanilla extract)

¾ cup strong hot coffee (see Note)

Hazelnut-Coffee Frosting (recipe follows)

Chocolate sprinkles for decorating

1. Preheat the oven to 350°F. Line a muffin tin with baking cups.

2. Sift the sugar, flour, cocoa, baking powder, baking soda, and salt into a medium bowl. Make a well in the center, and in the following order add: eggs, milk, oil, and Kahlúa. Beat with an electric mixer on low speed until the dry ingredients are incorporated. Increase the speed to medium and beat for 2 minutes more. Add ½ cup of the coffee, reserving the rest for the frosting, and beat on low speed just until blended. Pour the batter (it is quite thin) into a large measuring cup with a spout then into the baking cups, to a little over three-quarters full.

3. Bake in the oven for 20 to 25 minutes, until a toothpick inserted into the center of a cupcake comes out with only a few moist crumbs stuck to it. Let cool thoroughly before frosting. Frost with Hazelnut-Coffee Frosting. Sprinkle with chocolate sprinkles.

Note: *If you don't want the caffeine jolt, use decaf instead of regular coffee.*

Hazelnut-Coffee Frosting

Makes enough to frost 1 dozen cupcakes

> **6 tablespoons (¾ stick) unsalted butter, very soft**
> **1-pound box confectioners' sugar, sifted**
> **1½ tablespoons Frangelico (you can substitute 2 teaspoons vanilla extract)**
> **½ cup reserved coffee from the cupcakes, cooled**

Cream the softened butter in a medium bowl with an electric mixer. Add ½ pound (2 cups) of the confectioners' sugar, the Frangelico, and half of the reserved coffee. Beat on low speed, adding the remaining sugar a cup at a time, and dribbling in as much of the remaining coffee as needed, until spreading consistency.

Special Occasion Cakes
and Cheesecakes

That reminded Daphne. She reached for the shopping bag stowed beneath the table—something her sister had sent for him to give their mother. Handing it to the lawyer, she said, "Tell her it's from Kitty."

He peered into the bag at the pink cardboard box wrapped in string. "Anything I should know about?" he asked, only half teasing.

"Like a file or a hacksaw, you mean?" Daphne indulged in a brittle laugh. "No, I'm afraid not. It's a cake. My sister baked her a cake. Mother's favorite kind."

"What kind is that?"

"Lady Baltimore," she said.

Daphne didn't add that it was the same kind her mother had planned on serving at the party for her fortieth wedding anniversary.

—From One Last Dance

Lady Baltimore Cake with Tutti-Frutti Meringue Frosting

*I*n my novel One Last Dance, *Kitty Seagrave bakes this cake for her mother, Lydia, who's in jail for murdering Kitty's father. And though I doubt it would make up for being behind bars, this cake might remove some of the sting. For the life of me, I can't imagine why this once popular cake has fallen out of favor (except in the South, from whence it originated). It's light as a cloud (a cliché, I know, but in this case it happens to be true) and deserves to be front and center. I've adapted the original recipe by substituting chopped candied fruits for dried fruits in the meringue frosting; it adds a colorful, festive touch that makes this cake perfect for the holidays.* **Makes three 8-inch rounds, serving 10 to 12**

1 cup (2 sticks) unsalted butter, softened
2 cups superfine sugar (or sifted granulated sugar)
3½ cups cake flour
4 teaspoons baking powder
¼ teaspoon salt
1 cup milk
2 teaspoons vanilla extract
½ teaspoon almond extract
8 large egg whites, at room temperature
Tutti-Frutti Meringue Frosting (recipe follows)

1. Preheat the oven to 350°F. Grease three 8-inch round cake pans, and line the bottoms with parchment.

2. Cream the softened butter in a large bowl with an electric mixer. Add the sugar a scoop (about ¼ cup) at a time, beating until pale and fluffy (about 3 minutes total). Sift the flour together with the baking powder and salt. In a small bowl or measuring cup, stir the extracts into the milk. To the creamed mixture, add in the following order, beating on low speed after each addition just until incorporated: a third of the flour mixture; half of the milk mixture; half of the remaining flour mixture; the remaining milk mixture; then the remaining flour mixture. Set aside.

3. In a large bowl, beat the egg whites until stiff with an electric mixer on high speed. Add about a cup of the batter to the whites, folding gently just until blended. Add to the remaining batter and fold, cutting down the middle and up the sides with a spatula, *just until blended.* (Too much mixing will result in a heavier cake.) Place in the pans, smoothing the top with a spatula or the back of a spoon.

4. Bake in the oven for 20 to 25 minutes, until golden and a toothpick inserted into the center of one layer comes out clean. Let cool in the pans for 10 minutes before inverting onto wire racks. When completely cool, frost with Tutti-Frutti Meringue Frosting.

Tutti-Frutti Meringue Frosting

Makes enough to fill and frost 3 layers

2 cups sugar
4 large egg whites
Pinch of salt
1 cup walnuts or pecans, finely chopped
1 cup finely chopped candied fruit
1 teaspoon brandy (optional)

Combine the sugar and ½ cup of water in a medium saucepan. Cook over medium-high heat, stirring occasionally, until it comes to a boil. Lower the heat to medium and continue cooking for 3 minutes more. Meanwhile, beat the egg whites with the salt in a large bowl until frothy. Place the syrup in a Pyrex measuring cup with a spout and pour over the whites in a thin, steady stream, continuing to beat as you do so, until stiff peaks form. Fold in the chopped nuts, candied fruits, and brandy, if using.

Eileen's Birthday Banana Cake with Buttercream Frosting or Seven-Minute Frosting

When I was born, on the Fourth of July, my parents sent a telegram to my grandmother that read simply "Double celebration!" Mimi nearly fainted, thinking they'd meant twins. Happily, I have my birthday all to myself. Better yet, it's always a holiday, which in my family meant a picnic at the beach. My mother would pack marinated shish kebabs that we'd roast over a driftwood fire, and the meal would be capped with this cake—my all-time favorite. The only time it was less than successful was the year sparklers were substituted for the candles, which I don't recommend—they cast an unappetizing gray film over the top—though it didn't stop us from eating the cake.   *Makes two 8- or 9-inch rounds, serving 8 to 10*

½ cup (1 stick) unsalted butter, softened

1½ cups sugar

1 teaspoon vanilla extract

2 large eggs, at room temperature

2¼ cups all-purpose flour

½ teaspoon baking powder

¾ teaspoon baking soda

½ teaspoon salt

2 very ripe bananas (skins should be generously freckled), lightly mashed to equal 1 cup

¼ cup buttermilk

Buttercream Frosting or Seven-Minute Frosting (recipes follow)

1. Preheat the oven to 350°F. Grease and flour two 8- or 9-inch round cake pans, and line the bottoms with parchment.

2. Cream the softened butter in a large bowl with an electric mixer on medium speed. Gradually add the sugar, a scoop (about ¼ cup) at a time, beating until pale and fluffy. Blend in the vanilla. Add the eggs one at a time, beating well after each addition. Sift the flour together with the baking powder, baking soda, and salt. In a small bowl, combine the mashed bananas and buttermilk. To the creamed mixture add in the following order, beating on low speed after each addition just until blended: A third of the flour mixture, half of the banana mixture, half of the remaining flour mixture, the remaining banana mixture; then the remaining flour mixture.

3. Spoon the batter into the pans, and smooth the top with a spatula or the back of a spoon. Bake in the oven for 25 to 30 minutes, until a toothpick inserted into the center of one layer comes out clean. Let cool in the pans for 5 to 10 minutes before inverting onto wire racks. Cool completely before frosting. Frost with Buttercream Frosting or Seven-Minute Frosting.

Buttercream Frosting

Makes enough to fill and frost two 8- or 9-inch layers

> ⅓ cup unsalted butter, very soft
> 4 cups confectioners' sugar, sifted
> 1 teaspoon vanilla extract
> 1 to 4 tablespoons half-and-half

Cream the softened butter in a large bowl with an electric mixer. Gradually add the sifted confectioners' sugar, beating well. Add the vanilla and 1 tablespoon of the half-and-half, and beat until the frosting is spreading consistency. If it's too thick, dribble in more half-and-half as you continue beating, until spreading consistency.

Seven–Minute Frosting

This frosting holds up well for picnics, as it doesn't require refrigeration.

Makes enough to fill and frost two 8- or 9-inch layers

> 2 large egg whites
> 1½ cups sugar
> 1½ teaspoons light corn syrup (or ¼ teaspoon cream of tartar)
> Dash of salt
> 1 teaspoon vanilla extract

(continued)

Eileen's Birthday Banana Cake *(continued)*

Place all the ingredients except the vanilla in the top of a double boiler, and stir in ⅓ cup of cold water. Away from the heat, while waiting for the water in the bottom to come to a boil, beat the mixture for 1 minute with an electric mixer on medium speed. Place *over* the boiling water (make sure the bottom of the pan isn't touching the water), and continue beating until the mixture forms stiff peaks (about 5 minutes). (Don't overcook, or it will become difficult to work with and crusty as it dries.) Remove from the boiling water. Add the vanilla, and beat until the frosting is spreading consistency, 2 to 3 minutes more.

Blue-Ribbon Chocolate Cake with Chocolate Satin Frosting or White Chocolate–Cream Cheese Frosting

Where there is life, there is chocolate cake. Birthdays wouldn't be the same without it. At county fairs, you'll often find one proudly bearing a ribbon. And no self-respecting restaurant's dessert menu would be complete without some form of chocolate cake. This classic recipe comes out perfect every time, moist and just dense enough without being too fudgy. It was one of my dad's favorites.

Makes three 9-inch rounds, serving 10 to 12

6 ounces unsweetened chocolate

1 cup (2 sticks) unsalted butter, softened

2 cups sugar

2 teaspoons vanilla extract

5 large eggs, at room temperature

2¼ cups all-purpose flour, sifted

1 teaspoon baking soda

1 teaspoon salt

1½ cups buttermilk

Chocolate Satin Frosting or White Chocolate–Cream Cheese Frosting (recipes follow)

1. Preheat the oven to 350°F. Grease and flour three 9-inch round cake pans, and line the bottoms with parchment.

2. Place the chocolate in a microwave-safe bowl; heat in the microwave for 30 seconds at a time, stirring after each interval, until melted (about 1½ minutes total). Alternate method: Place the chocolate in a heat-resistant bowl and set *over* (not in) water that's been brought to a boil then removed from the heat; stir occasionally until melted. Set aside to cool.

(continued)

3. Meanwhile, cream the softened butter in a large bowl with an electric mixer. Add the sugar a scoop (about ¼ cup) at a time, beating until pale and fluffy. Blend in the vanilla. Add the eggs one at a time, beating well after each addition. Blend in the cooled chocolate, and continue beating for several minutes more.

4. Re-sift the flour together with the baking soda and salt. To the creamed mixture, add in the following order, beating after each addition just until incorporated: a third of the flour mixture; half of the buttermilk; half of the remaining flour mixture; the remaining buttermilk; then the remaining flour mixture. Spoon the batter into the pans, smoothing with a spatula or the back of a spoon. Bake in the oven for 25 to 30 minutes, until a toothpick inserted into the center of one layer comes out clean (see Note). Cool the layers in the pans for 5 minutes before inverting onto wire racks. Cool completely before frosting with Chocolate Satin Frosting or White Chocolate–Cream Cheese Frosting.

Note: Many ovens won't comfortably accommodate three 9-inch pans on a single rack. Since crowding or placing on racks at different levels will create uneven results, I find it's best to hold off on baking the third layer until the first two are out of the oven.

Chocolate Satin Frosting

Makes enough to fill and frost three 9-inch layers

> 4½ ounces unsweetened chocolate
>
> 4 cups sifted confectioners' sugar
>
> 4½ to 5 tablespoons hot coffee
>
> 1 large egg plus 1 yolk
>
> ½ cup plus 2 tablespoons unsalted butter, softened
>
> 2 teaspoons vanilla extract

1. Place the chocolate in a microwave-safe bowl; heat in the microwave for 30 seconds at a time, stirring after each interval, until melted (about 1½ minutes total). Alternate method: Place the chocolate in a heat-resistant bowl and set *over* (not in) water that's been brought to a boil then removed from the heat; stir occasionally until melted. Set aside to cool.

2. Blend together the confectioners' sugar, cooled chocolate, and coffee in a large bowl, with an electric mixer. Beat in the egg and yolk, then the softened butter and vanilla. If the frosting is too thin, nest the bowl in a larger bowl partially filled with ice water and beat until spreading consistency.

Note: You might be uneasy about the raw egg in the frosting. I settle it by using eggs from free-range hens fed on organic grain, for which incidences of salmonella are reportedly quite low (though admittedly there is still a small risk). If you want to be one hundred percent safe, frost with White Chocolate–Cream Cheese Frosting instead.

White Chocolate–Cream Cheese Frosting

Sinfully rich!   *Makes enough to fill and frost three 8- or 9-inch layers*

8 ounces white chocolate
½ cup plus 2 tablespoons unsalted butter, softened
10 ounces cream cheese, softened
2½ tablespoons lemon juice
1½ cups sifted confectioners' sugar

1. Place the chocolate in a small heat-resistant bowl. Set the bowl in a pan of water that's been brought to a boil then removed from the heat; stir occasionally until melted. Remove the bowl from the pan and set aside to cool.

2. Beat the softened butter for 5 minutes in a large bowl with an electric mixer on medium speed. Add the softened cream cheese and beat for 5 minutes more. Blend in the lemon juice. Add the cooled chocolate and confectioners' sugar, and beat until the frosting is spreading consistency. If it's too thick, dribble in a little milk or cream, continuing to beat as you do so, until spreading consistency.

Red Velvet Cake with Mocha Buttercream Frosting

The mystery of this cake isn't its deep red color, but how anything this rich could possibly be low-fat (minus the frosting, of course). Amazingly it contains no butter, milk, or eggs! The original recipe is a holdover from World War II, when chocolate was in short supply, but it's no secret as to why it's remained a favorite in the decades since. It's so moist a dusting of confectioners' sugar is all that's needed (though I've included a recipe for frosting). Note: You need a food processor for this. *Makes two 8-inch rounds, serving 8 to 10*

3 cups all-purpose flour, sifted

2 cups sugar

⅓ cup unsweetened cocoa (not Dutch-process)

2 teaspoons baking soda

¾ teaspoon salt

½ cup vegetable oil or coconut oil

1 tablespoon vanilla extract

One 1-ounce jar red food coloring

2 tablespoons lemon juice

Confectioners' sugar for dusting or Mocha Buttercream Frosting (recipe follows)

1. Preheat the oven to 350°F. Grease and flour two 8-inch round cake pans, and line the bottoms with parchment.

2. Place the flour, sugar, cocoa, baking soda, and salt in a food processor, and whir to combine. Whisk together 2 cups of cold water, the oil, vanilla, food coloring, and lemon juice. Pour over the dry ingredients, and whir just until blended. Pour into the pans, and drop each pan onto a hard surface (such as the kitchen counter) from a height of about 6 inches to release the bubbles (you may need to do this a couple of times).

3. Bake in the oven for 25 to 30 minutes, until a toothpick inserted into the center of one layer comes out clean. Cool in the pans for several minutes before inverting onto wire racks. Dust with confectioners' sugar, or frost with Mocha Buttercream Frosting.

Mocha Buttercream Frosting

Makes enough to fill and frost two 8- or 9-inch layers

2 ounces unsweetened chocolate

1 cup (2 sticks) unsalted butter, softened

4 cups confectioners' sugar, sifted

2 to 4 tablespoons strong coffee, at room temperature

1. Place the chocolate in a microwave-safe bowl; heat in the microwave for 30 seconds at a time, stirring after each interval, until it's melted (about 1 minute total). Set aside to cool.

2. Cream the butter (it should be *very* soft) in a large bowl, with an electric mixer, until pale and fluffy. Gradually add the sugar (¼ cup at a time), mixing until well blended. Add the melted chocolate and beat until blended. Dribble in the coffee a tablespoon at a time, beating until the frosting is spreading consistency.

Orange Layer Cake with Orange Filling and Seven-Minute Frosting

I make this for my husband every year on his birthday. Under a snowy cap of Seven-Minute Frosting sprinkled with toasted coconut, it seems to float like a cloud. For fancy occasions, you can spread the Orange Filling between the layers. Another option: As a summertime treat, when strawberries are in season, stack unfrosted layers with whipped cream and lightly sweetened strawberry slices. **Makes three 9-inch rounds, serving 10 to 12**

1 cup (2 sticks) unsalted butter, softened

2 cups sugar

2 teaspoons vanilla extract

4 large eggs, at room temperature

1 tablespoon orange zest

4 cups cake flour, sifted

2 teaspoons baking powder

1½ teaspoons baking soda

½ teaspoon salt

2 cups buttermilk

Orange Filling (recipe follows)

Seven-Minute Frosting (page 53–4)

Sweetened flaked coconut for garnish

1. Preheat the oven to 350°F. Grease and flour three 9-inch round cake pans, and line the bottoms with parchment.

2. Cream the softened butter in a large bowl with an electric mixer on medium speed. Gradually add the sugar (about ¼ cup at a time), beating until pale and fluffy. Blend in the vanilla, and mix well. Add the eggs one at a time, beating well after each addition. Continue beating for several more minutes. Blend in the zest. Re-sift the flour together with the baking powder, baking soda, and salt. To the creamed mixture, add in the following order, beating after each addition just until incorporated: a third of the flour mixture; half of the buttermilk; half of the remaining flour mixture; the remaining buttermilk; then the remaining flour mixture. Spoon into the pans, smoothing the tops with a spatula or the back of a spoon.

3. Bake in the oven (see Note) for 30 minutes, until a toothpick inserted into the center of one layer comes out clean. Fill with Orange Filling and frost with Seven-Minute Frosting. Sprinkle the top and sides of the frosted cake with the sweetened flaked coconut.

Note: Many ovens won't comfortably accommodate three 9-inch pans on a single rack. Since crowding or placing on racks at different heights will create uneven results, it's best to hold off on baking the third layer until the first two are out of the oven.

Orange Filling

Makes about 1 cup; enough to fill 2 layers

> ¾ **cup sugar**
> 2 **tablespoons cornstarch**
> **Dash of salt**
> ¾ **cup fresh orange juice**
> 1 **tablespoon fresh lemon juice**
> 1 **teaspoon orange zest**
> 2 **large egg yolks, lightly beaten, at room temperature**
> 1 **tablespoon unsalted butter**

Combine the sugar, cornstarch, and salt in a small saucepan. Gradually whisk in the juices. Cook over medium heat, stirring constantly, until the mixture thickens and turns clear (it should be translucent and generously coat the back of a spoon). Whisk a small amount of the hot mixture into the egg yolks, then whisk the yolks into the remaining hot mixture in the pan. Remove from the heat and add in the zest and butter, stirring until melted. Scrape into a bowl, and set aside to cool.

Maple Chiffon Cake with Maple–Cream Cheese Frosting

*T*his was another of my dad's favorites. I've made it many times for my husband as well. Sandy spent summers in Vermont when he was growing up—where you'd better love maple or risk getting run out of the state—and for him this cake is a trip down memory lane. Frosted with Maple–Cream Cheese Frosting, it's a double-whammy for maple lovers. Note: You have to beat the egg whites until very *stiff*—that's what makes this cake so ethereal.

Serves 10 to 12

2¼ cups cake flour, sifted
¾ cup granulated sugar
¾ cup dark brown sugar
1 tablespoon baking powder
1 scant teaspoon salt
½ cup vegetable oil or coconut oil
5 large egg yolks, lightly beaten, at room temperature
2 teaspoons maple flavoring
1 cup (8 large) egg whites, at room temperature
½ teaspoon cream of tartar
1 cup finely chopped walnuts (optional)
Maple–Cream Cheese Frosting (page 39), doubled

1. Preheat the oven to 325°F.

2. In a large bowl, combine the sifted flour, sugars, baking powder, and salt. Make a well in the dry ingredients and add, in the following order: the oil, yolks, ¾ cup of water, and the maple flavoring. Blend with an electric mixer at medium speed until very smooth. Set aside.

3. In a separate bowl, beat the egg whites and cream of tartar with an electric mixer on high speed until *very* stiff peaks form (stiffer than for meringue or for angel cake). Drizzle the batter in a thin stream over the beaten whites in a crisscrossing motion, gently folding and cutting with a spatula down the center and up one side just until blended. Don't over-mix! Fold in the nuts, if using.

4. Spoon into an ungreased 10-inch tube pan with a removable bottom, and bake in the oven for 55 minutes. Increase the heat to 350°F and bake for 10 to 15 minutes more, until a toothpick inserted into the center comes out clean. Invert while still in the pan (my mother inverts hers on a bottle neck), and let the cake cool thoroughly before removing from the pan. Frost with the Maple–Cream Cheese Frosting.

Mom's Angel Food Cake with Lemon Glaze

T he perfect light dessert after a heavy meal. When my mother makes this in the summer-time, she spoons whipped cream and sliced strawberries sweetened with a little sugar over the top. I drizzle a lemon glaze over the cake.   *Serves 10 to 12*

1 cup cake flour, sifted
1¼ cups confectioners' sugar, sifted
12 large egg whites (1½ cups), at room temperature
1½ teaspoons cream of tartar
1½ teaspoons vanilla extract
¼ teaspoon almond extract
1 cup superfine sugar
Lemon Glaze (recipe follows)

1. Preheat the oven to 375°F.

2. Re-sift the flour with the confectioners' sugar; set aside.

3. Place the egg whites, cream of tartar, and vanilla and almond extracts in a large bowl. Beat with an electric mixer on high speed until soft peaks form. Add the sugar a few tablespoons at a time, beating until stiff peaks form.

4. Place the flour-sugar mixture in a fine-mesh sieve, ¼ cup at a time, and shake over the beaten whites, gently folding after each addition, just until incorporated.

5. Spoon into an ungreased 10-inch tube pan, and bake in the oven for 30 to 40 minutes, until golden and the cracks on top look dry. While still in the pan, invert the cake on a bottleneck or wire rack (this will prevent it from falling as it cools). When completely cool, remove from the pan and ice with Lemon Glaze.

Lemon Glaze

Makes enough to glaze one 10-inch angel food cake

> 3 tablespoons unsalted butter, melted
> 1½ cups confectioners' sugar, sifted
> 4 to 5 tablespoons lemon juice
> ¾ teaspoon lemon zest

In a medium bowl, place the butter, confectioners' sugar, 4 tablespoons of the lemon juice, and zest. Whisk until smooth, dribbling in the remaining tablespoon of lemon juice, if needed (the glaze is thin). Drizzle over the top and sides of the cooled cake. Allow the glaze to set before serving.

Tennessee Jam Cake with Brown Sugar Frosting

*M*y mother's family is from the South, where this recipe is as traditional as pecan pie. For a slightly less sweet cake, use preserves sweetened with fruit juice (such as Polaner).

Makes three 9-inch rounds, serving 10 to 12

1 cup (2 sticks) unsalted butter, softened
1½ cups sugar
One 13-ounce jar fruit preserves (I use apricot)
4 large eggs, at room temperature
2½ cups all-purpose flour
1 teaspoon baking soda
¼ teaspoon salt
1 teaspoon ground cinnamon
½ teaspoon ground nutmeg
½ teaspoon ground cloves
1 cup buttermilk
1½ cups chopped pecans (optional)
Brown Sugar Frosting (recipe follows)

1. Preheat the oven to 350°F. Line the bottoms of three 9-inch round cake pans with parchment; grease and flour the sides.

2. Cream the softened butter in a large bowl with an electric mixer on medium speed. Gradually add the sugar, beating until pale and fluffy. Set aside ½ cup of the preserves, and add the remaining preserves to the creamed mixture, blending well. Add the eggs one at a time, beating for 1 minute after each addition.

3. Sift the flour together with the baking soda, salt, cinnamon, nutmeg, and cloves. To the creamed mixture, add in the following order, beating on low speed after each addition just until incorporated: a third of the flour mixture; half of the buttermilk; half of the remaining flour mixture; the remaining buttermilk; then the remaining flour mixture. Stir in the chopped pecans, if using. Spoon the batter into the pans.

4. Bake in the oven for 30 to 35 minutes (see Note), until a toothpick inserted into the center of one layer comes out clean. Cool in the pans for 10 minutes before inverting onto wire racks. Cool thoroughly, and spread 2 of the layers with the remaining ½ cup of preserves, to within ½ inch of the edges. Stack them, placing the unfilled layer on top. Frost with Brown Sugar Frosting.

Note: Many ovens won't comfortably accommodate three 9-inch pans on a single rack. Since crowding or placing on racks at different heights will create uneven results, it's best to hold off baking the third layer until the first two are out of the oven.

Brown Sugar Frosting

Makes 2½ cups, enough to fill and frost three 9-inch layers

> 1 cup packed dark brown sugar
> ½ cup (1 stick) unsalted butter
> ⅔ cup half-and-half
> 4 cups confectioners' sugar

1. In a small saucepan, combine the brown sugar, butter, and half-and-half. Cook over the lowest heat, stirring constantly, until the butter is melted and the sugar is dissolved.

2. Sift the confectioners' sugar into a medium bowl and nest in a larger bowl partially filled with ice water. Gradually pour in the hot syrup while beating with an electric mixer on low speed. Beat for 3 to 4 minutes more, until the frosting is spreading consistency.

Coconut Cake with Coconut Filling and Seven-Minute Frosting

I f you take this to a picnic, you'll need ballast to keep it from blowing away with the first stiff breeze. It requires a little extra effort, but the results are so spectacular, it's well worth it. Recently I wrapped up a piece for my friend Nick to take home with him. It never made it that far; he called from his car to rave as he was licking the frosting from the wrapper.

Makes two 8 or 9-inch rounds, serving 8 to 10

2¼ cups cake flour, sifted

1 tablespoon baking powder

1 scant teaspoon salt

1½ cups granulated sugar

⅔ cup canned coconut milk

⅓ cup milk

⅓ cup vegetable oil or coconut oil

1 teaspoon lemon extract

2 large eggs, separated, at room temperature

½ cup confectioners' sugar, sifted

Coconut Filling (recipe follows)

Seven-Minute Frosting (page 53–4)

Sweetened flaked coconut for garnish

1. Preheat the oven to 375°F. Line two 8 or 9-inch round cake pans with parchment, and grease and flour the pans, including the parchment.

2. In a large bowl, sift the flour together with the baking powder, salt, and granulated sugar. In a measuring cup, stir together the coconut milk and regular milk. Make a well in the center of the dry ingredients and, in the following order, then add: the oil, half of the milk mixture, and the lemon extract. Beat with an electric mixer on low speed until blended, then on medium speed for 1 minute, until the batter is smooth, constantly scraping the bowl with a spatula as you go along. Add the remaining milk mixture and the egg yolks. Beat for 1 more minute, until smooth.

3. In a separate bowl, beat the egg whites until soft peaks form. Gradually add the confectioners' sugar as you continue beating, until stiff peaks form. Carefully fold into the batter, repeatedly cutting down the center with a spatula and up one side, just until blended. Scrape into the pans, smoothing the tops with the spatula or the back of a spoon.

4. Bake in the oven for 20 to 25 minutes, until a toothpick inserted into the center of one layer comes out clean. Let cool in the pans for 5 minutes before inverting onto wire racks. When completely cool, fill with Coconut Filling and frost with Seven-Minute Frosting. Sprinkle the top and sides with sweetened flaked coconut.

Coconut Filling

Makes 1¾ cups, enough to fill four 8-inch layers

⅔ cup evaporated milk
⅔ cup sugar
¼ cup (½ stick) unsalted butter
1 large egg, beaten
Dash of salt
1 teaspoon vanilla extract
1⅔ cups sweetened flaked coconut

In a small saucepan combine the evaporated milk, sugar, butter, egg, and salt. Cook over low heat until the mixture thickens and begins to boil, stirring constantly. Remove from the heat. Stir in the vanilla and coconut. Set aside to cool. Use half of the filling for the cake, and freeze what's left for later use.

Caramel Banana-Walnut Torte

This is worthy of a pastry chef—vanilla custard and banana slices sandwiched between layers of banana cake with a baked-on caramelized topping, piled with whipped cream. Whereas a simple banana cake garners quiet praise, this fancy torte truly makes a statement. It takes a little extra effort, but doesn't require any particular skill. Make it for company, and your guests will be swooning. ***Makes one three-layer torte, serving 10 to 12***

For the cake

1 cup firmly packed dark brown sugar

1 cup (2 sticks) unsalted butter

¼ cup heavy cream

1 cup chopped walnuts

1½ cups granulated sugar

2 very ripe bananas (skins should be generously freckled), mashed to equal 1 cup

1 teaspoon vanilla extract

3 large eggs, at room temperature

2½ cups all-purpose flour, sifted

1¼ teaspoons baking powder

1 teaspoon baking soda

½ teaspoon salt

¾ cup buttermilk

For the filling

½ cup sugar

3 tablespoons all-purpose flour

¼ teaspoon salt

1 cup low-fat milk

1 large egg, beaten

1 teaspoon vanilla extract

1 tablespoon unsalted butter

2 medium firm-ripe bananas, sliced

For the topping

½ **cup heavy cream**

2 **tablespoons confectioners' sugar**

1. Preheat the oven to 350°F. Grease the sides only of three 8-inch round cake pans.

2. Combine the brown sugar, ½ cup of the butter, and cream in a small saucepan. Cook over low heat just until the butter is melted, stirring constantly. Pour into the pans, tilting to cover the bottoms. Sprinkle with the chopped walnuts.

3. In a large bowl, cream the remaining ½ cup of butter, softened to room temperature, with an electric mixer on medium speed. Add the granulated sugar a little at a time, beating until pale and fluffy. Add the mashed bananas and vanilla, and beat until well blended, about 1 minute. Add the eggs one at a time, beating well after each addition.

4. In a separate bowl, combine the sifted flour, baking powder, baking soda, and salt. Add half of the dry ingredients to the creamed mixture, and beat at low speed just until blended, scraping the bowl with a spatula as you go along. Add the buttermilk, beating just until incorporated. Then add the remaining dry ingredients, and beat just until blended. Spoon the batter into the pans to cover the brown sugar mixture, smoothing it with the spatula.

5. Bake in the oven for 30 minutes, until a toothpick inserted into the center of one layer comes out clean (see Note). Let the layers cool in the pans for 5 minutes, then loosen the edges with the tip of a sharp knife and invert on wire racks placed over wax paper to catch the drips.

6. *To prepare the filling:* In a medium saucepan, combine the sugar, flour, and salt. Gradually stir in the milk. Cook over medium heat, stirring constantly, until the mixture thickens and starts to boil. Remove from the heat and pour a small amount into the beaten egg. Whisk to combine. Return to the hot mixture in the pan and cook, stirring constantly, until it starts to bubble. Remove from the heat. Add the vanilla and butter, and stir until the butter is melted. Scrape into a clean bowl and refrigerate, uncovered, while the cake layers are cooling.

7. To assemble the torte, place one cake layer, caramelized side up, on a serving plate. Spoon half the cooled filling over it, smoothing to within ½ inch of the edges. Arrange half the banana slices over the filling. Repeat the process with the second layer, ending with the

(continued)

Caramel Banana-Walnut Torte *(continued)*

third layer placed caramelized side up. Whip the cream for the topping until soft peaks form. Add the confectioners' sugar, and beat until stiff peaks form. Spoon or pipe over the top layer of the torte. Refrigerate it until ready to serve.

Note: Many ovens won't accommodate three pans on a single rack. Since crowding or baking on separate racks will create uneven results, hold off on baking the third layer until the first two are out of the oven.

Chocolate-Pecan Torte

*E*very year at Christmas my husband's parents in Georgia send us several pounds of chocolate-covered pecans. I created this nearly flourless torte in an effort to duplicate that delightful combination. Glazed with chocolate and garnished with whipped cream, it satisfies on
every level.   ***Makes one 8-inch torte, serving 8 to 10***

½ cup (1 stick) unsalted butter

8 ounces semisweet chocolate

3 large eggs, separated, at room temperature

½ cup granulated sugar

1 teaspoon vanilla extract

½ cup finely chopped pecans

2 tablespoons all-purpose flour

1 teaspoon vegetable shortening or lard

½ cup heavy cream

2 tablespoons confectioners' sugar

Chocolate curls or pecan halves for garnish

1. Preheat the oven to 375°F. Grease and flour the bottom only of an 8-inch springform
pan with a removable rim.

2. Melt the butter and 7 ounces of the chocolate in a small saucepan over the lowest heat,
stirring constantly. Set aside to cool.

3. In a medium bowl, beat the egg whites with an electric mixer on high speed until
medium peaks form. Set aside.

4. Place the cooled chocolate-butter mixture, the granulated sugar, ½ teaspoon of the
vanilla, and the chopped pecans in a separate bowl. Beat until well blended. Add the egg
yolks one at a time, beating for 1 minute after each addition, and scraping the bowl as you
go along. Add the flour, and beat just until blended. Carefully fold in the beaten egg whites,
repeatedly cutting down the middle and up one side with a spatula, just until blended.
Spoon into the pan.

(continued)

Chocolate-Pecan Torte *(continued)*

5. Bake in the oven for 20 to 25 minutes, until the torte is set in the center. (It should no longer jiggle when the pan is gently shaken.) Cool thoroughly before removing the rim of the pan.

6. Meanwhile, melt the shortening with the remaining 1 ounce of chocolate in a small saucepan over the lowest heat. Drizzle over the cooled torte, using the back of a spoon to evenly cover the top, and letting it dribble down the sides.

7. In a medium bowl, whip the cream with the confectioners' sugar and remaining ½ teaspoon of vanilla until stiff peaks form. Spoon or pipe around the edges of the torte. Garnish with chocolate curls or pecan halves, if desired.

Classic Cheesecake with Pineapple Glaze

*T*his is my mother's recipe, the only cheesecake she ever made, as far as I know. When something is this good, why look elsewhere? More substantial than most, it's perfect for large parties. You can even make it a week or so in advance: Freeze the cake without the topping, and thaw it in the refrigerator overnight. Add the topping just before serving.　　***Serves 14 to 16***

For the crust

1 cup all-purpose flour, sifted

¼ cup sugar

1 teaspoon lemon zest

½ cup (1 stick) unsalted butter, cut into chunks

1 large egg yolk, lightly beaten

¼ teaspoon vanilla extract

For the filling

Five 8-ounce packages cream cheese, softened

1¾ cups sugar

3 tablespoons all-purpose flour

1 teaspoon lemon zest

¼ teaspoon salt

¼ teaspoon vanilla extract

5 large eggs, plus 2 yolks, at room temperature

¼ cup heavy cream

Pineapple Glaze (recipe follows)

1. Preheat the oven to 400°F. Grease the *rim only* of a 9-inch springform pan.

2. *For the crust:* In a food processor combine the flour, sugar, and zest. Add the butter and pulse until the mixture is crumbly. Alternate method: Combine the above ingredients in a bowl and, with your fingers or a pastry cutter, work in the butter until the mixture is

(continued)

crumbly. Add the egg yolk and vanilla; pulse or blend until dough forms. Press one-third of the dough over the ungreased bottom of a 9-inch springform pan with the sides removed. Bake in the oven for 5 minutes, until lightly golden. Let cool. Attach the greased sides to the crust-lined bottom, and press the remaining dough evenly over the sides to a height of about 2 inches. Set aside while you prepare the filling:

3. Increase the oven temperature to 500°F.

4. *For the filling:* In a large bowl, beat the softened cream cheese with an electric mixer until fluffy. In a separate bowl, combine the sugar, flour, zest, and salt. Gradually blend the flour mixture into the cream cheese until thoroughly incorporated. Add the eggs and yolks one at a time, beating after each addition just until smooth (too much air will cause the surface of the cheesecake to crack). Gently stir in the cream. (If there are lumps, a hand-held immersion blender is the quickest way to remove them. Just be careful not to overbeat.)

5. Turn into the crust-lined pan. Bake in the oven for 5 to 7 minutes, until the top has begun to brown. Reduce the heat to 300°F, and bake for 1 hour more, until the sides are set and the center jiggles slightly when the pan is gently shaken. Turn off the heat and leave the cake in the oven, the door propped open (with a wooden spoon or oven mitt), for 1 hour. Remove from the oven and let it cool at room temperature for 2 hours more. Before removing the side of the pan, carefully run the tip of a sharp knife around it to loosen the crust. Refrigerate for 6 to 8 hours, or overnight.

6. Two hours before serving, glaze with Pineapple Glaze.

Pineapple Glaze

Makes a little over ¾ cup

> **3 tablespoons sugar**
> **1 tablespoon cornstarch**
> **1 cup unsweetened pineapple juice**
> **½ teaspoon lemon zest**
> **Canned pineapple rings for garnish**

In a small saucepan, combine the sugar and cornstarch. Stir in the pineapple juice and zest, whisking to remove any lumps. Bring to a boil over medium heat, stirring constantly. Lower the heat and continue cooking until the mixture is clear and just beginning to thicken (it should generously coat the back of a spoon). Set aside to cool. Spread over the cooled cheesecake. Just before serving, top with halved canned pineapple rings arranged in a pinwheel pattern. Or spoon 1 to 2 cups of fresh strawberries, raspberries, or blueberries, sweetened to taste, over the top. Refrigerate for 2 hours before serving.

Cranberry Cheesecake

I can't think of anything more festive for the holidays than this no-bake refrigerator cheese-cake. Easy to make, it sparkles jewel-like at the center of any table. I once served it at a Christmas party, and several of my guests called the next day to request the recipe. Serve it at Thanksgiving when you want a break from the usual fare. **Serves 12 to 14**

¾ **cup graham cracker crumbs**

3 tablespoons unsalted butter, melted

3 cups cranberry juice cocktail

3 envelopes unflavored gelatin

2 cups heavy cream

Four 8-ounce packages cream cheese, softened

2 cups sugar

4 teaspoons lemon juice

2 cups fresh or unthawed frozen cranberries

1. *For the crust:* In small bowl, combine the graham cracker crumbs and melted butter. Press firmly over the bottom of an ungreased 9-inch springform pan. Place in the refrigerator to chill while you prepare the filling (you can do this earlier in the day).

2. Pour 2 cups of the cranberry juice cocktail into a small saucepan; sprinkle with 2 envelopes of the gelatin. Cook over low heat, stirring until the gelatin is dissolved. Remove from the heat, and set aside.

3. In medium bowl, beat the cream until soft peaks form (see Note).

4. In a large bowl, beat the softened cream cheese and 1 cup of the sugar with an electric mixer until smooth. Gradually beat in the gelatin mixture and lemon juice until well blended. Fold in the whipped cream, repeatedly cutting down the center and up one side with a spatula, just until blended. Pour the mixture into the pan, and place in the refrigerator to chill.

5. *For the topping:* In a medium saucepan, combine the cranberries, the remaining 1 cup of sugar, and ¾ cup of the cranberry juice cocktail. Cook over high heat until it comes to a boil, stirring occasionally. Reduce the heat to medium, and cook 5 minutes more, stirring occasionally. While the cranberry mixture is simmering, place the remaining ¼ cup of cranberry juice cocktail in a small bowl or measuring cup and sprinkle with the remaining envelope of gelatin. When soft, add to the hot cranberry mixture, and stir until dissolved. Refrigerate until it begins to set—it should form a soft mound when dropped from a spoon (the consistency of very soft pudding)—30 to 60 minutes. Spoon the cranberry mixture over the cheesecake, and chill until set, about 4 hours. Remove the side of the pan, and serve.

Note: *Cream will whip faster if the bowl is chilled: Half an hour or so beforehand, place a clean mixing bowl in the freezer. Pour the cream into the chilled bowl when ready, and whip.*

Raspberry Marzipan Cheesecake

T he combination of flavors in this cheesecake is marvelous, yet subtle. And since it's best made a day in advance (it needs to set at least 12 hours in the refrigerator), it's perfect for parties when you have to prepare ahead of time. It also freezes well. Just thaw in the refrigerator several hours or overnight.

Serves 12 to 14

For the crust

Vanilla wafers (about 53), enough for 1½ cups crumbs

6 tablespoons (¾ stick) unsalted butter

½ cup finely chopped almonds

For the filling

Two 8-ounce packages cream cheese, softened

7 ounces almond paste

1 cup sugar

3 large eggs, at room temperature

1½ teaspoons almond extract

3 cups sour cream

6 tablespoons seedless raspberry preserves

1 teaspoon lemon juice

Whipped cream and raspberries for garnish (optional)

1. Preheat the oven to 325°F. (Place a sheet of aluminum foil on the rack below to catch drips.) Grease a 9- or 10-inch springform pan.

2. *For the crust:* Whir the vanilla wafers in a blender or food processor until finely ground. Transfer to a small bowl, and stir in the melted butter and chopped almonds. Press the mixture over the bottom of the springform pan. Bake in the oven for 10 minutes, or until golden. Set aside to cool while you prepare the filling.

3. *For the filling:* Place the softened cream cheese in a large bowl. Crumble in the almond paste (it's easier if you soften it first in the microwave for 20 to 30 seconds), and beat with an electric mixer on medium speed until smooth. Add the sugar a little at a time as you continue beating. Add the eggs one at a time, beating after each addition just until blended while constantly scraping the sides and bottom of the bowl with a spatula. Stir in the almond extract and sour cream. Pour into the crust-lined pan.

4. Mix the raspberry preserves with the lemon juice. Drop by teaspoonfuls onto the batter, using the tip of a sharp knife to swirl into a decorative pattern.

5. Bake in the oven for 1 hour and 20 minutes, until the edges are set and the center jiggles when the pan is gently shaken. Let it cool in the oven for 1 hour, with the heat turned off and the door propped open with a wooden spoon or oven mitt. Remove from the oven and, using the tip of a sharp knife, gently loosen the crust from the side of the pan without removing the side of the pan. Cover with aluminum foil; refrigerate overnight. Just before serving, remove the side of the pan. Garnish with whipped cream and fresh raspberries, if desired.

Cappuccino Cheesecake

C *lose your eyes and imagine you're in a café in Italy sipping a cappuccino—not the vapid brew that often passes for such here in the States, but the real deal: a thimbleful of dense, dark espresso that tastes as if it were made from beans roasted no more than an hour ago, capped with a foamy crown of steamed milk as thick as whipped cream, lightly sprinkled with bits of shaved chocolate. Now imagine that cappuccino in cheesecake form and you have this sublime dessert. It's in another realm from other coffee-flavored cheesecakes I've tried.*

Serves 12 to 14

⅓ cup dark-roasted coffee beans, regular or decaf

½ cup heavy cream

6 ounces chocolate wafers

3 tablespoons unsalted butter, melted

Three 8-ounce packages cream cheese, softened

1¼ cups sugar

4 large eggs, at room temperature

2 teaspoons vanilla extract

Whipped cream and shaved chocolate for garnish (optional)

1. An hour or so in advance: Grind the coffee beans coarsely (coarser than for an automatic drip coffeemaker). In a small saucepan, combine the cream and the ground coffee. Cook over low heat just until the mixture starts to simmer. Set aside to cool for at least 1 hour.

2. Meanwhile, place the chocolate wafers in a food processor or blender; whir until fine (crumbs should equal 1½ cups). Scrape into a small bowl and combine with the melted butter. Press the mixture over the bottom and side of an ungreased 9-inch springform pan, to a height of about 1 inch.

3. Preheat the oven to 300°F.

4. In a large bowl, beat the softened cream cheese with an electric mixer until fluffy. Add the sugar a few tablespoons at a time as you continue beating. Add the eggs one at a time, beating after each addition until smooth while continuously scraping the sides of the bowl with a spatula.

5. Strain the cream mixture through a fine-mesh strainer, pushing with the back of a spoon to extract as much of the liquid as possible (don't worry about any fine grains that might pass through). Add the liquid to the cheese mixture, along with the vanilla, discarding the grounds, and beat just until blended. (If there are lumps, blend with an immersion blender or place in a food processor and whir a few times until smooth—the trick with cheesecakes is not to incorporate too much air through overbeating). Pour into the crust-lined pan.

6. Bake in the oven for 55 to 60 minutes, until the edges are set and the center jiggles slightly when the pan is gently shaken. Remove from the oven and carefully run a thin-bladed sharp knife between the crust and the side of the pan, as the cake will contract as it cools. Without removing the side, cool to room temperature, then cover with aluminum foil and chill for at least 3 hours, or overnight. Just before serving, remove the side of the pan. Carefully run a thin, sharp-bladed knife between the crust and the bottom of the pan before removing. Transfer the cake to a serving plate. Garnish with whipped cream and shaved chocolate, if desired.

Patsy's Lemon Ricotta Cheesecake with Candied Citrus Peel

*P*atsy's restaurant is a New York City institution. It was Frank Sinatra's favorite hangout, and through the years it's been a watering hole for a host of other celebrities as well—Tony Bennett, Rosemary Clooney, and more recently her nephew George Clooney, to name a few. You understand its appeal the minute you walk through the door, where famous or not, you're greeted by Joey Scognamillo, son of the original founder, and his wife, Rose, as if you were an honored guest in their home. Their son Sal is the executive chef, and what comes out of his kitchen is every bit as good as in Ol' Blue Eyes's day, judging from the throngs of diners that flock there every night. Luckily for my husband, the WINS newsroom, where he works, is only a few blocks away, so he often stops by to schmooze with Joey or Sal, or to pick up something to go. On special occasions, we reserve a table at Patsy's. I always save room for a slice of Sal's lemon ricotta cheesecake. The recipe was brought over from Italy by his grandfather Patsy. Its magic is in its simplicity, proof that's it's often the easiest desserts, with the fewest ingredients, that are the best. Sal was kind enough to share it with me, so I'm passing it on to you. If you care to dress it up a bit, you can spoon strawberries over the top or sprinkle it with candied citrus peel.

Serves 12 to 14

3 pounds (6 cups) whole-milk ricotta (don't substitute skim)
1⅔ cups sugar
4 large eggs, at room temperature
¾ teaspoon vanilla extract
Zest from 1 lemon
Strawberries or candied lemon or orange peel (recipe follows) for garnish (optional)

1. Preheat the oven to 400°F. Grease and flour a 9-inch springform pan.

2. In a large bowl, blend the ricotta, sugar, eggs, vanilla, and zest with an electric mixer until smooth. Pour into the prepared pan, and place on a foil-lined baking sheet to catch the drips. Set it on the lowest rack of the oven, and bake for 50 to 55 minutes, until the edges

are set and the center jiggles slightly when the pan is gently shaken. Leave it in the oven to cool for 1 hour, with the heat turned off and the door propped open with a wooden spoon or oven mitt. Chill for several hours or overnight before removing the side of the pan. Spoon sliced strawberries, sweetened to taste, over individual servings, or sprinkle with slivers of candied lemon or orange peel, if desired.

Candied Citrus Peel

Makes 1 pound

> 12 ounces (about ¾ cup) rinsed, quartered citrus peels
> 1½ cups granulated sugar
> ¼ cup light corn syrup
> ¼ to ⅓ cup superfine sugar

Place the peels in a medium saucepan and pour in just enough water to cover them. Bring to a boil over high heat, uncovered, and let boil for 1 minute. Reduce the heat to its lowest setting and simmer for 30 minutes more. Drain. Repeat the process twice more. Drain the peels in a colander, and set aside to cool. When cool enough to handle, scrape away any white pith. Cut the peels lengthwise into ¼-inch strips. Set aside. In a medium saucepan, place the granulated sugar, corn syrup, and 1½ cups of cold water. Cook over medium heat until the sugar is dissolved, stirring occasionally. Add the peels, and reduce the heat to its lowest setting. Simmer, stirring occasionally, for approximately 1 hour, until translucent. Drain, and spread the peels over a wire rack set over a sheet of wax paper. Let stand until barely moist to touch, about 2 hours. Place in a large covered plastic container with the superfine sugar, and shake until the peels are coated. Spread over a wire rack and let dry thoroughly, 8 hours or overnight (see Note).

Note: *Whatever you don't use immediately can be stored in an airtight container, covered in sugar, for up to 2 months.*

Cookies and Bars

She was cutting the crusts from sandwiches and arranging them on the lovely old Meissen platter Sam had given Claire when she looked up and said, "Your kitchen smells like my grandma's. I used to love spending the night at her house when I was little. We always made sugar cookies. She had all these cookie cutters in the shapes of animals."

Claire wordlessly walked over to the long cupboard by the fridge, rummaging inside until she found what she was looking for: a battered shoebox that made a faint, tinny rattling as she carried it over to the table. "My housewarming gift from your grandmother," she said.

Andie pried off the lid, reaching inside to finger a cookie cutter in the shape of a bear. She smiled at the memories it evoked. "They'd be perfect for kids' parties."

"Kids' parties. Now there's an idea." Claire could envision it: birthday teas for preteen girls, like grown-up versions of the pretend tea parties they played at when they were little. "How would you like to be in charge? We could split the profits down the middle, fifty-fifty."

—From *Taste of Honey*

Chocolate-Molasses Crinkles

I used to keep a cookie jar on the counter when my kids were growing up. These cookies went so fast, I always made a double batch. They were also the most oft-requested cookie for care packages when the kids were away at school. The chocolate and molasses make for an inspired blend. *Makes 3½ to 4 dozen cookies*

3 ounces unsweetened chocolate
½ cup (1 stick) unsalted butter, softened
¾ cup granulated sugar
6 tablespoons dark brown sugar
3 tablespoons molasses
1 large egg
1 teaspoon vanilla extract
2 cups all-purpose flour
¾ teaspoon baking soda
1½ teaspoons ground ginger
¼ teaspoon salt
Confectioners' sugar for rolling

1. Preheat the oven to 350°F. Grease 2 baking sheets.

2. Place the chocolate in a small microwave-safe bowl; heat in the microwave for 30 seconds at a time, stirring after each interval, until melted (about 1½ minutes total). Set aside to cool.

3. In a large bowl, cream the softened butter with an electric mixer on medium speed. Drizzle in the cooled chocolate, beating constantly, until well blended. Add the granulated sugar, brown sugar, molasses, and egg. Beat for 3 minutes more. Blend in the vanilla.

4. Sift together the flour, baking soda, ginger, and salt. Add to the creamed mixture and beat on low speed just until incorporated (don't overmix).

5. Shape the dough into 1-inch balls and lightly roll in confectioners' sugar. Place 2 inches apart on the baking sheets. Bake in the oven for 10 to 12 minutes, until the edges are firm

and the centers are still soft (see Notes). Let cool on the sheet for a minute or two before transferring to a wire rack.

Notes: *Many ovens won't comfortably accommodate more than one baking sheet at a time. For best results, bake separately.*

When baking cookies, such as these, that yield more than 2 dozen, you don't need more than 2 baking sheets. Simply re-use the ones you have after each batch comes out of the oven, making sure to let the baking sheet cool first.

Oatmeal–Chocolate Chip Cookies

If you took a poll, my guess is that the top two favorite cookies in America would be Tollhouse and oatmeal. So what better than a cross between the two? I make these dense, chewy cookies for the children in my life, including the Big Kid, otherwise known as my husband. Note: They travel well, and at bake sales they're always among the first offerings to go.

Makes 4 dozen cookies

1 cup (2 sticks) unsalted butter, softened

1 cup granulated sugar

1 cup firmly packed dark brown sugar

2 teaspoons vanilla extract

2 tablespoons milk

2 large eggs

2 cups all-purpose flour

1 teaspoon baking soda

1 teaspoon baking powder

Scant 1 teaspoon salt

2½ cups rolled oats

12 ounces semisweet chocolate chips

1½ cups chopped walnuts or pecans

1. Preheat the oven to 350°F. Grease 2 baking sheets.

2. In a large bowl, cream the softened butter with an electric mixer on medium speed. Add the granulated sugar and brown sugar, and mix until thoroughly blended. Blend in the vanilla, milk, and eggs. In a small bowl, combine the flour, baking powder, baking soda, and salt. Add to the creamed mixture and blend on low speed until incorporated. Stir in the oats, chocolate chips, and chopped nuts.

3. Scoop by rounded tablespoons onto the baking sheets, placing 2 inches apart. Bake in the oven for 10 to 12 minutes, until the edges start to brown. Let cool slightly on the sheet before transferring to a wire rack.

Notes: *Many ovens won't comfortably accommodate more than one baking sheet at a time. For best results, bake separately.*

When baking cookies, such as these, that yield more than 2 dozen, you don't need more than two baking sheets. Simply re-use the ones you have after each batch comes out of the oven, making sure to let the baking sheet cool first.

Pecan Sandies

This was my dad's favorite cookie. For his birthday and for Christmas, my sister Patty would often make him a batch, which she'd put into a shoebox lined with wax paper. He'd store them in the freezer and thaw them out one or two at a time to eat. Coincidentally, they're my husband's favorite cookie, too. If you don't want to go to the trouble of dipping them in chocolate, you can make a variation known as Mexican Wedding Cakes (see Variation).

Makes 3 dozen cookies

1 cup (2 sticks) unsalted butter, softened

⅓ cup granulated sugar

2 teaspoons vanilla extract

2 cups all-purpose flour, sifted

¼ teaspoon salt

1 cup chopped pecans (you can substitute walnuts)

About 1 cup confectioners' sugar

3 ounces unsweetened or semisweet chocolate

1. In a large bowl, cream the softened butter and sugar with an electric mixer on medium speed. Add the vanilla and 2 teaspoons of water, and beat until blended. Add the flour and salt, and mix on low speed until incorporated, then increase speed to medium and mix until well blended, working in with your hands if the dough becomes too stiff.

2. Cover the bowl with plastic wrap, and chill for at least 30 minutes. Preheat the oven to 325°F and lightly grease 2 baking sheets.

3. Shape the chilled dough into fingers roughly 1 inch thick and 3 inches long. Place 2 inches apart on the baking sheets. Bake in the oven for 20 minutes, or until lightly golden. Let cool slightly on the sheet before transferring to a wire rack.

4. Place the chocolate in a small microwave-safe bowl; heat in the microwave for 30 seconds at a time, stirring after each interval, until melted (about 1½ minutes total). Alternate method: Place the chocolate in a bowl *over* (not in) a pan of boiling water removed from the heat; stir occasionally until melted.

5. While the cookies are still warm, roll them in confectioners' sugar. Dip one end of each cookie into the melted chocolate, and place on a wire rack over a sheet of wax paper. The chocolate will harden as it cools.

Variation: For Mexican Wedding Cakes, roll the chilled dough into 1-inch balls instead of fingers. Bake according to the recipe, and roll them in the confectioners' sugar while warm. Omit the chocolate.

Corn Flake Macaroons

*M*y mother used to make these when we were growing up—I think she got the recipe off the Kellogg's Corn Flakes box. We kids loved the unbaked dough almost as much as we did the cookies. Once my sister Patty snitched a handful when my mother was out of the kitchen and stuffed it into a plastic bag that she shoved down the front of her pedal pushers. Unfortunately, the bag burst, and Mom walked in to find batter oozing down Patty's leg. Talk about busted! *Makes 3 dozen cookies*

Whites from 4 large eggs
¼ teaspoon cream of tartar
1 teaspoon vanilla extract
1⅓ cups sugar
1 cup chopped walnuts or pecans
1 cup sweetened flaked coconut
3 cups Corn Flakes

1. Preheat the oven to 325°F. Generously grease 2 baking sheets or line with parchment.

2. In a large bowl, beat the egg whites with an electric mixer on high speed, until foamy. Add the cream of tartar and vanilla. Gradually add the sugar, beating constantly, until stiff, glossy peaks form. Fold in the chopped nuts, coconut, and Corn Flakes. Drop by rounded tablespoons onto the baking sheets, about 2 inches apart. Bake in the oven for 20 minutes, or until lightly browned.

3. Immediately transfer to wire racks to cool.

Notes: *Many ovens won't comfortably accommodate more than one baking sheet at a time. For best results, bake separately.*

When baking cookies, such as these, that yield more than 2 dozen, you don't need more than two baking sheets. Simple re-use the ones you have after each batch comes out of the oven, making sure to let the baking sheet cool first.

Coconut-Cranberry Cookies

These cookies are so festive—perfect for the holidays—and they taste as good as they look. For large parties or holiday cookie tins, double the recipe.   **Makes 3 dozen cookies**

¾ cup (1½ sticks) unsalted butter, softened
1 cup sugar
1½ teaspoons orange zest
1 teaspoon vanilla extract
1½ cups all-purpose flour
½ teaspoon baking powder
Pinch of salt
¾ cup dried cranberries
¾ cup sweetened flaked coconut

1. Preheat the oven to 350°F. Grease 2 baking sheets.

2. In a large bowl, cream the softened butter with an electric mixer on medium speed. Add the sugar a little at a time (¼ cup), beating until the mixture is pale and fluffy. Blend in the zest and vanilla. In a small bowl, combine the flour, baking powder, and salt. Add to the creamed mixture, and beat on low speed until the dry ingredients are incorporated. Increase the speed to medium and continue beating until it comes together in a dough. Stir in the cranberries and coconut.

3. With floured fingers, shape the dough into 1-inch balls, placing them 2 inches apart on the baking sheets. Bake in the oven for 8 to 10 minutes, just until the edges start to brown. Let cool on the sheet for several minutes before transferring to a wire rack.

Notes: Many ovens won't comfortably accommodate more than one baking sheet at a time. For best results, bake separately.

When baking cookies, such as these, that yield more than 2 dozen, you don't need more than two baking sheets. Simply re-use the ones you have after each batch comes out of the oven, making sure to let the baking sheet cool first.

Cherry Winks

*T*hese cookies have stood the test of time—home cooks have been baking them since the fifties—and once you've tasted them, you'll know why. Recently, I sent a batch to the newsroom where my husband Sandy works. One of his coworkers commented that he'd like to "live inside" them. **Makes about 5 dozen cookies**

¾ cup (1½ sticks) unsalted butter, softened

1 cup sugar

2 large eggs

2 tablespoons milk

1 teaspoon vanilla extract

2¼ cups all-purpose flour

2 teaspoons baking powder

½ teaspoon salt

1 cup chopped walnuts or pecans

1 cup pitted, chopped dates

⅓ cup finely chopped candied cherries, plus 15 whole cherries

1⅓ cups crushed Corn Flakes

1. Preheat the oven to 375°F. Grease 2 baking sheets.

2. In a large bowl, cream the softened butter with an electric mixer on medium speed. Gradually add the sugar, beating until pale and fluffy. Add the eggs one at a time, beating well after each addition. Blend in the milk and vanilla.

3. In a small bowl, combine the flour, baking powder, and salt. Add to the creamed mixture, and mix on low speed just until incorporated; increase the speed to medium and beat until smooth. Stir in the chopped nuts, dates, and the ⅓ cup of chopped cherries. Shape into balls roughly 1½ inches in diameter. Roll in the crushed Corn Flakes. Place them 2 inches apart on the baking sheets. Cut the remaining 15 cherries into quarters, and press 1

quarter into the top of each unbaked cookie. Bake in the oven for 10 minutes, until lightly browned. Immediately transfer to wire racks.

Notes: *Many ovens won't comfortably accommodate more than one baking sheet at a time. For best results, bake separately.*

When baking cookies, such as these, that yield more than 2 dozen, you don't need more than two baking sheets. Simply re-use the ones you have after each batch comes out of the oven, making sure to let the baking sheet cool first.

Sesame Seed Cookies

These cookies were a favorite in our house when I was growing up. When I went away to college, a care package wasn't complete without a batch. The combination of toasted sesame seeds and coconut make for a unique taste and crunchy-chewy texture that's positively addictive.

Makes 40 cookies

1 cup hulled sesame seeds (available in most well-stocked health food stores)
½ cup unsweetened shredded coconut (available in most well-stocked health food stores)
2 cups all-purpose flour
1 teaspoon baking powder
1 teaspoon baking soda
½ teaspoon salt
¾ cup vegetable oil or coconut oil
1 cup dark brown sugar
1 large egg
1 teaspoon almond extract

1. Preheat the oven to 350°F.

2. Spread the sesame seeds and coconut over an ungreased baking sheet, and bake in the oven, stirring once or twice, until lightly golden, about 6 to 8 minutes. (Keep a close watch so they don't get too dark!) Grease 2 baking sheets.

3. Sift together the flour, baking powder, baking soda, and salt.

4. In a large bowl, with an electric mixer on medium speed, cream the oil with the brown sugar. Add the egg, almond extract, and toasted sesame seed–coconut mixture. Beat until smooth. Add the flour mixture, and blend at low speed until incorporated; increase the speed to medium and mix until well blended.

5. Shape the dough into balls roughly 1 inch in diameter, and place them 2 inches apart on the baking sheets. Flatten the cookies with a fork or the bottom of a glass dipped in granu-

lated sugar. Bake in the oven for 8 to 10 minutes, until lightly golden. Let cool on the sheet for a minute or two before transferring to a wire rack.

Notes: *Many ovens won't comfortably accommodate more than one baking sheet at a time. For best results, bake separately.*

When baking cookies, such as these, that yield more than 2 dozen, you don't need more than two baking sheets. Simply re-use the ones you have after each batch comes out of the oven, making sure to let the baking sheet cool first.

Snickerdoodles

*A*nother classic, one that originated in New England in the 1800s. The name is a nonsense word for something thrown together in a hurry. Crunchy, coated with cinnamon-sugar, these cookies are the perfect thing to go with a mug of hot cocoa on a cold day.

Makes about 3 dozen cookies

4 tablespoons unsalted butter, softened (see Notes)

4 tablespoons vegetable shortening or lard

1½ cups plus 2 tablespoons sugar

1 teaspoon vanilla extract

2 large eggs

2¾ cups all-purpose flour

1 teaspoon cream of tartar

½ teaspoon baking soda

¼ teaspoon salt

2 teaspoons ground cinnamon

1. Preheat the oven to 400°F. Grease 2 baking sheets.

2. In a large bowl, with an electric mixer on medium speed, cream the softened butter and shortening with 1½ cups of the sugar, beating until pale and fluffy. Blend in the vanilla. Add the eggs one at a time, beating well after each addition. In a small bowl, combine the flour, cream of tartar, baking soda, and salt. Add to the creamed mixture and beat on low speed until incorporated; increase the speed to medium and beat until well blended.

3. Combine the remaining 2 tablespoons of sugar and the cinnamon.

4. Scoop the dough by level tablespoons and shape into balls (they will be about 1¼ inches in diameter); roll in the sugar-cinnamon mixture. Place them 2 inches apart on the baking sheets. Bake in the oven for 8 to 10 minutes, until the edges start to brown. Transfer to a wire rack to cool.

Notes: *You can use all butter, if you like. The only difference, besides taste, is that the cookies will be a little flatter.*

Many ovens won't comfortably accommodate more than one baking sheet at a time. For best results, bake separately.

When baking cookies, such as these, that yield more than 2 dozen, you don't need more than two baking sheets. Simply re-use the ones you have after each batch comes out of the oven, making sure to let the baking sheet cool first.

Chinese Almond Cookies

For me, a meal in Chinatown isn't complete without an almond cookie for dessert. I like these homemade ones even better than the giant, crumbly kind sold in Chinese bakeries. Delicate and more manageable in size, with a subtle almond flavor, they go well with any cuisine.

Makes about 4 dozen cookies

1 cup (2 sticks) unsalted butter, softened
1 cup sugar
1 large egg, plus 1 yolk
1 teaspoon almond extract
2½ cups all-purpose flour
1 teaspoon baking powder
Pinch of salt
1 tablespoon heavy cream
About ⅓ cup whole blanched almonds

1. In a large bowl, cream the softened butter and sugar with an electric mixer on medium speed. Blend in the egg and almond extract. In a small bowl, combine the flour, baking powder, and salt. Add to the creamed mixture, and beat on low speed until incorporated; increase the speed to medium and beat until it comes together in a soft dough. Cover the bowl tightly with plastic wrap and chill for at least 30 minutes.

2. Shortly before taking the dough out of the refrigerator, preheat the oven to 325°F and grease 2 baking sheets.

3. With floured fingers, shape the dough into 1-inch balls and place them about 2 inches apart on the baking sheets. With the bottom of a glass dipped in sugar, gently flatten the cookies.

4. Whisk the egg yolk with the cream. Brush over the unbaked cookies, and press 1 whole blanched almond into each one. Bake in the oven for 15 to 20 minutes, until lightly browned. Let cool slightly on the sheet before transferring to a wire rack.

Notes: *Many ovens won't comfortably accommodate more than one baking sheet at a time. For best results, bake separately.*

When baking cookies, such as these, that yield more than 2 dozen, you don't need more than two baking sheets. Simply re-use the ones you have after each batch comes out of the oven, making sure to let the baking sheet cool first.

Walnut Shortbread Cookies

I made these one year at Christmas for the cookie tins I give out to the important people in my life. Nearly everyone who thanked me afterward remarked on these cookies in particular. They're more buttery than sweet, with a hint of maple. If you in live in New England, you'll no doubt have ready access to maple sugar, which is sold in most stores. If not, you can find it in well-stocked specialty stores, or you can buy it on-line (see Sources). **Makes 30 cookies**

1¼ cups walnuts
2 cups all-purpose flour
⅔ cup maple sugar (or ⅔ cup granulated sugar plus ½ teaspoon maple extract)
¼ teaspoon baking powder
¼ teaspoon salt
1 cup (2 sticks) unsalted butter, softened and cut into chunks
½ teaspoon almond extract

1. In a food processor, place the walnuts and 1 tablespoon of the flour. Whir until the nuts are finely chopped. Add the remaining flour, baking powder and salt, and the maple sugar (if substituting granulated sugar, add the maple extract at the same time); pulse to combine. Add the almond extract and butter. Whir a few seconds, then pulse just until the dough comes together (don't overprocess!). Scrape onto a sheet of plastic wrap. Wrap tightly and chill for at least 30 minutes.

2. Shortly before taking the dough out of the refrigerator, preheat the oven to 325°F.

3. Shape the chilled dough into 1½-inch balls and place about 2 inches apart on ungreased baking sheets. With the bottom of a glass dipped in maple or granulated sugar, slightly flatten each cookie. Bake in the oven for 20 to 25 minutes, until lightly golden. Let cool on the sheet for a minute or two before transferring to a wire rack.

Notes: *Many ovens won't comfortably accommodate more than one baking sheet at a time. For best results, bake separately.*

When baking cookies, such as these, that yield more than 2 dozen, you don't need more than two baking sheets. Simply re-use the ones you have after each batch comes out of the oven, making sure to let the baking sheet cool first.

Lime-Pistachio Cookies

On a recent trip to Victoria, British Columbia, my husband and I were lucky enough to snag a table at the popular Rebar Restaurant, known for its wholesome food and toothsome baked goods. I was quite taken with this cookie in particular, which I adapted using pistachio nuts in place of the pumpkin seeds called for in the original recipe.   **Makes 3½ dozen large cookies**

½ cup roughly chopped unsalted shelled pistachios

½ cup (1 stick) unsalted butter, softened

2 tablespoons vegetable oil or coconut oil

2 cups sugar

Zest from 2 limes

2 large eggs

4 tablespoons lime juice

3½ cups unbleached flour

1 teaspoon baking soda

1 teaspoon salt

1. Preheat the oven to 350°F. Grease 2 baking sheets.

2. Place the pistachios on an ungreased baking sheet, and toast in the oven for 3 to 4 minutes, until lightly golden. Set aside to cool while you prepare the dough.

3. In a large bowl, with an electric mixer on medium speed, cream the softened butter and oil with the sugar and zest. Add the eggs and lime juice, beating until well blended. In a small bowl, combine the flour, baking soda, and salt. Add to the creamed mixture, beating on low speed until incorporated; increase the speed to medium and beat until well blended. Stir in the chopped nuts.

4. Scoop by rounded tablespoons onto the baking sheets, placing about 2 inches apart. Flatten each slightly with the bottom of a glass dipped in sugar. Bake in the oven for 8 to 10 minutes, until very lightly golden. Let cool slightly on the sheet before transferring to a wire rack.

Note: *Most ovens won't comfortably accommodate more than one baking sheet at a time. For best results, bake separately.*

Gingerbread Cookies

I used to make these around the holidays when my kids were little. We'd cut them into shapes, decorate them, then wrap them in plastic wrap and hang them on the Christmas tree. For days afterward, the house would be filled with the mingled scents of gingerbread and evergreen. The only trick was to keep the ones on the lower branches from being eaten.

Makes about 3 dozen 3- to 4-inch cookies

¾ cup molasses
½ cup vegetable oil or coconut oil
⅓ cup firmly packed dark brown sugar
1 large egg
2¾ cups all-purpose flour
1 tablespoon baking powder
½ teaspoon salt
1 tablespoon ground cinnamon
1 tablespoon ground ginger
½ teaspoon ground cloves

1. In a large bowl, beat together the molasses, oil, brown sugar, and egg with an electric mixer on low speed. In a small bowl, combine the flour, baking powder, salt, cinnamon, ginger, and cloves. Add to the wet mixture, and beat at low speed just until the dry ingredients are incorporated; increase the speed to medium and mix until well blended, using your hands if the dough becomes stiff to beat. Cover the bowl tightly with plastic wrap and chill for several hours or overnight.

2. Shortly before rolling out the dough, preheat the oven to 350°F and grease 2 baking sheets.

3. Divide the dough in half and roll each half into a ball. Return 1 ball to the refrigerator while you roll out the other one. Place on a floured pastry cloth and press with the heel of your hand, shaping the edges to keep them even, to form about a 1-inch thick round. Roll out to a thickness of about ¼ inch. With a biscuit cutter or cookie cutters, cut into rounds or shapes. Repeat with the remaining ball of dough. Gather up the scraps; roll out and cut as above.

4. Set about 2 inches apart on the baking sheet, and bake in the oven for 8 to 10 minutes, just until the edges start to brown. Let the cookies cool slightly on the sheet before transferring to a wire rack.

Notes: Many ovens won't comfortably accommodate more than one baking sheet at a time. For best results, bake separately.

When baking cookies, such as these, that yield more than 2 dozen, you don't need more than two baking sheets. Simply re-use the ones you have after each batch comes out of the oven, making sure to let the baking sheet cool first.

Chocolate Sandwich Cookies

I think of these as grownup Oreos, with chocolate instead of cream filling. They're also good with a mint-cream filling, for those who remember Girl Scout cookies fondly. They require a little extra work, but you can enlist any kids on hand to help cut out the cookies and fill them once they're baked.   ***Makes 2 dozen sandwich cookies***

For the cookies

2 ounces unsweetened chocolate

½ cup (1 stick) unsalted butter, softened

½ cup sugar

1 large egg

3 tablespoons milk

1¾ cups all-purpose flour, sifted

1½ teaspoons baking powder

½ teaspoon salt

For the filling

1¾ cups confectioners' sugar, sifted

¼ cup unsweetened cocoa

½ teaspoon vanilla extract

3 to 4 tablespoons heavy cream

1. Place the chocolate in a small, microwave-safe bowl; heat in the microwave for 30 seconds at a time, stirring after each interval, until melted (about 1 minute total). Alternate method: Place in a bowl *over* (not in) boiling water removed from the heat, stirring occasionally until melted. Set aside to cool.

2. In a large bowl, cream the softened butter and sugar with an electric mixer on medium speed. Add the egg, and blend well. Add the milk and cooled chocolate, and beat until smooth. Combine the sifted flour, baking powder, and salt. Add to the creamed mixture, and stir or beat on low speed until it's incorporated; increase the speed to medium and beat until a dough forms. Gather the dough into a ball, cover tightly in plastic wrap, and chill for several hours or overnight.

3. Shortly before rolling out the dough, preheat the oven to 400°F.

4. Divide the dough in half, and shape each half into a ball. Return 1 ball to the refrigerator while you roll out the other one: Place on a floured pastry cloth and press with the heel of your hand, shaping the edges to keep them even, to form about a 1-inch thick round. Roll to a thickness of about ⅛ inch. With a floured 2-inch biscuit cutter, cut into rounds. Repeat with the remaining ball of dough. Gather up the scraps; roll and cut as above.

5. Set about 2 inches apart on ungreased baking sheets, and bake in the oven for 10 to 12 minutes, just until the edges begin to brown. Transfer to a wire rack. While the cookies are cooling, prepare the filling:

6. In a medium bowl, combine the confectioners' sugar and cocoa. Add the vanilla and 3 tablespoons of the cream, and beat with an electric mixer on low speed until it's incorporated. Increase the speed to medium and beat until smooth, dribbling in the remaining cream until spreading consistency. Place a dollop of filling on the *bottom* of 1 cookie, and sandwich with another cookie (bottoms together). Use just enough to create a generous filling that won't ooze out the sides when the cookie layers are gently pressed together. Repeat with the remaining cookies.

Variation: *For a mint-cream filling, eliminate the cocoa in the chocolate filling and increase the confectioners' sugar to 2 cups. Substitute ¼ teaspoon mint extract for the vanilla extract.*

Note: *Many ovens won't comfortably accommodate more than one baking sheet at a time. For best results, bake separately.*

Maple-Cream Sandwich Cookies

T hese cookies remind me of Christmas mornings growing up, when there was always a maple Santa in my stocking. They're a maple lover's dream, and so professional looking, anyone would think they came from a bakery. I make them only on special occasions, otherwise I'd be tempted to eat too many.

Makes 32 cookies

For the cookies

2¾ cups all-purpose flour

½ teaspoon baking soda

1 teaspoon salt

1 cup firmly packed light brown sugar

2 large eggs

1½ teaspoons maple extract

1 cup (2 sticks) unsalted butter, softened and cut into chunks

For the filling

2 cups confectioners' sugar

1 teaspoon maple extract

4 to 5 tablespoons heavy cream

1. *For the cookies:* Place the flour, baking soda, salt, and brown sugar in a food processor; whir to combine. Add the eggs, maple extract, and softened butter. Pulse just until the dough comes together. Scrape into a bowl, cover tightly with plastic wrap, and chill for several hours.

2. Alternate method: In a large bowl, cream the butter and sugar with an electric mixer on medium speed. Add the eggs one at a time, beating well after each addition. Blend in the maple extract. Combine the flour, baking soda, and salt. Add to the creamed mixture, and beat on low speed until it's incorporated; increase the speed to medium and beat until a dough forms. Chill as above.

3. Shortly before rolling out the dough, preheat the oven to 400°F.

4. Divide the dough in half, and shape each half into a ball. Return 1 ball to the refrigerator while you roll out the other one: Place on a floured pastry cloth and press with the heel of your hand, shaping the edges to keep them even, to form about a 1-inch thick round. Roll to a thickness of about ⅛ inch. With a floured 2-inch biscuit cutter, cut into rounds. Repeat with the remaining ball of dough. Gather up the scraps; roll and cut as above.

5. Bake in the oven for 7 to 10 minutes, until lightly golden. Transfer to a wire rack to cool.

6. *Meanwhile, prepare the filling:* In a medium bowl, with an electric mixer on low speed, blend the confectioners' sugar, maple extract, and 4 tablespoons of the cream. Increase the speed to medium, and beat until smooth, dribbling in the remaining cream until the filling is spreading consistency. Place a dollop of filling on the *bottom* of 1 cookie, and sandwich with another cookie (bottoms together). Use just enough to create a generous filling that won't ooze out the sides when the cookie layers are gently pressed together. Repeat with the remaining cookies.

Crunchy Peanut Cookies

B*eware: These cookies are addictive. I like them better than peanut-butter cookies because they contain whole, salted peanuts, a taste reminiscent of beer nuts. Adults and kids alike adore them.*   ***Makes 3½ dozen cookies***

1 cup (2 sticks) unsalted butter, softened

1½ cups firmly packed dark brown sugar

2 large eggs

2 teaspoons vanilla extract

3 cups all-purpose flour

½ teaspoon baking soda

½ teaspoon salt

10 ounces (2 cups) whole roasted, salted peanuts

Granulated sugar for garnish

1. In a large bowl, cream the softened butter and brown sugar with an electric mixer on medium speed. Add the eggs and vanilla, and beat until smooth. In another bowl, sift together the flour, baking soda, and salt. Add to the creamed mixture, beating on low speed until it's incorporated; increase the speed to medium and beat until smooth. Stir in the peanuts. Cover the bowl tightly with plastic wrap and chill for at least 15 minutes.

2. Shortly before taking the dough out of the refrigerator, preheat the oven to 375°F and grease 2 baking sheets.

3. Drop by rounded tablespoons about 2 inches apart onto the baking sheets. Flatten each with the bottom of a glass dipped in granulated sugar. Bake in the oven for 8 to 10 minutes, until lightly golden. Let cool slightly on the sheets before transferring to a wire rack.

Notes: *Many ovens won't comfortably accommodate more than one baking sheet at a time. For best results, bake separately.*

When baking cookies, such as these, that yield more than 2 dozen, you don't need more than two baking sheets. Simply re-use the ones you have after each batch comes out of the oven, making sure to let the baking sheet cool first.

Chocolate–Macadamia Nut Clusters

*I*f ever there was a cookie made for chocoholics, it's this one. Whole macadamia nuts and sweetened flaked coconut add crunch to this dense, candy bar–like treat that one of my tasters declared the best cookie he'd ever eaten.   *Makes 3½ dozen cookies*

8 ounces bittersweet or semisweet chocolate, chopped

¼ cup (½ stick) unsalted butter

1 cup sugar

2 large eggs

1½ teaspoons vanilla extract

3 tablespoons all-purpose flour

¼ teaspoon baking powder

8 ounces (1½ cups) whole unsalted macadamia nuts

1 cup semisweet chocolate chips

1 cup sweetened flaked coconut

1. Preheat the oven to 350°F. Grease 2 baking sheets.

2. Place the chocolate and butter in a small, microwave-safe bowl; heat covered, in the microwave for 30 seconds at a time, stirring after each interval (about 1½ minutes total), until melted. Alternate method: Place in a bowl over (not in) a pan of boiling water removed from the heat, stirring occasionally, until the chocolate and butter are melted. Set aside to cool.

3. In a large bowl, beat the sugar, eggs, and vanilla with an electric mixer on medium speed, until well blended. Add the cooled chocolate mixture, and beat until smooth. Mix in the flour and baking powder, and beat just until blended. Stir in the macadamia nuts, chocolate chips, and coconut.

4. Drop the dough by rounded tablespoons about 2 inches apart on the baking sheets. Bake in the oven for 8 to 10 minutes, until the edges are done and the centers are still soft (a

(continued)

Chocolate–Macadamia Nut Clusters *(continued)*

cookie should hold a depression when lightly pressed). Don't overbake, or you'll end up with chocolate rocks! The secret to these cookies is their chewy, fudge-like consistency. Let cool for a few minutes on the sheets before transferring to a wire rack.

Notes: *Many ovens won't comfortably accommodate more than one baking sheet at a time. For best results, bake separately.*

When baking cookies, such as these, that yield more than 2 dozen, you don't need more than two baking sheets. Simply re-use the ones you have after each batch comes out of the oven, making sure to let the baking sheet cool first.

Apricot Bars

This is my favorite kind of baked good—easy to make, yet so impressive-looking, it might have come from a Viennese pastry shop. The buttery shortbread crust is topped with a mousse-like apricot layer sprinkled with sliced almonds. Perfect for a fancy tea.

Makes 32 to 35 bars

⅔ cup dried apricots

½ cup (1 stick) unsalted butter, softened

1⅓ cups all-purpose flour

1¼ cups granulated sugar

½ teaspoon baking powder

¼ teaspoon salt

2 large eggs

½ teaspoon almond extract

¾ cup sliced or slivered almonds

Confectioners' sugar for dusting

1. Preheat the oven to 350°F. Line the bottom and 2 sides of an 8-inch square pan with aluminum foil cut to leave a 3- to 4-inch overhang at either end. Lightly grease the pan, including the foil.

2. Rinse the apricots well. Place them in a small bowl, and cover with boiling water. Let them soak while you prepare the crust.

3. Place the butter, 1 cup of the flour, and ¼ cup of the granulated sugar in a food processor. Whir until crumbly, just before the dough starts to stick together. Press firmly over the bottom of the prepared pan. Bake in the oven for 18 to 20 minutes, until lightly golden. Set aside to cool.

4. Place the remaining ⅓ cup of flour, 1 cup of sugar, the baking powder, salt, eggs, almond extract, and ½ cup of the almonds in the food processor (no need to wash it after the first use). Drain the apricots in a sieve (press with the back of a spoon to extract the liquid), and

(continued)

Apricot Bars *(continued)*

add to the flour mixture. Whir until smooth, about 1 minute. Spread over the cooled crust, and sprinkle with the remaining ¼ cup of almonds.

5. Return to the oven and bake for 20 to 25 minutes, until golden. Let cool thoroughly in the pan before lifting out, using the foil overhang as handles. Dust with confectioners' sugar and cut into squares.

Chocolate-Orange Bars

*I*f you love chocolate-covered orange peels, you'll love these bars. The crunchy shortbread crust infused with coffee flavor goes perfectly with the marmalade center and chocolate topping, making for that rarest of treats, the kind that blooms in your mouth, revealing itself layer by layer.

Makes about 2 dozen bars

½ cup (1 stick) unsalted butter, softened

¾ cup sugar

1 large egg yolk

1 cup all-purpose flour

1½ tablespoons finely ground coffee

½ teaspoon baking powder

¼ teaspoon salt

¾ cup orange marmalade

6 ounces semisweet or bittersweet chocolate, chopped

3 tablespoons heavy cream

1. Preheat the oven to 325°F.

2. In a large bowl, cream the butter and sugar with an electric mixer on medium speed. Add the egg yolk, and blend until smooth. In a small bowl, combine the flour, coffee, baking powder, and salt. Add to the creamed mixture, beating on low speed until incorporated; increase the speed to medium and beat until well blended. Press firmly over the bottom of an ungreased 9 × 12-inch baking pan (it forms a very thin layer that increases in volume as it bakes). Bake in the oven for 15 to 18 minutes, until golden.

3. Let the crust cool for 5 minutes, then spread with the marmalade. Let cool thoroughly.

4. In a small microwave-safe bowl, place the chopped chocolate (it doesn't have to be finely chopped; rough chunks are okay) and cream. Heat in the microwave for 30 seconds at a time, stirring after each interval (about 1½ minutes total), until melted. Alternate method: Place in a bowl *over* (not in) a pan of boiling water removed from the heat, stirring occasionally, until melted. (It's okay if some of the chunks aren't completely melted; they will continue melting as the mixture cools.) Spread evenly over the marmalade filling, working quickly before the chocolate mixture sets. Chill for 1 hour. Bring to room temperature before cutting into 2-inch bars or squares.

Date Bars

I've made and eaten many date bars in my time, and these are the best, bar none (no pun intended). I usually have half a dozen different kinds of cookies stored in the freezer at any given time, and when my husband is in the mood for something sweet, this is the first one he'll reach for. Thawed in the microwave, they're nearly as good as fresh from the oven.

Makes 3 dozen bars

1½ cups firmly packed dark brown sugar

1 tablespoon cornstarch

1½ cups finely chopped pitted dates (see Note)

1 cup sour cream

½ cup heavy cream

1 teaspoon maple extract

3 large egg yolks

1¼ cups all-purpose flour

2 cups quick-cooking rolled oats

½ teaspoon baking soda

¾ cup (1½ sticks) unsalted butter, cut into chunks

1. Preheat the oven to 350°F. Grease a 9 × 12-inch baking pan.

2. In a medium saucepan, combine ¾ cup of the brown sugar, the cornstarch, chopped dates, sour cream, heavy cream, maple extract, and egg yolks. Cook over medium heat, stirring constantly, until thickened. Remove from the heat, and let cool while you prepare the base/topping:

3. Place the flour, rolled oats, baking soda, and remaining ¾ cup brown sugar in a food processor; whir to combine. Add the butter, and pulse until the mixture is the consistency of coarse meal (the butter should be the size of small peas). Set aside 1½ cups, and press the remaining mixture over the bottom of the prepared pan. Bake in the oven for 10 minutes, until lightly golden. Set aside to cool.

4. Meanwhile, scrape the cooled filling into the food processor (no need to wash it after the first use); whir until smooth. Spread evenly over the cooled base. Sprinkle with the reserved flour-oat mixture. Return to the oven and bake for 20 to 30 minutes more, until golden brown. Allow to cool completely in the pan before cutting into bars.

Note: *If using a food processor to chop the dates, you can clean the blade and bowl easily afterward by whirring a slice of bread in it.*

Toffee-Almond Bars

T hese are so rich and chewy, they're almost a candy bar. A little bit goes a long way, so cut them small.   *Makes about 3 dozen bars*

1 cup (2 sticks) unsalted butter, softened
½ cup sugar
2 cups all-purpose flour
1¾ cups Skor English Toffee Bits
¾ cup light corn syrup
1 cup sliced almonds
¾ cup sweetened flaked coconut

1. Preheat the oven to 350°F. Grease the sides only of a 9 × 12-inch baking pan.

2. *For the crust:* In a large bowl, cream the butter and sugar with an electric mixer at medium speed. Add the flour, and beat at low speed until it's incorporated; increase the speed to medium, and beat until well blended. Press evenly over the bottom of the prepared pan. Bake in the oven for 15 to 20 minutes, until lightly golden.

3. *Meanwhile, prepare the topping:* In a medium saucepan, combine the toffee bits and corn syrup. Cook over low heat, stirring constantly, until the toffee bits are melted, 10 to 12 minutes. Remove from the heat, and stir in ½ cup of the almonds and ½ cup of the coconut. Spread evenly over the cooled crust to within ¼ inch of the edges (it spreads as it bakes). Sprinkle with the remaining ½ cup of almonds and ¼ cup of coconut. Return to the oven for 15 minutes more, and bake until bubbly. Cool thoroughly in the pan before cutting into bars.

Rainforest Bars

These are one of those everything-but-the-kitchen-sink bars—dense, chewy, and crunchy all at once. Put out a plate of these at any large gathering and they'll be gone before you can blink.

Makes about 2 dozen bars

½ cup (1 stick) plus 2 tablespoons unsalted butter, softened

4 cups (1 pound) light brown sugar

3 large eggs

2¾ cups all-purpose flour

2½ teaspoons baking powder

½ teaspoon salt

1 cup semisweet chocolate chips

⅔ cup chopped walnuts or pecans

½ cup sweetened flaked coconut

1. Preheat the oven to 325°F. Grease a 9 × 12-inch baking pan.

2. In a large bowl, cream the softened butter and light brown sugar with an electric mixer at medium speed. Add the eggs, and blend well. In a small bowl, combine the flour, baking powder, and salt. Add to the creamed mixture, mixing on low speed until incorporated; increase the speed to medium and beat until well blended. Stir in the chocolate chips, chopped nuts, and coconut. Press evenly over the bottom of the prepared pan. Bake in the oven for 30 to 35 minutes, until lightly golden but still soft. Cool slightly in the pan. Cut into squares while still warm. Cool thoroughly before removing from the pan.

Pecan Squares

*T*his recipe was sent to me by one of my readers, Annette Collier. I've tried other pecan squares, but I like these best—they're almost as dense and nutty as pecan pie. In fact, if you don't want to go to the trouble of baking a pie for Thanksgiving, make these squares instead.   ***Makes about 2 dozen 2-inch squares***

1 cup (2 sticks) unsalted butter, softened

1 cup light brown sugar

2 cups plus 1 tablespoon all-purpose flour

5 large eggs

2 cups dark brown sugar

1 tablespoon all-purpose flour

1 teaspoon vanilla extract

4 cups coarsely chopped pecans

1. Preheat the oven to 350°F. Grease a 9 × 12-inch baking pan.

2. *For the crust:* In a large bowl, cream the softened butter and light brown sugar with an electric mixer on medium speed. Add 2 cups of the flour, and mix on low speed until incorporated; increase the speed to medium, and mix until well-blended. With floured fingers, press evenly over the bottom of the pan. Bake in the oven for 20 minutes, until lightly golden. Set aside to cool.

3. *Meanwhile, prepare the topping:* In the same bowl (no need to wash it after the first use), place the eggs, dark brown sugar, remaining 1 tablespoon of flour, and the vanilla. Blend with the electric mixer on low speed until smooth. Stir in the chopped pecans. Pour the topping over the cooled crust, and return to the oven for 25 to 35 minutes more, until bubbly (the top will be quite brown). Cool thoroughly in the pan before cutting into 2-inch squares.

Ultimate Lemon Squares

There are many recipes for lemon squares, but this one stands out from the pack—it's the right balance of tart and sweet, with enough filling in proportion to the crust. My daughter, Mary, bakes them whenever she's over at our house. They're perfect for large parties.

Makes about 20 2-inch squares

½ cup (1 stick) unsalted butter, softened

⅓ cup confectioners' sugar, plus more for dusting

1 cup plus 2½ teaspoons all-purpose flour

3 large eggs, lightly beaten

1½ cups granulated sugar

6 tablespoons lemon juice

1 teaspoon lemon zest

1. Preheat the oven to 350°F. Grease an 8-inch square baking pan.

2. *For the crust:* In a medium bowl, cream the softened butter with an electric mixer on medium speed. Add the confectioners' sugar and 1 cup of the flour, and beat on low speed until incorporated; increase the speed to medium, and beat until well blended. Press the dough firmly over the bottom of the pan. Bake in the oven for 15 minutes, until lightly golden. Set aside to cool.

3. *Meanwhile, prepare the topping:* In a medium bowl, combine the eggs, granulated sugar, remaining 2½ teaspoons of flour, the lemon juice, and zest. Beat with the electric mixer on low speed until well blended. Spread over the cooled crust and return to the oven for 20 to 25 minutes more, until set. Let cool thoroughly in the pan before cutting into 2-inch squares. Dust with confectioners' sugar.

Raspberry-Marzipan Meringue Squares

*D*on't be fooled by the fluffy meringue topping: These squares pack a mean punch. The *unique blend of flavors and textures put them at the top of my list of favorites.*

Makes about 35 2-inch squares

1 cup (2 sticks) unsalted butter, softened

7 ounces almond paste

½ cup firmly packed light brown sugar

1 large egg

½ teaspoon almond extract

2 cups all-purpose flour

¾ cup raspberry jam

3 large egg whites

½ teaspoon cream of tartar

⅔ cup superfine sugar

1. Preheat the oven to 350°F. Line the bottom and 2 sides of a 9 × 12-inch baking pan with aluminum foil, leaving several inches of overhang on either side. Lightly grease the foil.

2. Place the butter, almond paste, and light brown sugar in a food processor; whir until smooth. Add the egg and almond extract, and whir to blend. Add the flour, and pulse just until a dough forms (don't overprocess!). Scrape into the pan, and spread evenly over the bottom.

3. Bake in the oven for 20 to 25 minutes, until lightly golden. Cool for 5 minutes, then spread with the jam.

4. Reduce the oven heat to 325°F.

5. In a large bowl, beat the egg whites and cream of tartar with an electric mixer on high speed until foamy. Add the superfine sugar a little at a time, beating until soft peaks form. Spread over the raspberry filling, swirling into peaks. Return to the oven and bake for 20 minutes more, until the meringue is set and golden. Let it cool completely before lifting it out of the pan, using the foil overhang as handles. Cut into 2-inch squares.

Note: Whatever you don't serve right away, place in an airtight container in the refrigerator, making sure the lid of the container isn't touching the meringue topping. Don't cover with plastic wrap! Place them in the freezer if storing for more than a few days.

Fudge Meltaways

A Goudge family favorite, these no-bake squares are more of a candy than a cookie. I used to make them for school bake sales, when I was growing up and when my kids were little, and they were always among the first offerings to go. Kids love them, as do adults with a sweet tooth.

Makes about 3 dozen 1-inch squares

¾ cup (1½ sticks) unsalted butter
3½ ounces unsweetened chocolate
¼ cup granulated sugar
2 teaspoons vanilla extract
1 large egg, lightly beaten
2 cups graham cracker crumbs
1 cup sweetened flaked coconut
½ cup chopped walnuts or pecans
2 cups sifted confectioners' sugar
1 tablespoon milk

1. *For the crust:* Place ½ cup of the butter and 1 ounce of the chocolate in a medium microwave-safe bowl; heat, covered, in the microwave for 30 seconds at a time, stirring after each interval (about 1½ minutes total), until melted. Alternate method: Place in a bowl *over* (not in) a pan of boiling water removed from the heat, stirring occasionally, until the butter and chocolate are melted. Add the granulated sugar, 1 teaspoon of the vanilla, the egg, graham cracker crumbs, coconut, and chopped nuts; stir until well blended. Press evenly over the bottom of an ungreased 9 × 12-inch baking pan. Chill while you prepare the topping.

2. In the same bowl (no need to wash it after the first use), place the remaining ¼ cup of butter, softened. Add the confectioners' sugar, milk, and remaining teaspoon of vanilla. Beat with the mixer on low speed until incorporated; increase the speed to medium and beat until well blended. Spread evenly over the chilled crust. Return to the refrigerator, and chill until firm.

3. *Meanwhile, prepare the chocolate glaze:* Melt the remaining 2½ ounces of chocolate and spread it over the filling. Chill until almost firm. Cut into 1-inch squares, and chill until completely firm.

Triple-Threat Brownies

This recipe was sent to me by a reader, Jolene Hampton White, and they're as heavenly as she promised. Though a little more work than plain brownies, they're well worth the effort. Note: You can tint the filling with food coloring, if you like—red or green at Christmastime makes them especially festive. ***Makes 2 to 2½ dozen brownies***

¾ cup (1½ sticks) plus 3 tablespoons unsalted butter

4 ounces unsweetened chocolate

3 large eggs

1½ cups granulated sugar

1 teaspoon instant espresso powder

1½ teaspoons vanilla extract

1 cup all-purpose flour

½ teaspoon salt

2½ cups confectioners' sugar

1½ to 3 tablespoons milk

½ teaspoon almond extract

¾ cup semisweet chocolate chips

1. Preheat the oven to 350°F. Grease a 9-inch square baking pan.

2. Place the unsweetened chocolate and ½ cup of the butter in a medium microwave-safe bowl; heat, covered, in the microwave for 30 seconds at a time, stirring after each interval (about 1½ minutes total), until melted. Alternate method: Place in a bowl *over* (not in) a pan of boiling water removed from the heat, stirring occasionally until melted. Set aside to cool.

3. Meanwhile, beat the eggs and granulated sugar with an electric mixer on low speed. Mix the espresso powder with 1 teaspoon of boiling water to form a sludge. Add to the sugar-egg mixture along with the cooled chocolate mixture and vanilla. Beat until smooth. Add the flour and salt, and beat on low speed until incorporated; increase the speed to medium and beat until smooth. Pour into the pan. Bake in the oven for 20 to 25 minutes,

(continued)

Triple-Threat Brownies *(continued)*

until a toothpick inserted into the center comes out with only a few moist crumbs stuck to it. Let cool thoroughly in the pan, at least 1 hour.

4. In a small bowl, with the electric mixer on low speed, cream ¼ cup of the remaining butter, softened, with the confectioners' sugar. Dribble in the milk as you continue beating until the filling is spreading consistency. Blend in the almond extract. Spread evenly over the cooled brownie base and chill for 1 hour.

5. Melt the semisweet chocolate chips and the remaining 3 tablespoons of butter using the same method as for the unsweetened chocolate. Working quickly, spread the mixture evenly over the filling. Chill until firm, about 30 to 45 minutes. Let the brownies come to room temperature before cutting into squares. Use a sharp knife, dipped in hot water then wiped dry, to make nice clean cuts.

Kahlúa Brownies with Homemade Kahlúa

I've gotten more feedback on these brownies than for any other recipe on my Web site, except my banana bread. They're a cinch to make, yet they live long in memory. Plus, they keep well—they're even better a day or two later. If you're feeling particularly adventurous, you can even make your own Kahlúa (see the recipe below), which requires just a few simple steps and some patience. Around the holidays, when I have time, I put up a gallon or so of homemade Kahlúa, which I then transfer to inexpensive, decorative bottles from Pier 1 Imports to give away as gifts. The rest I save for baking. **Makes about 2 dozen brownies**

¾ cup (1½ sticks) unsalted butter

4 ounces unsweetened chocolate

4 large eggs

2 cups granulated sugar

¼ cup Kahlúa or other coffee-flavored liqueur

1¼ cups all-purpose flour

½ teaspoon baking powder

½ teaspoon salt

Confectioners' sugar for dusting

1 cup chopped walnuts or pecans (optional)

1. Preheat the oven to 350°F. Grease a 9 × 12-inch baking pan.

2. Place the butter and chocolate in a medium microwave-safe bowl; heat in the microwave, covered, for 30 seconds at a time, stirring after each interval (about 1½ minutes total), until melted. Alternate method: Place in a bowl *over* (not in) a pan of boiling water removed from the heat, stirring occasionally, until melted. Set aside to cool.

3. Meanwhile, beat the eggs and sugar with an electric mixer on low speed until pale and lemon-colored. Blend in the Kahlúa and cooled chocolate mixture, beating until smooth. Add the flour, baking powder, and salt. Beat on low speed until incorporated; increase the

(continued)

speed to medium and beat *just until blended*. Don't overmix! Stir in the chopped nuts, if using.

4. Pour into the pan, smoothing even with a spatula. Bake in the oven for 25 to 30 minutes, until a toothpick inserted into the center comes out with only a few moist crumbs stuck to it. Cool in the pan before cutting into squares. Dust with confectioners' sugar.

Homemade Kahlúa

Makes ½ gallon; allow 4 weeks to cure

4 cups sugar
2-ounce jar instant coffee crystals
Fifth of vodka

In a stockpot or 4-quart saucepan, combine the sugar and 4 cups of cold water. Bring to a boil over high heat. Add the coffee crystals a little at a time, stirring until dissolved. Lower the heat and simmer, uncovered, for about 2 hours, until syrupy. Let it cool several hours or overnight, until room temperature. Pour the cooled syrup into a clean glass gallon jug. Add the vodka and swirl gently to blend. Let it stand undisturbed in a cool, dark place for a minimum of 4 weeks.

Pies and Tarts

"Not even an itty bitty taste?" Clive gazed longingly at the pie in Erin's hands.

"The next one will have your name on it," she promised.

"Cruelty, thy name is woman." The landlord heaved a sigh of resignation. One of his more eccentric traits was dressing up in uniforms, of which he had an extensive collection. Today's was an Italian garde's, complete with crimson beret that sat at a rakish angle atop his ivory mane. Though with his blue eyes heavily lined with kohl the effect was more that of an aging silent film star. "Did anyone ever tell you you'd make a great dominatrix?"

"No. But if I don't find a job soon, it's something to keep in mind," she replied with a laugh.

—From *Otherwise Engaged*

A Word About Fruit Pies

When it comes to fruit, I have a simple rule: Buy in season. Fruits like cherries and apricots—even those shipped from sunnier climes—taste more like wax fruit if you buy them in January, and, to add insult to injury, they cost an arm and a leg. Even with produce that's in season you have to be selective, especially in supermarkets where much of the fruit is picked green and shipped long distances (which is why I buy fruit at our local greenmarket whenever possible): If it doesn't pass the sniff test, pass it up. A peach or melon without a trace of scent will be equally tasteless. Appearances can also be deceiving: Chances are that shiny red apple won't be as crisp and sweet as the misshapen one with the dusky bloom from the farmstand down the road.

For obvious reasons, summer is my favorite time of the year for baking fruit pies. But what to do with that bushel of peaches all ripening at once? If you have limited freezer space, like me, freezing whole pies isn't really an option. How then to enjoy an apricot or peach pie in winter? Simple: Freeze just the filling. Line a pie plate with aluminum foil, placing the same size sheet of plastic wrap over the foil (to keep the filling from sticking to it), and making sure there's enough overhang to bring the ends together to form a seal. Prepare the filling as called for in the recipe, only instead of placing it in an unbaked crust, spoon it directly into the foil and plastic wrap–lined pie plate. Freeze several hours or overnight, then remove the filling from the pie plate, and place it in a zip-top freezer bag. The rounds can then be stacked in your freezer like Frisbees. (Be sure to label them.) When you have unexpected company or you're in the mood for a pie, all you have to do is prepare and roll out the dough (for a two-crust pie), pop in the round of frozen filling, and bake. Note: Add an extra half hour to the baking time when using frozen filling.

Never-Fail Pie Dough   ✎

*T*he key to a stellar pie is its crust, and this recipe lives up to its name: It delivers a perfect crust every time. I make a double batch whenever I have free time and freeze it for later use. Note: Don't be put off by the use of lard; it's lower in fat and cholesterol than butter and the non-hydrogenated kind contains none of the bad trans-fatty acids. It also makes for the flakiest crusts known to mankind. For the healthiest alternative, buy non-hydrogenated whenever possible (see Sources).   **Makes enough for one 9-inch double-crust pie**

2 cups all-purpose flour
¾ teaspoon salt
1 tablespoon sugar
1½ teaspoons baking powder
¾ cup (6 ounces) chilled lard or 6 tablespoons lard
    and 6 tablespoons unsalted butter (see Note), chilled
1½ teaspoons cider vinegar
1 large egg, beaten

1. Place the flour, salt, sugar, and baking powder in a food processor, and whir to combine. Add the lard, in chunks. Whir for several seconds, then pulse until crumbly but not pulverized. Dump into a large bowl. Alternate method: Place the above ingredients in a large bowl, and cut with a pastry cutter until crumbly.

2. Whisk the vinegar and beaten egg with 3½ tablespoons of cold water. Add to the flour mixture all at once. Whisk vigorously with a fork *just until the dough comes together* (be very careful not to overmix, as this will result in a tough crust). Shape into a ball. Cut in half, and gently shape each half into a ball. Wrap individually in plastic wrap and chill for at least 30 minutes. (It keeps well in the refrigerator for up to a week; in the freezer for several

(continued)

Never-Fail Pie Dough *(continued)*

months.) When thawing frozen dough, place in the refrigerator overnight, then leave at room temperature for 30 minutes before rolling out.

Notes: *You can make this dough with a combination of half lard, half butter, or all butter, if you wish. If neither is available, vegetable shortening (such as Crisco stick shortening) will suffice, either as a substitute for the lard or in combination with the butter.*

To make enough for two double-crust pies, double all the ingredients except the egg and increase the water to ½ cup.

A Word About Crumb Crusts

A nifty trick for delivering the perfect crumb crust every time is one I learned from baking maven Maida Heatter, who generously permitted me to use it herein. Though advance preparation is required, it takes very little extra work. The bonus is that it simplifies the serving process, which is key when entertaining, and ensures a beautiful presentation.

Flip a pie plate over so that the bottom side is facing up. Cover it with a 12-inch square of aluminum foil, shiny side down, and mold the foil to the shape of the pie plate. Remove and turn the pie plate right side up. Gently, without bending the foil shell, place it in the pie plate, turning the edges under to fit the rim while holding it anchored with a folded dishtowel.

Make the crust according to the recipe, only instead of pressing the crumbs directly onto the pie plate, press them onto the foil shell, using the following method: Distribute the crumbs evenly, pressing firmly with your fingertips over the sides to a height of about ½ inch above the rim before pressing over the bottom, making sure there are no loose crumbs. Bake as directed.

When the crust is cooled, cover lightly with plastic wrap and place in the freezer. Freeze for several hours or preferably overnight, until solid. Remove from the freezer and carefully lift the shell from the pie plate. Holding it from underneath with the flat of one hand, carefully rotate while peeling off the foil shell; it should come away in one piece, not in strips. (If the crust is frozen solid, it won't crumble.) Gently lower the crust into the pie plate, and proceed according to the recipe.

If you don't have the time for advance preparation, butter the pie plate before pressing the crumbs onto it. This will keep the finished crust from sticking when you serve the pie.

Perfect Apple Pie

*I*s it any wonder that eight out of ten Americans name apple pie as their favorite dessert? Over the years I've made dozens, and with each one I've tweaked the recipe a bit more, until now it's about as close to perfect as an apple pie can get: one that's generously filled and not overly sweet, with the caramelized taste of a tarte Tatin and a flaky crust that holds up at both ends. *Makes one 9-inch double-crust pie, serving 6 to 8*

8 cups peeled, cored, and sliced apples (tart varieties such as McIntosh,
    Jonathan, Greening, and Granny Smith yield the best texture and flavor.
    Whenever possible, I use a combination of the above), about 8 to 10 large apples
1 tablespoon lemon juice
1 cup Sucanat, Demerara, or turbinado sugar (I prefer Sucanat, which is richer
    in molasses flavor). If none of the above are available, substitute 1 cup dark brown sugar,
    or 1 cup granulated sugar plus 1 tablespoon molasses
4 to 5 tablespoons all-purpose flour (depending on the juiciness of the apples)
1 teaspoon ground cinnamon
1/8 teaspoon ground nutmeg, preferably freshly grated
1 large egg
Never-Fail Pie Dough (page 133–4) for a double 9-inch crust
1 tablespoon unsalted butter, chilled
Granulated sugar for garnish

1. In a large bowl, toss the apple slices with the lemon juice. Add the Sucanat, flour, cinnamon, and nutmeg. With a large spoon or spatula (I use my hands), toss until the apples are coated.

2. Place the dough for the bottom crust on a floured pastry cloth. Flatten by pressing down with the heel of your hand, shaping the edges to keep them from becoming ragged, until it forms about an inch or so thick round. With a rolling pin, roll (from the center outward) into a circle roughly 11 inches in diameter. Carefully fold in half, then again, to form a triangle. Place in an ungreased 9-inch pie plate, positioning it so the point of the triangle is in the center of the pie plate. Gently unfold. Trim the edges to within 1½ inches or so of the rim.

3. Whisk the egg with 1 teaspoon of water. Lightly brush over the bottom and sides of the rolled dough with a pastry brush, just enough to glaze it. Spoon in the filling, and pat it into a mound. Dot with the chilled butter.

4. Roll out the top crust the same as for the bottom crust. Transfer to the pie plate, and with a sharp knife or kitchen shears, trim the overhang to within an 1 inch or so of the rim. Roll the bottom and top edges inward, pressing lightly to seal; with your thumb, indent at regular intervals to form a single fluted edge. With the tip of a sharp knife, cut vents in the center of the top crust (I make mine in a four-pointed star pattern).

5. Preheat the oven to 375°F.

6. Place the pie in the freezer for at least 15 minutes (it freezes well for up to a month), until the dough is firm (for longer storage, wrap tightly in plastic wrap once it's firm). Using aluminum foil cut into 2-inch strips, form a collar around the fluted edge of the dough (this will keep it from browning too quickly), crimping it to hold it in place. Brush with the remaining egg glaze (you won't need it all). Sprinkle with granulated sugar, just enough to lend some sparkle.

7. Bake in the oven for 15 minutes (see Note). Lower the temperature to 350°F and bake for 50 to 55 minutes more, or until the filling is tender but not mushy (it should give way when the tip of a sharp knife is inserted in one of the vents). If it's browning too quickly, place a sheet of aluminum foil lightly over the top. The foil "collar" remains in place throughout baking; the fluted edge bakes perfectly underneath. Place on a wire rack to cool. When cool enough to handle, gently peel away the foil strips. Serve warm or at room temperature.

Note: If the pie is frozen solid, add an additional 30 minutes to the baking time. Lightly cover with foil halfway through baking.

Berry Medley Pie

What says summer more than a berry pie? I haunt our local greenmarket during the summer months, pouncing on whatever's in season. On a recent trip to the San Juan Islands, in Washington state, where blackberries grow wild alongside the road, I thought I'd died and gone to heaven. I prevailed upon the owners of the bed and breakfast my husband and I were staying at to let me use their kitchen so I could bake a pie. To Charles and Valerie Binford of The Place at Cayou Cove, on Orcas Island, I will be eternally grateful.

Makes one 9-inch double-crust pie, serving 6 to 8

**2 cups each fresh or unthawed frozen blueberries, blackberries, and
      raspberries (you can substitute sliced strawberries for one of the berries,
      or use 3 cups each of just two kinds of berries)**
1½ cups sugar
3½ tablespoons Minute Tapioca or tapioca starch (see Notes)
¼ teaspoon salt
⅛ teaspoon ground cinnamon
2 tablespoons lemon juice
Never-Fail Pie Dough (page 133–4) for a double 9-inch crust
1 large egg
1 tablespoon unsalted butter, chilled

1. Place the washed and well-drained berries in a large bowl. If using frozen berries, don't wash them; simply break them up with your hands (this is easier if you let them thaw at room temperature for 10 minutes or so).

2. Add the sugar, tapioca, salt, cinnamon, and lemon juice to the berries and gently toss (I use my fingers) until the berries are coated. Let them stand for 15 to 20 minutes, gently stirring once or twice to keep tapioca lumps from forming. (Eliminate this step if using tapioca starch.)

3. Meanwhile, place the dough for the bottom crust on a floured pastry cloth. Flatten by pressing down with the heel of your hand, shaping the edges to keep them from becoming ragged, until it forms about an inch or so thick round. With a rolling pin, roll (from the center outward) into a circle roughly 11 inches in diameter. Carefully fold in half, then again, to form a triangle. Place in an ungreased 9-inch pie plate, positioning it so the point of the triangle is in the center of the pie plate. Gently unfold. Trim the overhang to within 1½ inches or so of the rim.

4. Whisk the egg with 1 teaspoon of water. Lightly brush over the bottom and sides of the rolled dough with a pastry brush, just enough to glaze it. Spoon in the filling. Dot with the chilled butter.

5. For a latticed top crust: Follow the directions for rolling out the bottom crust. Cut the round into strips ½- to ¾-inch wide. Gently transfer half the strips, one at a time, to the filling, placing them about ¾ to 1 inch apart, using the longer ones for the center and the shorter ones for the sides. Rotate the pie, and repeat with the remaining strips at the opposite angle to create a lattice. With a sharp knife or kitchen shears, trim the overhang to within 1 inch or so of the rim; fold the bottom and top edges inward, and press lightly to seal; with your thumb, indent at regular intervals to create a single fluted edge.

6. Preheat the oven to 375°F.

7. Place the pie in the freezer for at least 15 minutes (it freezes well for up to a month), until the dough is firm (if freezing for a longer period, wrap tightly in plastic wrap once it's firm). Using aluminum foil cut into 2-inch wide strips, form a collar around the fluted edge (this will keep it from browning too quickly), crimping it to hold it in place. Brush the lattice top with the remaining egg mixture (you won't need it all). Lightly sprinkle with granulated sugar, if desired.

8. Bake in the oven for 1¼ hours (1½ hours, if you're using frozen berries) until the syrup bubbling up through the lattice forms heavy bubbles that don't burst. If it's browning too quickly, cover lightly with aluminum foil the last 15 minutes of baking (see Notes). Place on a wire rack to cool. When cool enough to handle, gently peel away the foil strips. Serve at room temperature.

Notes: I prefer tapioca starch to Minute Tapioca. It thickens the filling nicely without the risk of lumps forming. If it's not available in your area, you can buy it on-line at kalustyans.com (see Sources).

The foil "collar" can remain on throughout baking; the fluted edge bakes perfectly underneath.

Blackberry-Peach Pie

*P**eaches and blackberries are two of my favorite fruits, so what better than a combination of the two? This pie is one of my more inspired creations, according to those who've tried it. You don't even have to wait until peaches and berries are in season; it tastes equally good when made with frozen fruit. My friend Jon loves it, so he baked it for Thanksgiving.*

Makes one 9-inch double-crust pie, serving 6 to 8

3 cups peeled and sliced fresh, or unthawed frozen, peaches

3 cups fresh or unthawed frozen blackberries

1½ cups sugar

3½ tablespoons Minute Tapioca or tapioca starch (see Notes)

¼ teaspoon salt

2 tablespoons lemon juice

Never Fail Pie Dough (page 133–4) for a double 9-inch crust

1 large egg

1 tablespoon unsalted butter, chilled

1. Place the sliced peaches and blackberries in a large bowl. If using frozen fruit, don't wash it; simply break it apart (this is easier if you let it thaw at room temperature for 10 minutes or so) and cut up the larger peach slices into smaller ones.

2. Add the sugar, tapioca, salt, and lemon juice, and gently toss (I use my fingers) until the fruit is coated. Let it stand for 15 to 20 minutes, gently stirring once or twice to keep tapioca lumps from forming. (Eliminate this step if using tapioca starch.)

3. Meanwhile, place the dough for the bottom crust on a floured pastry cloth. Flatten by pressing down with the heel of your hand, shaping the edges to keep them from becoming ragged, until it forms about an inch or so thick round. With a rolling pin, roll (from the center outward) into a circle roughly 11 inches in diameter. Carefully fold in half, then again, to form a triangle. Place in an ungreased 9-inch pie plate, positioning it so the point of the triangle is in the center of the pie plate. Gently unfold. Trim the overhang to within 1½ inches or so of the rim.

4. Whisk the egg with 1 teaspoon of water. Lightly brush over the bottom and sides of the rolled dough with a pastry brush, just enough to glaze it. Spoon in the filling. Dot with the chilled butter.

5. For a latticed top crust: Follow the directions for rolling out the bottom crust. Cut the round into strips ½- to ¾-inch wide. Gently transfer half the strips, one at a time, to the filling, placing them about ¾ to 1 inch apart, using the longer ones for the center and the shorter ones for the sides. Rotate the pie, and repeat with the remaining strips at the opposite angle to create a lattice. With a sharp knife or kitchen shears, trim the overhang to within 1 inch or so of the rim; roll the bottom and top edges inward, and press lightly to seal; with your thumb, indent at regular intervals to create a single fluted edge.

6. Preheat the oven to 375°F.

7. Place the pie in the freezer for at least 15 minutes (it freezes well for up to a month), until the dough is firm (if freezing for a longer period, wrap tightly in plastic wrap once it's firm). Using aluminum foil cut into 2-inch wide strips, form a collar around the fluted edge (this will keep it from browning too quickly), crimping it to hold it in place. Brush the lattice with the remaining egg mixture (you won't need it all). Lightly sprinkle with granulated sugar, if desired.

8. Bake in the oven for 1¼ hours (1½ hours, if you're using frozen fruit), until the syrup bubbling up through the lattice forms heavy bubbles that don't burst. Cover lightly with aluminum foil the last 15 minutes of baking if browning too quickly (see Notes). Place on a wire rack to cool. When cool enough to handle, gently peel away the foil strips. Serve at room temperature.

Notes: I prefer tapioca starch to Minute Tapioca. It thickens the filling nicely without the risk of lumps forming. If it's unavailable in your area, you can order it on-line at kalustyans.com (see Sources).

The foil "collar" can remain on throughout baking; the fluted edge bakes perfectly underneath.

Strawberry-Rhubarb Pie

*I*n a previous life, when I was a young bride living in British Columbia with my first hus-band, I discovered to my delight that the pesky "weed" that kept cropping up in my backyard was, in fact, rhubarb. Though nothing beats rhubarb fresh from the garden, any kind, even frozen, tastes pretty darn good in a pie (just be sure to discard the leafy tops, which are poison-ous). Combined with strawberries, you have a marriage made in pie heaven.

Makes one 9-inch double-crust pie, serving 6 to 8

4 cups rhubarb (preferably fresh) cut into 1-inch pieces

2 cups hulled and sliced strawberries (see Notes)

1½ cups sugar

3½ tablespoons Minute Tapioca or tapioca starch (see Notes)

¼ teaspoon salt

2 teaspoons lemon juice

Never-Fail Pie Dough (page 133–4) for a double 9-inch crust

1 large egg

1 tablespoon unsalted butter, chilled

1. Place the rhubarb and strawberries in a large bowl. Add the sugar, tapioca, salt, and lemon juice, and gently toss (I use my fingers) until the fruit is coated. Let it stand for 15 to 20 minutes, gently stirring it once or twice to keep tapioca lumps from forming. (Eliminate this step if using tapioca starch.)

2. Meanwhile, place the dough for the bottom crust on a floured pastry cloth. Flatten it by pressing down with the heel of your hand, shaping the edges to keep them from becoming ragged, until it forms about an inch or so thick round. With a rolling pin, roll (from the center outward) into a circle roughly 11 inches in diameter. Carefully fold in half, then again, to form a triangle. Place in an ungreased 9-inch pie plate, positioning it so the point of the triangle is in the center of the pie plate. Gently unfold. Trim the overhang to within 1½ inches or so of the rim.

3. Whisk the egg with 1 teaspoon of water. Lightly brush over the bottom and sides of the rolled dough with a pastry brush, just enough to glaze it. Spoon in the filling. Dot with the butter.

4. For a latticed top crust, follow the directions for rolling out the bottom crust. Cut the round into strips ½- to ¾-inch wide. Gently transfer half the strips, one at a time, to the filling, placing them about ¾ to 1 inch apart, using the longer ones for the center and the shorter ones for the sides. Rotate the pie, and repeat with the remaining strips at the opposite angle to create a lattice. With a sharp knife or kitchen shears, trim the overhang to within 1 inch or so of the rim; roll the bottom and top edges inward, press lightly to seal; with your thumb, indent around at regular intervals to create a single fluted edge.

5. Preheat the oven to 375°F.

6. Place the pie in the freezer for at least 15 minutes (it freezes well for up to a month), until the dough is firm (if freezing for a longer period, wrap tightly in plastic wrap once it's firm). Using aluminum foil cut into 2-inch wide strips, form a collar around the fluted edge (this will keep it from browning too quickly), crimping it to hold it in place. Brush the lattice with the remaining egg mixture (you won't need it all). Lightly sprinkle with granulated sugar, if desired.

7. Bake in the oven for 1¼ hours (1½ hours, if the pie is frozen), until the syrup bubbling up through the lattice forms heavy bubbles that don't burst. If it's browning too quickly, cover lightly with aluminum foil the last 15 minutes of baking (see Notes). Place on a wire rack to cool. When cool enough to handle, gently peel away the foil strips. Serve at room temperature.

Notes: A nifty way to hull strawberries is to push a drinking straw through the bottom (pointy end) of each and out through the top; the stem and leaves pop right off.

I prefer tapioca starch to Minute Tapioca. It thickens the filling nicely without the risk of lumps forming. If it's unavailable in your area, you can order it on-line at kalustyans.com (see Sources).

The foil "collar" can remain on throughout baking; the fluted edge bakes perfectly underneath.

Farmstand Cherry Pie

For my husband, this cherry pie brings back memories of his childhood summers in Vermont. The really nice thing about it is that you can have it any time of the year, since it's made with jarred sour cherries.   *Makes one 9-inch double-crust pie, serving 6 to 8*

Two 24-ounce jars sour cherries (about 5 cups)
1¼ cups granulated sugar
4 tablespoons Minute Tapioca or tapioca starch (see Notes)
1½ teaspoons red food coloring
½ teaspoon almond extract
Never-Fail Pie Dough (page 133–4) for a double 9-inch crust
1 large egg
1 tablespoon unsalted butter, chilled

1. Drain the cherries, reserving 1 cup of the juice. Place in a large bowl, and stir in the sugar, tapioca, food coloring, and almond extract. Let it stand for 15 to 20 minutes, stirring once or twice to keep tapioca lumps from forming. (You can eliminate this step if using tapioca starch.)

2. Meanwhile, place the dough for the bottom crust on a floured pastry cloth. Flatten it by pressing down with the heel of your hand, shaping the edges to keep them from becoming ragged, until it forms about an inch or so thick round. With a rolling pin, roll (from the center outward) into a circle roughly 11 inches in diameter. Carefully fold in half, then again, to form a triangle. Place in an ungreased 9-inch pie plate, positioning it so the point of the triangle is in the center of the pie plate. Gently unfold. Trim the overhang to within 1½ inches or so of the rim.

3. Whisk the egg with 1 teaspoon of water. Lightly brush over the bottom and sides of the rolled dough with a pastry brush, just enough to glaze it. Spoon in the filling. Dot with the chilled butter.

4. For a latticed top crust, follow the directions for rolling out the bottom crust. Cut the round into strips ½- to ¾-inch wide. Gently transfer half the strips, one at a time, to the filling, placing them about ¾ to 1 inch apart, using the longer ones for the center and the shorter ones for the sides. Rotate the pie, and repeat with the remaining strips at the opposite angle to create a lattice. With a sharp knife or kitchen shears, trim the overhang to within 1 inch or so of the rim; roll the bottom and top edges inward, and press lightly to seal; with your thumb, indent around at regular intervals to create a single fluted edge.

5. Preheat the oven to 375°F.

6. Place the pie in the freezer for at least 15 minutes (it freezes well for up to a month), until the dough is firm (if freezing for a longer period, wrap tightly in plastic wrap once it's firm). Using aluminum foil cut into 2-inch wide strips, form a collar around the fluted edge (this will keep it from browning too quickly), crimping it to hold it in place. Brush the lattice with the remaining egg mixture (you won't need it all). Lightly sprinkle with granulated sugar, if desired.

7. Bake in the oven for 1 to 1¼ hours (1½ hours, if the pie is frozen), until the syrup bubbling up through the lattice forms heavy bubbles that don't burst. If it's browning too quickly, cover lightly with foil the last 15 minutes of baking (see Notes). Place on a wire rack to cool. When cool enough to handle, gently peel away the foil strips. Serve at room temperature.

Notes: *I prefer tapioca starch to Minute Tapioca. It thickens nicely without the risk of lumps forming. If it's unavailable in your area, you can order it on-line at kalustyans.com (see Sources).*

The foil "collar" can remain on throughout baking; the fluted edge bakes perfectly underneath.

Chilled Peach Pie

A *"sink" peach is one so juicy you have to eat it over a sink to keep the juices from running down your chin. With peaches that luscious, it seems almost a shame to bake them. Try this chilled variation instead, which takes full advantage of peach season in all its glory.*

Makes one 9-inch single-crust pie, serving 6 to 8

For the crust

1½ cups graham cracker crumbs

3 tablespoons sugar

⅛ teaspoon ground cinnamon

Pinch of ground nutmeg

4 tablespoons unsalted butter, melted

For the filling

5 cups peeled, sliced firm-ripe peaches (see Note)

¾ cup orange juice, preferably fresh

¼ cup cornstarch

¾ cup granulated sugar (a bit less, if the peaches are especially sweet)

¼ cup lemon juice

One 8-ounce package cream cheese, softened

½ cup confectioners' sugar

1. Preheat the oven to 375°F. Lightly butter a 9-inch pie plate.

2. *For the crust:* In a small bowl, combine the graham cracker crumbs, the sugar, cinnamon, nutmeg, and melted butter. Press the mixture firmly over the bottom and sides of the pie plate (or use the method on page 135). Bake in the oven for 6 to 8 minutes, until lightly golden. Set it aside to cool while you prepare the filling.

3. *For the filling:* In a blender, whir together 1 cup of the sliced peaches, the orange juice, cornstarch, and sugar. Place in a medium saucepan and cook over medium-high heat, stirring constantly, until the mixture boils and thickens enough to generously coat a spoon (the consistency of baby food). Remove from the heat, and stir in the lemon juice. Let it cool to warm, then add the remaining peach slices; toss gently (I use my fingers). Set aside to cool until lukewarm, about 20 to 25 minutes.

4. Place the softened cream cheese and confectioners' sugar in a medium bowl; beat with an electric mixer at low speed just until blended. Increase the speed to medium and beat until well blended. Scrape into the cooled pie crust and smooth even. Scrape the cooled peach mixture over the cream cheese mixture. Chill, uncovered, for several hours or overnight.

Note: A quick and effective way to peel peaches is to blanch them first in a stockpot of boiling water for 2 to 3 minutes. Rinse them under cold water, and the skins will slip right off.

Lemon Chiffon Pie

When I was growing up, if my mother happened to drive by a house with a lemon tree in the yard—this was California, after all—she'd pull over, knock on the door, and ask the owner if she could buy some of his or her lemons. If it was a large enough tree, the owner was usually happy to have us pick as many as we liked, free of charge. I can still remember the scent of fresh-picked lemons filling our station wagon. This light, summery pie, one of my mom's oft-made recipes, is that memory made edible.   ***Makes one 9-inch single-crust pie, serving 6 to 8***

For the crust

1½ cups graham cracker crumbs

3 tablespoons sugar

⅛ teaspoon ground cinnamon

Pinch of ground nutmeg

4 tablespoons unsalted butter, melted

For the filling

1 envelope (2¼ teaspoons) unflavored gelatin

½ cup granulated sugar

Dash of salt

4 large eggs, separated (see Note)

½ cup fresh lemon juice

½ cup fresh orange juice

1 teaspoon lemon zest

⅓ cup confectioners' sugar

Lemon slices for garnish (optional)

1. Preheat the oven to 375°F. Lightly butter a 9-inch pie plate.

2. ***For the crust:*** Combine the graham cracker crumbs, sugar, cinnamon, nutmeg, and melted butter. Press the mixture firmly over the bottom and sides of the pie plate (or use the method on page 135). Bake in the oven for 6 to 8 minutes, or until lightly golden. Set it aside to cool while you prepare the filling.

3. *For the filling:* In a medium saucepan, combine the gelatin, sugar, and salt. In a small bowl, beat together the egg yolks, lemon juice, orange juice, and ¼ cup of water. Stir into the sugar-gelatin mixture. Cook over medium heat, stirring constantly, just until the mixture starts to boil. Remove from the heat and stir in the zest. Chill, stirring occasionally, until the mixture forms a soft mound when dropped from a spoon, 20 to 40 minutes. (Keep a close watch, as it gels quickly once it begins to set. If this happens, reheat the mixture and chill again.)

4. In a medium bowl, beat the egg whites with an electric mixer on high speed until soft peaks form. Gradually add the confectioners' sugar, beating until stiff peaks form. Gently fold in the chilled gelatin mixture, repeatedly cutting down the middle and up one side with a spatula. Pour into the cooled pie shell. Chill, uncovered, for several hours or overnight. Garnish with wafer-thin lemon slices cut into halves or fourths, if desired.

Note: It's easier to separate eggs when they're chilled.

Seedless Grape Chiffon Pie

This is one of only two desserts my sister Patty makes. With something this show-stopping, she insists she need not expand her repertoire. Once you've tried it, you'll see why. The vanilla wafer crust and chiffon filling studded with green grapes that crunch satisfyingly between your teeth make for an unusual and refreshing summertime dessert.

Makes one 9-inch single-crust pie, serving 6 to 8

For the crust

1 cup (35 wafers) vanilla wafers crumbs

3 tablespoons sugar

¼ cup (½ stick) unsalted butter, melted

For the filling

1 envelope (2¼ teaspoons) unflavored gelatin

6 ounces canned pineapple juice

½ cup sugar

¼ teaspoon salt

1½ teaspoons lemon juice

1 cup heavy cream

1½ cups seedless green grapes, washed and removed from stems
   (use pearl grapes, if available; with very large grapes,
   it's best to cut them in half)

Mint sprig for garnish (optional)

1. Preheat the oven to 400°F. Lightly grease a 9-inch pie plate.

2. *For the crust:* Combine the vanilla wafer crumbs, sugar, and melted butter. Press the mixture firmly over the bottom and sides of the pie plate (or use the method on page 135). Bake in the oven for 6 to 8 minutes, until golden. Set it aside to cool while you prepare the filling.

3. *For the filling:* Stir the gelatin into ¼ cup of water and set aside to soften. In a medium saucepan, combine the pineapple juice, sugar, and salt. Cook over medium-high

heat until the mixture starts to boil. Remove from the heat; add the softened gelatin and the lemon juice, stirring until the gelatin is dissolved.

4. Chill, stirring occasionally, until the mixture forms a soft mound when dropped from a spoon, 20 to 40 minutes. (Keep a close watch once it begins to set, as it gels quickly at this point. If this happens, reheat the mixture and chill again.)

5. In a large bowl, whip the cream with an electric mixer on high speed until stiff peaks form. Carefully fold in the chilled gelatin mixture along with 1 cup of the grapes, repeatedly cutting down the middle with a spatula and up one side, just until blended. Pour into the cooled crust, and sprinkle the remaining grapes over the top. Chill, uncovered, for several hours or overnight. Garnish with a mint sprig, if desired.

Pumpkin Chiffon Pie

I'd never been a big fan of pumpkin pie—until I discovered this recipe. It's as light as the traditional kind is dense, with a splash of rum to give it a nice kick. Since it's chilled, it makes a nice contrast on holidays when you're serving more than one pie. My daughter, Mary, always makes it when she comes for Thanksgiving.

Makes one 9-inch single-crust pie, serving 6 to 8

1½ cups gingersnap crumbs (I use Peek Freans Ginger Crisps)

⅔ cup plus 2 tablespoons sugar

5 tablespoons unsalted butter, melted

1 envelope (2¼ teaspoons) unflavored gelatin

3 large eggs, separated

½ teaspoon salt

½ teaspoon ground cinnamon

½ teaspoon ground nutmeg

½ teaspoon ground ginger

1¼ cups canned pumpkin (*not* pumpkin pie filling)

3 to 4 tablespoons dark rum, or 1 teaspoon rum extract

½ cup heavy cream

2 to 3 tablespoons slivered almonds (optional)

1 tablespoon minced candied ginger (optional)

1. Lightly butter a 9-inch pie plate.

2. *For the crust:* Combine the gingersnap crumbs, 2 tablespoons of the sugar, and the melted butter. Press the mixture firmly over the bottom and sides of the pie plate. Chill while you prepare the filling.

3. *For the filling:* Stir the gelatin into ¼ cup of hot water until dissolved; set aside. In the top of a double boiler, place the egg yolks and ⅓ cup of the remaining sugar, whisking until thoroughly blended. Add the salt, cinnamon, nutmeg, ginger, and dissolved gelatin. Set over boiling water (make sure the bottom of the pan isn't touching the water), and cook over medium heat, stirring constantly, until the mixture thickens enough to generously coat a spoon. Remove from the heat; add the pumpkin and rum (or rum extract), stirring vigorously to blend. Chill until the mixture forms a soft mound when dropped from a spoon, 30 to 40 minutes. (Keep a close watch once it begins to set, as it gels quickly at this point. If this happens, reheat the mixture and chill again.)

4. In a large bowl, beat the egg whites with an electric mixer on high speed until soft peaks form. Add the remaining ⅓ cup of sugar a few tablespoons at a time as you continue beating, until stiff peaks form.

5. In a separate bowl, whip the cream until medium peaks form (see Note).

6. Carefully fold the chilled pumpkin mixture into the whipped cream, then into the beaten egg whites, just until blended. Spoon the mixture into the pie shell. Chill, uncovered, for several hours or overnight. Just before serving, sprinkle with slivered almonds and/or candied ginger, if desired.

Note: Place the bowl in the freezer 10 to 15 minutes beforehand; cream whips faster when cold.

White Chocolate–Raspberry Pie

This recipe was sent to me by a fan, Pam Hoerner, who wrote that raspberries "are like gold here in Iowa," since they're available for only a short time in the summer. Wherever you reside, you'll love this luscious pie. Drizzled in white chocolate, it looks as sensational as it tastes.   **Makes one 9-inch single-crust pie, serving 6 to 8**

For the crust

   1 cup (35 wafers) vanilla wafer crumbs

   3 tablespoons sugar

   ¼ cup (½ stick) unsalted butter, melted

For the filling

   2 tablespoons milk

   6 ounces white chocolate, chopped

   4 ounces cream cheese, softened

   ⅓ cup confectioners' sugar

   1 teaspoon orange zest

   1 cup heavy cream

   2 pints fresh raspberries, washed, hulled, and dried

1. Preheat the oven to 400°F. Lightly butter a 9-inch pie plate.

2. *For the crust:* Combine the vanilla wafer crumbs with the sugar and melted butter. Press the mixture firmly over the bottom and sides of the pie plate (or use the method on page 135). Bake in the oven for 6 to 8 minutes, until golden. Set it aside to cool while you prepare the filling.

3. *For the filling:* In a small microwave-safe bowl, place the milk and 5 ounces of the chopped white chocolate. Heat in the microwave, covered, for 30 seconds at a time, stirring after each interval, until the chocolate is melted (about 1½ minutes total). Set aside to cool.

4. In a large bowl, beat the softened cream cheese with an electric mixer on medium speed until fluffy. Gradually blend in the confectioners' sugar and zest. Add the cooled chocolate mixture, and beat until smooth.

5. In a separate bowl, whip the cream with an electric mixer on high speed until stiff peaks form. Carefully fold it into the cream cheese mixture, repeatedly cutting down the middle with a spatula and up one side, just until blended. Spoon into the cooled pie shell. One at a time, place the raspberries (make sure they are *thoroughly* dry), tips up, in concentric rings over the filling, starting with the outer edge and working your way toward the center. Melt the remaining ounce of chocolate and drizzle it over the top (see Note). Chill the pie for at least 4 hours, or overnight.

Note: For easy drizzling, place the chocolate inside a zip-top freezer bag, and heat in the microwave for 30 seconds at a time, stopping after each interval to gently knead the bag so that the chocolate melts evenly. Let it cool slightly, then snip off one end of the bag to create a tiny opening. Squeeze the melted chocolate through the opening.

Pineapple Meringue Pie

I love lemon meringue pie, but my husband, Sandy, wasn't particularly fond of it when we met (which I chalked up to too many bad ones in greasy spoon diners). I've since brought him around with this variation. It's less tart than meringue pie made with lemons, but every bit as delicious.   *Makes one 9-inch single-crust pie, serving 6 to 8*

Never-Fail Dough (page 133–4) for a single 9-inch crust
    (you'll need only half the recipe)

For the filling

   3 large eggs
   One 20-ounce can crushed unsweetened pineapple, with juice
   1¼ cups canned pineapple juice
   1¼ cups sugar
   5 tablespoons cornstarch
   Dash of salt
   Zest from 1 lime
   2 tablespoons unsalted butter
   1 teaspoon lime juice

1. *For the crust:* Place the dough on a lightly floured pastry cloth and flatten with your hand into roughly a 1-inch thick round, shaping the edges to keep them even. With a rolling pin, roll from the center outward, until the round is about 11 inches in diameter. Carefully fold in half, then again to form a triangle. Transfer to an ungreased 9-inch pie plate, positioning it so the point is in the center of the plate. Carefully unfold. Trim with a sharp knife or kitchen shears, leaving an overhang of 1 inch or so. Fold the overhang under, and press with your thumb at regular intervals to form a fluted edge. Prick the bottom all over with a fork. Place in the freezer for at least 15 minutes, until firm.

2. Preheat the oven to 375°F. Line the unbaked shell with aluminum foil or parchment (not wax paper), and distribute pie weights (or dried beans) over the bottom. Bake in the oven for 15 to 20 minutes, until lightly golden. Remove from the oven, and reduce the oven temperature to 350°F. Set the crust aside to cool while you prepare the filling.

3. Separate the eggs and lightly beat the yolks. Set aside.

4. *For the filling:* In a medium saucepan, combine the crushed pineapple, pineapple juice, 1 cup of the sugar, the cornstarch, and salt, stirring to dissolve any lumps. Bring to a boil over medium heat, stirring constantly until it's thick enough to generously coat a spoon, about 5 minutes. Whisk a small amount (about ¼ cup) into the lightly beaten egg yolks, then return it to the hot mixture on the stove. Cook for 1 minute more. Remove from the heat; add the zest and butter, stirring until the butter is melted. Set aside while you prepare the topping.

5. In a medium bowl, beat the egg whites and lime juice with an electric mixer on high speed, until soft peaks form. Gradually add the remaining ¼ cup of sugar (a rounded tablespoon at a time), beating until stiff peaks form and the sugar is dissolved (rub a little between your fingers to test for graininess).

6. Spoon the filling into the cooled crust. Spread the meringue evenly over the top, swirling into peaks and making sure there are no gaps around the edges (or the meringue will pull away as it cools). Bake in the reduced-heat oven for 12 to 15 minutes, until the meringue is golden brown. Cool thoroughly before serving. If storing overnight, place in the refrigerator under a cake dome or large inverted bowl. *Don't cover with plastic wrap or foil.*

Margarita Pie

I used to have a house in Key West, Florida, where I often served this pie to my guests. It's been described alternately as a "souped-up Key lime pie" and as "the best margarita that doesn't come in a glass." Either way, it's a winner—lighter than Key lime pie, with a noticeable kick. For those who like a less spirited dessert, go easy on the tequila.

Makes one 9-inch single-crust pie, serving 6 to 8

For the crust

1½ cups graham cracker crumbs

3 tablespoons sugar

4 tablespoons unsalted butter, melted

For the filling

1 envelope (2¼ teaspoons) unflavored gelatin

½ cup fresh lime juice

4 large eggs, separated

1 cup sugar

¼ teaspoon salt

1 teaspoon lime zest

⅓ cup tequila

3 tablespoons triple sec

For the topping

1 cup heavy cream

2 tablespoons confectioners' sugar

1 to 2 limes, sliced thin

1. Preheat the oven to 375°F. Lightly butter a 9-inch pie plate.

2. *For the crust:* Combine the graham cracker crumbs, sugar, and melted butter. Press the mixture evenly over the bottom and sides of the pie plate (or use the method on page 135). Bake in the oven for 6 to 8 minutes, until golden. Set it aside to cool while you prepare the filling.

3. *For the filling:* Sprinkle the gelatin over the lime juice to soften it. In the top of a double boiler, whisk the egg yolks. Add the gelatin mixture and ½ cup of the sugar, and whisk to combine. Place over the water (make sure the bottom of the pan isn't touching the water) and cook over medium-high heat, stirring constantly, until the mixture thickens enough to generously coat a spoon. Remove from the heat. Add the salt, zest, tequila, and triple sec; whisk to combine. Chill for several minutes.

4. In a large bowl, beat the egg whites with an electric mixer on high speed, until soft peaks form. Gradually add the remaining ½ cup of sugar, beating until stiff peaks form. Carefully fold in the wet mixture (it will still be warm), repeatedly cutting down the middle with a spatula and up one side, just until blended. Pour into the cooled crust and chill for several hours or overnight.

5. *Just before serving, prepare the topping:* Whip the heavy cream with the confectioners' sugar and spread over the top of the pie. Garnish with the lime slices.

Banana Cream Pie

My friend Connie Sorensen made this once when we were teenagers and I was sleeping over at her house. We gorged ourselves, then rode our bikes around the neighborhood for hours to burn off the energy from all that sugar. I've since learned to eat sweets in moderation, but I still smile whenever I think of that banana cream pie. In recent years, it seems to have fallen out of favor, though I can't imagine why—it's the essence of comfort food.

Makes one 9-inch single-crust pie, serving 6 to 8

Never-Fail Pie Dough (page 133–4) for a single 9-inch crust
  (you'll need only half the recipe)

For the filling

  1 vanilla bean (you can substitute 1 teaspoon vanilla extract)
  1⅓ cups sugar
  ¼ cup cornstarch
  2¼ cups whole milk
  3 large eggs, separated
  3 firm-ripe bananas, peeled and sliced
  1 teaspoon vanilla extract
  ¼ teaspoon cream of tartar
  Dash of salt

1. *For the crust:* Place the dough on a lightly floured pastry cloth and flatten with your hand into about a 1-inch thick round, shaping the edges to keep them even. With a rolling pin, roll from the center outward, until the round is roughly 11 inches in diameter. Carefully fold it in half, then again to form a triangle. Transfer to an ungreased 9-inch pie plate, positioning it so the point is in the center of the plate. Carefully unfold. Trim with a sharp knife or kitchen shears, leaving about a 1-inch overhang. Fold the overhang under, and press with your thumb at regular intervals to form a fluted edge. Prick the bottom all over with a fork. Place in the freezer for 15 minutes, until firm.

2. Preheat the oven to 375°F.

3. Line the shell with aluminum foil or parchment (not wax paper), and distribute pie weights (or dried beans) over the bottom. Bake in the oven for 15 to 20 minutes, until lightly golden. Remove from the oven, and reduce the oven temperature to 350°F. Set the crust aside to cool while you prepare the filling.

4. *For the filling:* Split the vanilla bean. In a medium saucepan, combine 1 cup of the sugar and the cornstarch. Gradually add the milk, whisking to keep lumps from forming. Lightly beat the egg yolks, and whisk them into the milk mixture. Add both halves of the vanilla bean. Bring to a boil over medium heat, stirring constantly. Reduce the heat and simmer for 10 to 15 minutes, continuing to stir until the mixture thickens to the consistency of very soft pudding. Remove it from the heat (add the vanilla extract at this point if substituting it for the vanilla bean) and set it aside to cool until lukewarm. Remove the vanilla bean; rinse and freeze it for later use.

5. Distribute half of the banana slices evenly over the bottom of the cooled pie shell. Top with half of the filling, smoothing with the back of a spoon to cover the bananas. Repeat with the remaining banana slices and filling.

6. In a medium bowl, beat the egg whites and vanilla with an electric mixer on high speed until soft peaks form. Mix the cream of tartar, salt, and remaining ⅓ cup of sugar. Gradually add the mixture to the egg whites (a tablespoon at a time), beating until stiff peaks form and the sugar is dissolved (rub a little between your fingers to test for graininess). Spread it evenly over the filling, swirling into peaks and making sure there are no gaps around the edges, so the meringue won't pull away as it cools. Bake for 15 to 17 minutes in the reduced heat oven, or until the meringue is golden brown. Cool the pie thoroughly before serving. If chilling it overnight, place it under a cake dome or large inverted bowl (never use foil or plastic wrap), making sure it isn't touching the meringue.

Creamy Lemon Pie

T he distinctive blend of white chocolate, cream cheese, and lemon puts this pie in a class all its own. A little bit goes a long way, so go easy on the servings.

Makes one 9-inch single-crust pie, serving 8 to 10

For the crust

1 cup Zwieback toast crumbs

5 tablespoons sugar

¼ cup (½ stick) unsalted butter, melted

For the filling

1 cup granulated sugar

2 tablespoons cornstarch

2 tablespoons all-purpose flour

2 large egg yolks, lightly beaten

1 tablespoon unsalted butter

Zest from 1 lemon

¼ cup lemon juice

6 ounces white chocolate, chopped to equal 1 cup

8 ounces cream cheese, softened

½ cup heavy cream

3 tablespoons confectioners' sugar

1 lemon, thinly sliced (optional)

1. Preheat the oven to 375°F. Lightly butter a 9-inch pie plate.

2. *For the crust:* Combine the Zwieback toast crumbs with the sugar and melted butter. Press the mixture firmly over the bottom and sides of the pie plate (or use the method on page 135). Bake in the oven for 6 to 8 minutes, until lightly golden. Set it aside to cool while you prepare the filling.

3. *For the filling:* In a medium saucepan, combine the granulated sugar, cornstarch, and flour. Gradually stir in 1 cup of water, whisking until blended. Bring to a boil over medium heat, stirring constantly. Reduce the heat and simmer for 2 minutes more, stirring constantly, until the mixture thickens and becomes translucent. Remove from the heat. Mix a small amount (about ¼ cup) into the beaten egg yolks, then gradually return it to the hot mixture, whisking to keep lumps from forming. Simmer over low heat for 2 minutes more, stirring constantly (it is quite thick at this point). Remove from the heat, and stir in the butter, zest, and lemon juice. Set aside two-thirds of the mixture (from a total of 1¾ cups), leaving the remaining mixture in the saucepan. Add the chopped white chocolate to the hot mixture in the saucepan. Cook over the lowest heat, stirring constantly, just until the chocolate is melted.

4. In a small bowl, beat the softened cream cheese until fluffy. Gradually add the lemon-chocolate mixture, beating until well blended. Spread over the bottom of the cooled crust. Spread the reserved lemon mixture over the cream cheese layer. Chill for several hours or overnight.

5. Just before serving, whip the cream with an electric mixer on high speed until soft peaks form. Gradually add the confectioners' sugar and beat until stiff peaks form. Spoon around the edges of the pie. Garnish with lemon slices, if desired.

Ambrosia Pie

I *f you're a baby boomer like me, you'll recall that fifties standard, ambrosia salad, which has all but vanished in certain parts of the country. You'll find it reinvented here in a pie that tastes as heavenly as it looks (even if you don't love the salad). Take it to a company picnic or potluck and watch the line form.* ***Makes one 9-inch single-crust pie, serving 6 to 8***

For the crust

About 4 cups Rice Chex cereal

¼ cup packed light brown sugar

¼ teaspoon ground ginger

⅓ cup (5½ tablespoons) unsalted butter, melted

For the filling

1 envelope (2¼ teaspoons) unflavored gelatin

2 cups (1½-pound jar) mandarin orange segments

One 8-ounce can unsweetened crushed pineapple

About ½ cup fresh orange juice

½ cup plus 2 tablespoons sugar

½ teaspoon orange zest

⅔ cup heavy cream

3 ounces cream cheese, softened

¼ teaspoon ground ginger

1 tablespoon milk

½ cup mini marshmallows

½ cup sweetened flaked coconut

1. Preheat the oven to 375°F. Lightly butter a 9-inch pie plate.

2. *For the crust:* In a food processor or blender, grind the Rice Chex to fine crumbs equaling 1 cup (it may require a little more than 4 cups of cereal). Add the brown sugar and ginger; whir to blend. Add the melted butter, and pulse a few times, just until it's blended. Dump the mixture into the pie plate and press it firmly over the bottom and sides (or use the method on page 135). Bake in the oven for 6 to 8 minutes, until lightly golden. Set it aside to cool while you prepare the filling.

3. *For the filling:* Stir the gelatin into ¼ cup of cold water; set it aside to soften. Drain the orange segments and cut them into ½-inch pieces. Drain the crushed pineapple, reserving the juice. Combine the sliced orange segments with the drained crushed pineapple, and set aside. To the reserved pineapple juice, add enough orange juice to equal 1 cup total.

4. In a medium saucepan, stir together the juice and ½ cup of the sugar. Cook over medium heat, stirring continuously, until the mixture reaches a boil. Remove from the heat and stir in the softened gelatin and zest. Chill, stirring occasionally, until the mixture forms a soft mound when dropped from a spoon, 20 to 40 minutes. (Keep a close watch as it begins to set, as it gels quickly at this point. If this happens, reheat it and chill again.)

5. In a large bowl, beat the heavy cream with an electric mixer on high speed, until stiff peaks form. In a small bowl, beat the softened cream cheese, ginger, milk, and the remaining 2 tablespoons of sugar until smooth. Carefully fold the cream cheese mixture into the whipped cream, repeatedly cutting down the center with a spatula and up the sides, just until blended. Fold in the chilled orange mixture, orange segments and pineapple. Spoon into the cooled crust. Sprinkle with the marshmallows, then the coconut. Chill, uncovered, for several hours or overnight. (If chilling overnight, cover it with a cake dome or large inverted bowl.)

White Russian Pie

I adapted this coffee-flavored pie from a recipe given to me by one of my husband's coworkers at the WINS newsroom, a gentleman by the name of Jack Conceicao, who, in addition to being a fine news writer, is a connoisseur of baked goods. The headline is that it's as sinful as it looks.

Makes one 9-inch single-crust pie, serving 6 to 8

For the crust

    18 Oreo cookies, ground to equal about 1¼ cups crumbs

    2 tablespoons unsalted butter, melted

For the filling

    About 1 cup half-and-half

    ½ cup coarsely ground espresso beans

    ¼ cup (½ stick) unsalted butter, softened

    ⅓ cup granulated sugar

    1 teaspoon vanilla extract

    3 tablespoons all-purpose flour

    3 large eggs

    ½ cup plus 1 tablespoon Kahlúa or other coffee-flavored liqueur

    ⅓ cup dark corn syrup

    ½ cup Skor English Toffee Bits (available in most supermarkets)

    ½ cup chopped walnuts or pecans

    ½ cup heavy cream

    2 tablespoons confectioners' sugar

1. In a small saucepan, combine 1 cup of half-and-half for the filling with the coarsely ground espresso beans. Cook the mixture over medium heat until it starts to simmer. Immediately remove the pan from the heat, and set it aside to cool. When cool, pour the mixture through a fine-mesh strainer into a measuring cup, discarding the grounds. Add just enough additional half-and-half to equal ¾ cup (1 to 2 tablespoons).

2. Preheat the oven to 375°F and lightly butter a 9-inch pie plate.

3. *For the crust:* Combine the Oreo crumbs (see Note) and the melted butter. Press the mixture firmly over the bottom and sides of the pie plate; chill while you prepare the filling.

4. *For the filling:* In a large bowl, cream the softened butter with an electric mixer on medium speed. Add the granulated sugar, a little at a time, beating until pale and fluffy. Blend in the vanilla and flour. Add the eggs one at a time, beating well after each addition. With the electric mixer on low speed, gradually add ½ cup of the Kahlúa as you continue beating. Blend in the corn syrup and the half-and-half mixture. Stir in the toffee bits and chopped nuts.

5. Pour into the chilled crust, and place in the oven. Reduce the heat to 325°F, and bake for 40 to 45 minutes, until the edges are set and the center jiggles only slightly when the pie plate is gently shaken. Cool to room temperature then chill for several hours or overnight.

6. Just before serving, whip the cream with an electric mixer on high speed until soft peaks form. Add the confectioners' sugar and the remaining tablespoon of Kahlúa; beat until stiff peaks form. Spoon or pipe around the edges of the pie.

Note: *For best results, grind the Oreos in a food processor. You may need to process them a bit longer than wafer cookies.*

Mocha Buttercrunch Pie

More like a nutty chocolate candy bar, this pie is so rich, it oozes decadence with every bite. I suggest serving it after a light meal, when you can truly savor it. Note: You'll need a food processor for this.

Makes one 9-inch single-crust pie, serving 8 to 10

For the crust

1 cup all-purpose flour

¼ teaspoon salt

⅓ cup dark brown sugar

5½ tablespoons unsalted butter, chilled

3 tablespoons chopped semisweet or bittersweet chocolate

1 cup walnuts

1 teaspoon vanilla extract

For the filling

3 ounces unsweetened chocolate

1 cup (2 sticks) unsalted butter, softened

1 cup dark brown sugar

4 teaspoons coffee crystals, dissolved in 1 teaspoon boiling water

2 teaspoons vanilla extract

4 large eggs

For the topping

½ cup confectioners' sugar

2 tablespoons unsweetened cocoa

2 cups heavy cream

2 teaspoons Kahlúa, brandy, or dark rum

Shaved chocolate for garnish (optional)

1. Preheat the oven to 350°F. Lightly butter a 9-inch pie plate.

2. Place the chocolate for the filling in a microwave-safe bowl; heat in the microwave for 30 seconds at a time, stirring after each interval, until it's melted (about 1 to 1½ minutes

total). Alternate method: Place the chocolate in a bowl *over* (not in) boiling water that's been removed from the heat. Stir occasionally until it's melted. Set it aside to cool.

3. *For the crust:* In a food processor, place the flour, salt, dark brown sugar, chilled butter, chopped chocolate, walnuts, vanilla, and 2 teaspoons of water. Process until the mixture is thoroughly blended. With floured fingers, press it over the bottom and sides of the pie plate. Bake in the oven for 20 minutes. Set on a wire rack to cool while you prepare the filling.

4. *For the filling:* In a large bowl, cream the softened butter with an electric mixer on medium speed. Add the dark brown sugar a little at a time, beating until fluffy. Blend in the cooled, melted chocolate, coffee sludge, and vanilla, beating until smooth. Add the eggs one at a time, beating *very* well after each addition (2 to 3 minutes per egg). Pour the filling into the cooled pie shell. Chill for several hours or overnight.

5. *To prepare the topping:* Just before serving, sift together the confectioners' sugar and cocoa. In a chilled bowl, whip the cream to soft peaks with an electric mixer on high speed. Gradually add the sugar-cocoa mixture, beating until stiff peaks form. Blend in the liquor. Spoon the topping over the chilled pie, and garnish with shaved chocolate, if desired.

French Silk Pie

This is courtesy of my mother-in-law, Lindy Kenyon, and with its truffle-like filling and meringue shell, it's as seductive as the name implies. It's also flourless, which makes it an ideal choice for Passover or for those on a gluten-free diet.   *Serves 6 to 8*

For the shell

3 large egg whites

Pinch of salt

¼ teaspoon cream of tartar

½ teaspoon vanilla extract

¾ cup superfine sugar

⅓ cup finely chopped walnuts or pecans

For the filling

1 ounce unsweetened chocolate

½ cup (1 stick) unsalted butter, softened

¾ cup sugar

1 teaspoon vanilla extract

2 large eggs

For the topping

½ cup heavy cream

1 tablespoon crème de cacao

1 tablespoon unsweetened cocoa

1 tablespoon confectioners' sugar

Chocolate curls for garnish (optional)

1. Preheat the oven to 275°F. Grease a 9-inch pie plate.

2. *For the shell:* In a large bowl, beat the egg whites, salt, and cream of tartar with an electric mixer on high speed until soft peaks form. Blend in the vanilla. Add the superfine sugar a tablespoon at a time, beating on medium speed for 30 seconds after each addition, until stiff peaks form and the sugar is dissolved (test by rubbing a little between your fingers). Spread over the bottom and sides of the pie plate, using the back of a spoon to push the edges to a height of about 2 inches above the pie plate. Sprinkle with the chopped nuts. Bake in the oven for 1 hour. Turn off the heat, and let dry in the oven for 2 hours. Meanwhile, prepare the filling.

3. *For the filling:* Place the chocolate in a small microwave-safe bowl and heat in the microwave for 30 seconds at a time, stirring after each interval, until melted (about 1 minute total). Set it aside to cool.

4. In a large bowl, cream the softened butter with an electric mixer on medium speed. Gradually add the sugar and beat until light and fluffy. Add the cooled chocolate and vanilla; beat until smooth. Add the eggs one at a time, beating for 3 minutes after each addition. Scrape into the meringue shell, smoothing even with a spatula. Chill the pie for at least 2 hours.

5. *For the topping:* Just before serving the pie, beat the cream with an electric mixer on high speed until soft peaks form. Add the crème de cacao, cocoa, and confectioners' sugar. Beat until stiff peaks form. Heap the topping over the chilled pie. Garnish with chocolate curls, if desired.

Note: *You might be uneasy about the raw eggs. I settle it by using eggs from free-range hens fed on organic grain, for which the incidences of salmonella are reportedly quite low. If you want to be one hundred percent safe, use pasteurized eggs, which are treated to kill all bacteria. You can find them in the dairy case of many supermarkets.*

Sweet Potato Pie

*M*y family on my mother's side were originally from Alabama, and though the Masseys have since scattered to various parts of the country, we're linked to that heritage by the recipes handed down through the generations. What would Thanksgiving be without my mom's cornbread stuffing or pecan pie? A dessert synonymous with the South is sweet potato pie; you see it on menus everywhere south of the Mason-Dixon line. It's lighter than pumpkin pie, and in my opinion tastier. I would eat it every day of the week, if my waistline allowed. ***Makes one 9-inch single-crust pie, serving 6 to 8***

1¾ pounds sweet potatoes, to equal 1½ cups puree
Never-Fail Pie Dough (page 133–4) for a single 9-inch crust
    (you won't need the whole recipe)
1½ cups (12 ounces) evaporated milk
1 cup sugar
1 teaspoon ground cinnamon
¾ teaspoon ground nutmeg
½ teaspoon ground allspice
2 tablespoons dark rum
3 large eggs, lightly beaten
Whipped cream for garnish (optional)

1. Preheat the oven to 375°F.

2. Wash the sweet potatoes, scrubbing well to remove any dirt. Score the skins with a sharp knife, and place on a baking sheet in the oven. Bake for 40 to 45 minutes, until tender when pierced. When cool enough to handle, scoop out the pulp, discarding the skins. Puree in a blender or food processor until smooth. Set aside 1½ cups, and freeze excess for later use.

3. Place the dough on a lightly floured pastry cloth, and flatten it with your hand into about a 1-inch-thick round, shaping the edges to keep them even. With a rolling pin, roll from the center outward, until the round is roughly 11 inches in diameter. Carefully fold it in half, then again to form a triangle. Transfer it to an ungreased 9-inch pie plate, positioning it so the point is in the center of the plate. Carefully unfold. Trim the edges with a sharp knife or kitchen shears, leaving 1 inch or so of overhang. Fold the overhang under, and with your thumb press at regular intervals to form a fluted edge. Place the shell in the freezer for at least 15 minutes, until firm.

4. Increase the oven heat to 450°F.

5. Place the sweet potato puree, evaporated milk, sugar, cinnamon, nutmeg, allspice, and rum in a large bowl. Blend with an electric mixer on low speed until smooth. Add the eggs, and beat well. Remove the shell from the freezer. Using aluminum foil cut into 2-inch-wide strips, form a collar around the fluted edge, crimping to fix it in place (this will keep the edge from browning too quickly). Pour the filling into the shell. Rap the side of the plate sharply with a knife handle once or twice to get rid of any bubbles that might have formed. Bake in the oven for 10 minutes. Lower the oven heat to 350°F, and bake for 30 to 40 minutes more, until the center no longer jiggles when the plate is gently shaken. Serve at room temperature. Garnish with whipped cream, if desired.

Note: The foil "collar" can remain throughout baking; the fluted edge bakes perfectly underneath.

Pecan-Cranberry Pie

This is one of those Thanksgiving-wouldn't-be-the-same-without-it pies. If you find traditional pecan pie a tad too sweet, here is a nice compromise: The cranberries give it a welcome tartness and a jewel tone without sacrificing any of the caramel gooeyness. It's even good cold—the day after Thanksgiving, it's always the first leftover to go in our house.

Makes one 9-inch single-crust pie, serving 6 to 8

Never-Fail Pie Dough (page 133–4) for a single 9-inch crust
   (you won't need the whole recipe)
1¼ cups dark corn syrup
1 cup sugar
½ cup (1 stick) unsalted butter
4 large eggs
2 tablespoons all-purpose flour
¼ cup dark rum
6 ounces (about 1½ cups) pecan halves
1 cup fresh or unthawed frozen cranberries
Whipped cream for garnish (optional)

1. Place the dough on a lightly floured pastry cloth and flatten it with your hand into about a 1-inch-thick round, shaping the edges to keep them even. With a rolling pin, roll from the center outward, until roughly 11 inches in diameter. Carefully fold it in half, then again to form a triangle. Transfer it to an ungreased 9-inch pie plate, positioning it so the point is in the center of the plate. Carefully unfold it. Trim the edges with a sharp knife or kitchen shears, leaving 1 inch or so of overhang. Fold the overhang under, and press with your thumb at regular intervals to form a fluted edge. Place the shell in the freezer for at least 15 minutes, until it's firm.

2. Preheat the oven to 350°F.

3. In a medium saucepan bring the corn syrup and sugar to a full boil, stirring constantly. Remove from the heat and add the butter, stirring until melted.

4. In a medium bowl, blend the eggs, flour, and rum with an electric mixer on low speed. Add the syrup in a slow, steady drizzle as you continue beating, until the mixture is well blended.

5. Remove the shell from the freezer. Using aluminum foil cut into 2-inch wide strips, form a collar around the fluted edge, crimping to fix it in place (this will keep the edge from browning too quickly). Sprinkle the pecan halves and cranberries over the bottom. Pour in the filling, and bake in the oven for 45 minutes, or until the center jiggles only slightly when the pie plate is gently shaken. Let cool to room temperature before serving. Garnish with whipped cream, if desired.

Note: *The foil "collar" can remain on throughout baking; the fluted edge bakes perfectly underneath.*

Tangerine Tart

T his is my favorite kind of citrus dessert—not too sweet, with an intense orangey flavor I associate with everything I loved about growing up in California. Serve it after a heavy meal, when a light dessert is called for. Make the crust a day ahead of time, if you wish. Freeze it unbaked, covered tightly in plastic wrap.　　　*Makes one 11-inch tart, serving 6 to 8*

For the crust

2 cups all-purpose flour

¾ cup confectioners' sugar

2 teaspoons tangerine zest

7 ounces (1¾ sticks) unsalted butter, chilled

For the filling

3 large eggs

⅔ cup sugar

2 teaspoons tangerine zest

½ cup fresh tangerine juice

1½ tablespoons fresh lemon juice

½ cup half-and-half

For the topping

¾ cup heavy cream

2 tablespoons confectioners' sugar

1 teaspoon vanilla extract

1 teaspoon tangerine zest

1. *For the crust:* Place the flour, confectioners' sugar, and zest in a food processor, and whir to combine. Cut the butter into chunks and add it to the flour mixture. Pulse just until the mixture comes together in a mass (don't overprocess!) Scrape the dough into an ungreased 11-inch tart pan with a removable rim, and with floured fingers press it evenly over the bottom and sides. Place in the freezer while you prepare the filling.

2. Preheat the oven to 425°F.

3. *For the filling:* In a large bowl, whisk together the eggs and sugar until well blended. Add the zest, tangerine and lemon juices, and half-and-half. Whisk to blend. Pour the filling into the chilled shell. Bake in the oven for 30 to 40 minutes, until it's set (it no longer jiggles when the pan is gently shaken). Let it cool completely before removing the rim.

4. Just before serving: In a chilled bowl, whip the cream and confectioners' sugar with an electric mixer on high speed until soft peaks form. Blend in the vanilla and zest, and whip until medium peaks form. Place a dollop on each serving.

Jam Tart

*H*ere is a lovely alternative to tarts made with fresh fruit, one you can enjoy year round. Make it with any kind of jam you happen to have on hand, though I'm partial to apricot or berry. And if you prepare the crust a day in advance, the rest goes together in no time; the perfect dessert to make after work, on those evenings when you're having company.

Makes one 9-inch tart, serving 6

1¾ cups all-purpose flour
⅓ cup sugar
1 tablespoon lemon zest
½ teaspoon baking powder
½ teaspoon salt
¾ cup (1½ sticks) unsalted butter, chilled and cut into chunks
3 large eggs
1¾ cups fruit jam

1. Place the flour, sugar, zest, baking powder, and salt in a food processor, and whir to combine. Add the butter and whir for a few seconds, then pulse until the mixture resembles coarse meal (the butter should be the size of lentils). Alternate method: In a large bowl, combine the above ingredients and cut the butter in with a pastry cutter until the mixture is crumbly.

2. Lightly beat 2 of the eggs, and add them to the flour mixture. If you're using a food processor, pulse just until the dough begins to form. If you're using the alternate method, whisk the eggs into the flour mixture with a fork until it starts to come together in a mass. Gently gather the dough into a ball. Wrap tightly in plastic wrap, and chill for several hours or overnight. Let it sit at room temperature for 30 minutes before rolling it out.

3. Set aside a third of the dough. Place the remaining dough on a floured pastry cloth and flatten it with the heel of your hand into about a ½-inch round, shaping the edges to keep them even. Roll with a rolling pin, from the center outward, until the round is roughly 11 inches in diameter. Carefully fold it in half, then again, forming a triangle. Transfer it to a lightly buttered 9-inch tart pan with a removable rim, positioning it so the point of the triangle is at the center of the pan; carefully unfold it. Trim the overhang to within 1 inch or so of the rim, and fold under, pressing lightly to seal; indent with your thumb at regular intervals to create a fluted edge. Place in the freezer for at least 15 minutes.

4. Preheat the oven to 375°F.

5. Spread the jam evenly over the bottom of the chilled shell. Roll out the remaining dough and cut it into ½-inch-wide strips. Arrange half the strips over the filling, placing the longer ones in the middle and the shorter ones at the ends. Rotate the tart and arrange the remaining strips at the opposite angle to create a lattice. Beat the remaining egg with 1 teaspoon of water, and brush it over the top (you won't need it all). Bake in the oven for 40 to 45 minutes, until the crust is golden. Cool for at least 6 hours, until the jam is set, before removing the rim. Serve at room temperature.

Raspberry-Amaretto Tart

*O*n a recent trip to Washington state, my husband and I spent an evening with my friend and fellow author, Kristin Hannah, and her husband, Ben, at their home on Bainbridge Island. They cooked us a marvelous meal, which we ate out on the patio overlooking their pond and orchard. For dessert, Kristin prepared this tart, which was as scrumptious as it looked. She was kind enough to share the recipe with me. *Makes one 11-inch tart, serving 6 to 8*

For the crust

1¼ cups all-purpose flour

¼ cup confectioners' sugar

½ cup (1 stick) unsalted butter, chilled and cut into chunks

1 large egg yolk

2 tablespoons heavy cream

½ teaspoon lemon zest

1 tablespoon Amaretto

For the filling

1 pint (2 cups) fresh raspberries, washed, hulled, and dried

4 tablespoons Amaretto

8 ounces cream cheese, softened

⅓ cup sugar

2 large eggs

½ teaspoon almond extract

1. Toss the raspberries for the filling with 2 tablespoons of the Amaretto, and set aside, covered, for several hours.

2. *For the crust:* Place the flour and confectioners' sugar in a food processor and whir to combine. Add the butter and whir for a few seconds, then pulse until the mixture is the consistency of coarse meal. Dump it into a bowl. Alternate method: In a medium bowl, combine the above ingredients and cut the butter in with a pastry cutter until the mixture is the consistency of coarse meal. Whisk together the egg yolk, cream, zest, and Amaretto.

Add it to the flour mixture all at once, and whisk with a fork just until dough forms. Gather it into a ball, and wrap it tightly in plastic wrap. Chill for at least 1 hour.

3. Place the dough on a floured pastry cloth and flatten it with the heel of your hand into about a 1-inch thick round, shaping the edges to keep them even. With a rolling pin, roll from the center outward until the round is roughly 13 inches in diameter. Carefully fold it in half, then again, forming a triangle. Transfer it to an ungreased 11-inch tart pan with a removable rim, positioning it so the point of the triangle is at the center of the pan; carefully unfold it. Trim the overhang to fit the rim. Place the shell in the freezer for at least 15 minutes.

4. Preheat the oven to 375°F.

5. Line the shell with aluminum foil or parchment and distribute pie weights (or dried beans) over the bottom. Bake in the oven for 12 to 15 minutes. Remove the foil or parchment and the pie weights, and bake for 12 to 15 minutes more, until the crust is lightly golden. Set it aside to cool while you prepare the filling.

6. *For the filling:* In a large bowl, beat the softened cream cheese and sugar with an electric mixer on medium speed until fluffy. Add the eggs one at a time, beating after each addition just until blended. Mix in the almond extract and the remaining 2 tablespoons of Amaretto.

7. Spread the raspberries, including their juice, over the bottom of the cooled crust. Pour the cream cheese mixture over the top. Bake in the oven for 20 to 25 minutes, until the tip of a knife inserted into the center comes out clean. Let it cool thoroughly in the pan before removing the rim. Serve it at room temperature.

Apricot-Almond Tart

*W*hen I lived in California and used to can my own fruit, I always put a couple of pits into each jar of apricots, which lent a subtle almond flavor. This tart reminds me of those home-preserved apricots. It's good for brunch or for dessert.

Makes one 11-inch tart, serving 6 to 8

For the crust

1¼ cups all-purpose flour

¼ cup confectioners' sugar

½ cup (1 stick) unsalted butter, chilled and cut into chunks

1 large egg yolk

2 tablespoons heavy cream

½ teaspoon lemon zest

1 tablespoon Amaretto

For the filling

2 pounds 6 ounces (about 25 halves) canned or jarred apricots

1 cup finely ground almonds (I use Bob's Red Mill Almond Meal/Flour—see Sources)

¾ cup plus 1 tablespoon sugar

2½ teaspoons lemon zest

1 teaspoon almond extract

1 large egg plus 1 yolk

2 tablespoons unsalted butter

Confectioners' sugar for dusting

1. Drain the apricot halves and place them cut side down in a single layer on paper towels to absorb excess moisture.

2. *For the crust:* Place the flour and confectioners' sugar in a food processor, and whir to combine. Add the butter and whir for a few seconds, then pulse until the mixture is the consistency of coarse meal. Dump it into a bowl. Alternate method: In a medium bowl, combine the above ingredients and cut in the butter with a pastry cutter until the mixture is the consistency of coarse meal. Combine the yolk, cream, zest, and Amaretto, whisking with a fork to blend. Add to the flour mixture all at once, and whisk just until dough forms. Gather it into a ball, and wrap it tightly in plastic wrap. Chill for at least 1 hour.

3. Place the dough on a floured pastry cloth and flatten with the heel of your hand into about a 1-inch-thick round, shaping the edges to keep them even. With a rolling pin, roll from the center outward until the round is roughly 13 inches in diameter. Carefully fold it in half, then again, forming a triangle. Transfer it to an ungreased 11-inch tart pan with a removable rim, positioning it so the point of the triangle is at the center of the pan; carefully unfold it. Trim the overhang to fit the rim. Place the shell in the freezer for at least 15 minutes, until firm.

4. Preheat the oven to 350°F.

5. *Meanwhile, prepare the filling:* In a medium bowl, place the ground almonds, ¾ cup of the sugar, zest, almond extract, egg and yolk. Stir vigorously with a wooden spoon to blend. With your fingers, pat the filling evenly over the bottom of the chilled shell. Arrange the apricot halves over the filling, placing them cut side down. Dot them with butter and sprinkle with the remaining 1 tablespoon of sugar.

6. Bake in the oven for 55 to 65 minutes, until richly golden. Cool the tart thoroughly in the pan before removing the rim. Dust with confectioners' sugar. Serve at room temperature.

Red, White, and Blue Tart

For a Fourth of July picnic, I can't think of anything more dazzling, or patriotic, than this fresh fruit tart—it could upstage the fireworks! I make it with alternating double rings of blueberries and raspberries. It tastes as good with any kind of berry, so choose whatever's at peak ripeness. For ease of preparation, bake the crust a day in advance, and store it tightly wrapped at room temperature. **Makes one 11-inch tart, serving 6 to 8 (see Note)**

For the crust

2 cups all-purpose flour

⅓ cup confectioners' sugar

½ teaspoon salt

1 teaspoon lemon zest

½ cup (1 stick) unsalted butter, chilled and cut into chunks

3 tablespoons lard or vegetable shortening, chilled

3 large egg yolks

For the custard

¾ cup sugar

4 tablespoons cornstarch

¼ teaspoon salt

2 large egg yolks

2½ cups milk

¼ cup heavy cream

2 teaspoons vanilla extract

For the topping

1 pint (2 cups) each fresh blueberries and raspberries, washed, hulled, and dried

Confectioners' sugar for dusting (optional)

1. *For the crust:* Place the flour, confectioners' sugar, salt, and zest in a food processor and whir to blend. Add the butter, along with the lard or shortening. Pulse until the mixture resembles coarse meal. Dump into a medium bowl. Alternate method: Combine the above

ingredients in a bowl; cut with a pastry cutter until the mixture resembles coarse meal. Add the yolks, and whisk with a fork just until a dough forms. Gently gather into a ball and cover tightly with plastic wrap. Chill for at least 1 hour.

2. *For the custard:* In the top of a double boiler, combine the sugar, cornstarch, and salt. Lightly beat the egg yolks; add the milk and cream, and whisk until blended. Pour into the sugar-cornstarch mixture, whisking to remove any lumps. Cook over medium-low heat for about 8 minutes, stirring constantly and taking care not to let it boil, until the mixture is thick enough to generously coat a spoon. (You should be able to draw a fingertip over the back of the spoon and see a clean stripe.) Remove from the heat. Stir in the vanilla. Scrape into a bowl and set aside to cool to room temperature.

3. Place the dough on a floured pastry cloth and flatten it with the heel of your hand into about a 1-inch-thick round, shaping the edges to keep them even. With a rolling pin, roll from the center outward until the round is roughly 13 inches in diameter. Carefully fold it in half, then again, forming a triangle. Transfer it to an ungreased 11-inch tart pan with a removable rim, positioning it so the point of the triangle is at the center of the pan; carefully unfold it. Trim the overhang to fit the rim. Place the shell in the freezer for at least 15 minutes, until firm.

4. Preheat the oven to 425°F.

5. Line the chilled shell with aluminum foil or parchment (not wax paper), and distribute pie weights (or dried beans) over the bottom. Bake in the oven for 10 minutes. Remove the liner and pie weights. Lower the oven heat to 350°F, and bake for 10 to 15 minutes more, until lightly golden. Let it cool thoroughly before removing the rim.

6. Just before serving, spoon the cooled custard over the bottom of the crust, smoothing it even with the back of a spoon. (You won't need it all; save the excess to spoon over fresh fruit). Arrange the berries in rings, starting at the outer edge, as follows: Two rings of blueberries, then two rings of raspberries; repeat as you work your way toward the center. Dust the top with confectioners' sugar, if desired.

Note: If you have any leftover dough, gather it up and roll it out for a 4½-inch tart. Fill and decorate as with an 11-inch tart, only with single rings of berries.

Tip: If you have a convection oven, a neat trick for drying washed berries is to distribute them in a single layer over a baking sheet lined with paper towels and place them in the oven. Set the temperature control at zero, turning on only the convection control, which circulates air. The berries will dry in no time.

Chocolate Truffle Tart

Pure decadence, but worth every bite. The dense, truffle-like filling and cocoa-shortbread crust make for a truly memorable dessert that will satisfy even the most intense chocolate craving. When I made this tart for a coworker of my husband's in the WINS newsroom, Jack announced happily that his wife and daughter were on diets, so he'd have it all to himself. No such luck! All it took was one bite for those diets to go right out the window. Note: You'll need a food processor for this.   ***Makes one 11-inch tart, serving 8 to 10***

¾ cup all-purpose flour

½ cup confectioners' sugar

3 tablespoons unsweetened cocoa, plus more for dusting

¼ teaspoon ground cinnamon

¼ teaspoon salt

1 cup (2 sticks) unsalted butter (½ cup chilled and cut into chunks)

1 pound bittersweet or semisweet chocolate

½ cup granulated sugar

4 large eggs, lightly beaten

1 tablespoon Kahlúa or other coffee-flavored liqueur (see Note)

1. Preheat the oven to 350°F. Lightly grease an 11-inch tart pan with a removable rim.

2. Place the flour, confectioners' sugar, cocoa, cinnamon, and salt in a food processor and whir to combine. Add the chilled ½ cup of butter, and pulse until well blended. Scatter the mixture evenly over the pan (it's quite crumbly) before pressing it firmly with your fingers over the bottom and sides, starting with the sides and ending with the bottom. Bake in the oven for 15 to 18 minutes, until the crust starts to pull away from the rim. Set it aside to cool while you prepare the filling.

3. In a medium microwave-safe bowl, place half the chocolate and the remaining ½ cup of butter. Heat in the microwave, covered, for 30 seconds at a time, stirring after each interval, until melted (about 1½ minutes total). Stir in the granulated sugar. Set the mixture aside to cool for a few minutes. Add the beaten eggs, and blend with an electric mixer on low speed until smooth. Finely chop the remaining half of the chocolate, and stir it into the melted chocolate mixture along with the Kahlúa.

4. Pour the filling into the crust, and bake in the oven until the edges are set and the center jiggles slightly when the pan is gently shaken, about 20 minutes. Let it cool thoroughly in the pan, at least 2 hours, before removing the rim. Lightly dust the top with unsweetened cocoa before serving.

Note: *You can substitute another liqueur, such as Frangelico, Cointreau, Grand Marnier, or kirsch.*

Crustless Ricotta Tart with Blueberry Sauce

Nothing could be easier than this crustless tart. It takes no more than five minutes to throw together, yet it's fancy enough for company. Serve it with blueberry sauce, or sliced fruit sweetened with a little sugar or honey, for a scrumptious dessert that's low in calories.

Makes one 8-inch tart, serving 4 to 6

2½ cups ricotta
½ cup confectioners' sugar
⅛ teaspoon ground cinnamon
Dash of ground nutmeg
Dash of salt
2 extra-large egg whites, lightly beaten
Zest from 1 lemon
Blueberry Sauce (recipe follows)

1. Preheat the oven to 350°F. Lightly grease an 8-inch springform pan.

2. Place all the ingredients in a large bowl and mix with a wooden spoon until well blended. Scrape into the pan, smoothing even with the back of the spoon. Bake in the oven for 30 minutes, or until the top looks dry and is just starting to brown. Let it cool thoroughly in the pan before removing the rim. Serve with Blueberry Sauce.

Blueberry Sauce

You can make this while the tart is in the oven.   ***Makes about 1½ cups***

1 tablespoon cornstarch
¼ cup sugar
2 cups fresh or frozen blueberries

Place the cornstarch in a medium saucepan and gradually whisk in ⅓ cup of water, making sure no lumps form. Add the sugar and blueberries, and stir until blended. Cook over medium heat, stirring constantly, until the mixture comes to a boil and starts to thicken. Set it aside to cool. Serve it warm, or reheat it just before serving.

Pumpkin-Ginger Tart

This tart is similar to pumpkin pie, only creamier, with ginger preserves to lend a piquant touch.

Makes one 11-inch tart, serving 6 to 8

For the crust

2 cups all-purpose flour

¾ cup confectioners' sugar

1 teaspoon orange zest

¾ cup plus 2 tablespoons unsalted butter, chilled and cut into chunks

For the filling

One 15-ounce can (1¼ cups) pumpkin (*not* pumpkin pie filling)

1⅓ cups half-and-half

½ cup sugar

⅓ cup Dundee Ginger Preserve (or other brand)

2 extra-large eggs

½ teaspoon ground cinnamon

¼ teaspoon ground nutmeg

¼ teaspoon ground cloves

½ teaspoon salt

For the topping

½ cup heavy cream

2 tablespoons confectioners' sugar

1 to 2 tablespoons chopped candied ginger for garnish (optional)

1. *For the crust:* Place the flour, confectioners' sugar, and zest in a food processor and whir to combine. Add the butter and whir until the mixture forms moist crumbs. Scatter them evenly over the bottom of an 11-inch tart pan with a removable rim, and with your fingers press firmly over the bottom and sides, starting with the sides. Place the shell in the freezer for at least 15 minutes, until firm.

2. Preheat the oven to 425°F.

3. Line the chilled shell with aluminum foil or parchment (not wax paper) and distribute pie weights (or dried beans) over the bottom. Bake in the oven for 10 to 15 minutes, until it's just starting to brown around the edges. Remove the liner and pie weights and let the crust cool while you prepare the filling.

4. *For the filling:* Place the pumpkin, half-and-half, sugar, ginger preserves, eggs, cinnamon, nutmeg, cloves, and salt in a large bowl. Beat with an electric mixer on low speed until well blended. Pour into the partially baked crust (see Note). Lower the oven heat to 350°F, and bake for 40 to 50 minutes, until set (the tip of a sharp knife inserted in the center should come out clean). Cool the tart thoroughly in the pan before removing the rim.

5. *For the topping:* Just before serving, whip the cream with the confectioners' sugar until stiff peaks form. Spoon or pipe it around the edges of the tart. Sprinkle chopped candied ginger over the top.

Note: The filling is quite runny, so to keep it from spilling over as you transfer the pan to the oven, I recommend placing the pan on the oven rack before you pour it into the crust.

Pignoli Tart

In New York City, where I've lived for the past twenty years, the neighborhoods feel more like small towns loosely knitted together. Each has its own unique character, best defined by its food shops and eateries. In some, overlapping immigrant populations make for a curious mix—I'd never heard of Chinese-Latin cuisine until I moved here. In others, mainly the outer boroughs, are pockets of ethnicity so deeply rooted they defy change. Arthur Avenue, otherwise known as the Little Italy of the Bronx, is such a place—it's like a trip back in time. Old-world butcher shops and bakeries abound. In the Arthur Avenue Retail Market there's a booth where they roll cigars; and next to it one selling homemade ricotta and a variety of olives. Customers greet vendors like old friends. Transactions are carried on in both English and Italian. In the Arthur Avenue Café across the street, owned by the spry Nonna—Italian for Grandma—a customer asked if he could pay in Euros instead of dollars (she told him she'd trust him to come back later on with the dollars). At Pasquale's restaurant, where my husband and I feasted like kings for less than fifty dollars, we shared a slice of this sublime tart for dessert. Since no words can do it justice, I urge you to make it so you can see for yourself why people come from all over, often traveling some distance, to experience the culinary pleasures of Arthur Avenue.

Makes one 11-inch double-crust tart, serving 8 to 10

For the crust

  2 cups all-purpose flour
  6 tablespoons sugar
  1½ teaspoons baking powder
  ¼ teaspoon salt
  ¼ cup (½ stick) unsalted butter, chilled and cut into chunks
  ¼ cup (4 tablespoons) lard or vegetable shortening, chilled
  1 large egg, separated, plus 1 yolk

For the filling

  ¾ cup sugar
  3 tablespoons cornstarch
  2 cups whole milk

1 large egg, separated, plus 1 yolk

Zest from 1 lemon

1 teaspoon lemon juice

⅓ cup slivered almonds

⅓ cup pine nuts

Confectioners' sugar for dusting

1. *For the crust:* Place the flour, sugar, baking powder, and salt in a food processor and whir to combine. Add the butter and lard. Whir for a few seconds, then pulse until the mixture resembles coarse meal. Dump into a bowl. Alternate method: Place the above ingredients in a bowl and cut with a pastry cutter until the mixture resembles coarse meal. Whisk together the egg, yolk, and 5 tablespoons of cold water. Add to the flour mixture, and whisk with a fork just until dough forms. Gently gather into a ball, and wrap tightly in plastic wrap. Chill while you prepare the filling.

2. *For the filling:* In a medium saucepan, combine the sugar and cornstarch. Gradually pour in the milk, whisking to keep lumps from forming. Cook over medium heat, whisking constantly, until the mixture boils and thickens, 4 to 7 minutes. Remove from the heat. In a small bowl, lightly beat the 2 egg yolks. Stir a small amount of the hot mixture into the yolks, then return it to the hot mixture in the pan, cooking over low heat for 1 minute more while whisking constantly. Stir in the zest. Chill until lukewarm, stirring occasionally to prevent a skin from forming.

3. Place two-thirds of the dough, rolled into a ball, on a floured pastry cloth and flatten it with the heel of your hand into about a 1-inch-thick round, shaping the edges to keep them even. With a rolling pin, roll from the center outward until the round is roughly 13 inches in diameter. Carefully fold it in half, then again, forming a triangle. Transfer it to an ungreased 11-inch tart pan with a removable rim, positioning it so the point of the triangle is at the center of the pan; carefully unfold. Trim the overhang to fit the rim.

4. Spread with the filling. Roll out any leftover scraps of dough with the remaining third of dough as above, to form an 11-inch round. Place over the filling and press around the edges to seal. Chill in the freezer for at least 15 minutes, until firm.

5. Preheat the oven to 375°F.

6. Whisk together the egg white and lemon juice, and brush over the top. Sprinkle with the almonds and pine nuts. Bake in the oven for 30 to 40 minutes, until golden. Let cool in the pan for at least 1½ hours before removing the rim. Dust with confectioners' sugar just before serving.

Chocolate-Cherry Tart

The harmonious blend of chocolate and cherries will have you singing this tart's praises. My husband, Sandy, who keeps a box of chocolates on his desk at all times (he's naturally thin, which drives me crazy, as I have to watch every bite), says it reminds him of chocolate-covered cherries, only infinitely better. If you make it for company, they'll still be talking about it the next day. Top each serving with a dollop of sweetened whipped cream flavored with a teaspoon of kirsch, if desired. You'll need to soak the cherries a day in advance.

Makes one 11-inch tart, serving 8 to 10

For the crust

1 cup (2 sticks) unsalted butter, softened

½ cup sugar

1 large egg

1 teaspoon vanilla extract

2 cups all-purpose flour

5 tablespoons unsweetened cocoa

Scant ½ teaspoon salt

For the filling

1 cup sugar

1 cup dried sweet cherries, firmly packed

⅓ cup kirsch (or other cherry brandy)

3 large eggs

⅓ cup dark corn syrup

¼ cup (½ stick) unsalted butter, melted

1 teaspoon vanilla extract

Scant ½ teaspoon salt

6 ounces bittersweet or semisweet chocolate, chopped to equal 1 cup (see Note)

Confectioners' sugar for dusting

Unsweetened cocoa for dusting

1. A day in advance: In a small saucepan, combine ½ cup of the sugar for the filling with ½ cup of water. Bring to a boil over medium heat, occasionally tilting the pan so that the sugar dissolves. Remove from the heat, and stir in the dried cherries. Cool for 30 minutes. Stir in the kirsch. Let soak, covered, in the refrigerator overnight.

2. *For the crust:* In a large bowl, cream the softened butter with an electric mixer on medium speed. Add the sugar a little at a time, and beat until pale and fluffy. Blend in the egg and vanilla, beating until smooth. Sift together the flour, cocoa, and salt. Add to the creamed mixture, and beat on low speed just until blended. Press firmly over the bottom and sides of an ungreased 11-inch tart pan with a removable rim, starting with the sides and ending with the bottom. Place in the freezer while you prepare the filling.

3. Preheat the oven to 350°F.

4. Drain the cherries, reserving the syrup; set aside. In a large bowl, blend the eggs, corn syrup, melted butter, vanilla, and salt with an electric mixer on low speed. Add the remaining ½ cup of sugar for the filling and ¼ cup of the reserved cherry syrup. Beat until well blended. Stir in the chopped chocolate. Sprinkle the cherries over the bottom of the chilled shell. Pour in the filling. Bake in the oven for 55 to 60 minutes, until the edges are set and the center jiggles only slightly when the pan is gently shaken. Cool thoroughly in the pan before removing the rim. Dust with confectioners' sugar and cocoa.

Note: You can use a food processor for chopping chocolate; pulse until the chocolate is finely chopped but not ground.

Pineapple-Coconut Tartlets

*T*hese bite-size tarts are ideal for large parties when finger food is called for.

Makes 3 dozen 2-inch tarts

1¾ cups all-purpose flour

2 tablespoons cornstarch

½ cup confectioners' sugar

1 teaspoon vanilla extract

1 cup (2 sticks) unsalted butter, softened

1 large egg

½ cup granulated sugar

1½ cups unsweetened flaked coconut (see Notes)

1 cup Polaner pineapple preserves (or other brand)

1. Preheat the oven to 350°F.

2. Place the flour, cornstarch, and confectioners' sugar in a food processor and whir to combine. Add the vanilla and softened butter. Whir for a few seconds, then pulse just until a dough forms. Scrape into a bowl, cover tightly with plastic wrap, and chill for at least 30 minutes.

3. Meanwhile, whisk together the egg and granulated sugar. Add the coconut and stir to blend.

4. Shape the dough with your hands into 1-inch balls and place in ungreased miniature (2-inch cup) muffin tins (see Notes). With your thumb, press a ball over the bottom and sides of each cup to form a tart shell. Spoon 1 slightly rounded teaspoon of the pineapple preserves into each shell, and top with 1 teaspoon of the coconut-egg mixture. Bake in the oven for 20 to 30 minutes, until the edges are lightly golden. If the tops are browning too quickly, cover lightly with aluminum foil the last 5 to 10 minutes of baking. Let cool in the tins. When thoroughly cool, gently pry from the cups with a knife.

Notes: *If you have only one tin, you can bake the tarts in batches. Keep the unused dough chilled, covered in plastic wrap, until ready to use, and wash the tin between batches.*

If unsweetened coconut is unavailable, you can substitute sweetened flaked coconut.

Crisps, Cobblers, and Puddings

She'd been just shy of her thirtieth birthday, an age when most people begin to wonder if it might be worth taking a second look at life's map to see if they're headed in the right direction. Fired with inspiration, she set off in search of Nana's old cookbooks, conveniently stored away in a box in her parents' attic. Several months and dozens of trials later, armed with tentative orders from a handful of restaurants and delis, she had gone about recreating a sort of fifties-style kitchen. In the beginning, yes, her more sophisticated friends had laughed. Pineapple upside-down cake? Apple brown Betty? Rice Krispies treats? That wasn't what people wanted these days, they'd said. Black bottom pie had gone out with Hula Hoops and backyard bomb shelters.

Kitty had merely smiled and gone about filling her orders, which soon swelled to a flood . . .

—From *One Last Dance*

Apple Crisp

If I were stranded on a deserted island and had to pick just one dessert for the duration, it would probably be my mother's apple crisp. It evokes so many happy memories of growing up: Watching my mother peel apples and crumble the floury topping; Sunday dinners when all six of us children would trip over each other to clear the table, the better to snag that last crusty bit stuck to the pan. I went on to make it for my children when they were little and I didn't always have time for a pie. Now that they're grown, my husband is the happy beneficiary. I make it for those occasions when comfort food is called for, or when I have more apples than I know what to do with.

Serves 10 to 12

10 to 12 apples, preferably tart variety (such as McIntosh, Macoun, Greening, or Granny Smith)
Juice from 1 lemon
¾ cup all-purpose flour
1 cup dark brown sugar
1½ teaspoons ground cinnamon
¼ teaspoon ground nutmeg
½ cup (1 stick) unsalted butter, softened

1. Preheat the oven to 350°F. Grease a 9 × 12-inch baking pan.

2. Peel, core, and slice the apples. Toss with the lemon juice. Spread evenly in the pan.

3. Place the flour, dark brown sugar, cinnamon, and nutmeg in a food processor and pulse to combine. Add the butter and whir a few seconds, then pulse until the mixture is crumbly. Alternate method: Place the above ingredients in a bowl and crumble with your fingers or a pastry cutter. Spread evenly over the apple slices in the pan.

4. Bake in the oven for 45 to 55 minutes, until the apples are tender (they should give way when the tip of a sharp knife is inserted into the center). Serve warm or at room temperature.

Note: *You can't miss with a scoop of vanilla ice cream.*

Pear-Cranberry Crisp

*I*n this crisp, the cranberries provide just the right touch of tartness to balance the sweetness of the topping and give it a nice pink marbling throughout. Use firm-ripe pears only; any variety will do, or use a mixture. Served warm, with a scoop of vanilla ice cream, there's nothing more comforting on a cold night.   ***Serves 10 to 12***

8 cups pears (about 8 large pears) peeled, cored, and sliced

1 cup fresh or unthawed frozen cranberries

Juice from 1 lemon

1 tablespoon granulated sugar

¾ cup all-purpose flour

1 cup dark brown sugar

1 teaspoon ground cinnamon

¼ teaspoon ground ginger

¼ teaspoon ground nutmeg

½ cup (1 stick) unsalted butter, softened

1. Preheat the oven to 350°F. Grease a 9 × 12-inch baking pan.

2. Toss the pear slices and cranberries with the lemon juice and granulated sugar. Dump into the pan and pat even.

3. Place the flour, dark brown sugar, cinnamon, ginger, and nutmeg in a food processor and whir to combine. Add the butter, and whir a few seconds, then pulse until crumbly. Alternate method: Place the above ingredients in a bowl and crumble with your fingers or a pastry cutter. Sprinkle evenly over the pear-cranberry mixture in the pan.

4. Bake in the oven for 45 to 55 minutes, until tender when pierced with a knife. Serve warm or at room temperature.

Apple Brown Betty
with Lemon Sauce

This is one of those homespun favorites that never goes out of style. Traditionally it's made with breadcrumbs or graham cracker crumbs, but I've adapted it using gingersnap crumbs, which enhances the flavor of the apples.

Serves 6 to 8

4 to 5 medium apples, preferably tart variety (such as McIntosh, Macoun, Greening, or
    Granny Smith), peeled, cored, and sliced to equal 5 cups
1 tablespoon lemon juice
3 tablespoons unsalted butter
2 cups gingersnap crumbs (I use Peek Freans Ginger Crisps)
½ cup firmly packed dark brown sugar
½ teaspoon lemon zest
Lemon Sauce (recipe follows)

1. Preheat the oven to 375°F. Lightly grease an 8-inch square baking pan.

2. Toss the apples with the lemon juice and set aside.

3. Place the butter in a medium skillet and cook over the lowest heat until melted. Add the gingersnap crumbs and cook, stirring continuously, until lightly toasted, about 3 minutes. Scatter a third of the crumbs over the bottom of the pan. Arrange half of the apple slices over the crumbs in the pan.

4. Combine the dark brown sugar and zest; sprinkle half over the apple slices in the pan. Scatter with half of the remaining crumbs. Layer with the remaining apple slices, and scatter the remaining crumbs over the top. Carefully pour ⅓ cup of hot water over the top, disturbing the crumbs as little as possible.

5. Bake in the oven for 40 to 50 minutes, until tender when pierced with a knife. Serve warm, with Lemon Sauce.

Lemon Sauce

Makes 1⅓ cups

⅓ cup sugar
1 tablespoon cornstarch
Dash of salt
3 tablespoons unsalted butter, softened
1½ tablespoons lemon juice
1 teaspoon lemon zest

In the top of a double boiler, combine the sugar, cornstarch, and salt. Slowly stir in 1 cup of water. Place *over* boiling water (make sure the bottom of the pan isn't touching the water). Cook, stirring constantly, until the mixture thickens and becomes translucent (it should generously coat a spoon). Remove from the boiling water. Stir in the butter, lemon juice, and zest. Serve warm. (Reheat in a Pyrex measuring cup in the microwave just before serving, if necessary.)

Blackberry-Rhubarb Cobbler

*I*n summer, when my husband and I stay at our favorite inn on Orcas Island, The Place at Cayou Cove, we have access to the innkeepers' organic garden and all the pears, apples, and blackberries we can pick. I took advantage of the bounty to create this cobbler, which to my mind is just about the perfect summer dessert, with its hint of citrus and a jewel-like luster that's hard to describe (I encourage you to see for yourself!). If fresh blackberries aren't available, frozen berries work just as well.

Tip: When rhubarb is in season, buy extra and freeze it, sliced. It keeps well frozen for several months. The same for blackberries: If you're lucky enough to live in an area where they're plentiful, freeze them in single layers on baking sheets then place them in zip-top bags.

Serves 10 to 12

4 cups fresh or unthawed frozen blackberries

3 cups rhubarb cut into ½-inch slices

2 teaspoons lemon juice

1½ teaspoons orange zest

3½ tablespoons tapioca starch or cornstarch

1¼ cups sugar

2 cups all-purpose flour

2 teaspoons baking powder

½ teaspoon salt

½ cup (1 stick) unsalted butter, chilled and cut into chunks

½ cup milk

1. Preheat the oven to 425°F.

2. Gently toss (I use my hands) the blackberries and rhubarb with the lemon juice, zest, tapioca starch, and 1 cup of the sugar. Place in an ungreased 10 × 13-inch casserole dish or baking pan. Set aside while you prepare the topping.

3. Place the flour, remaining ¼ cup of sugar, baking powder, and salt in a food processor and whir to combine. Add the butter and whir for a few seconds, then pulse until the mix-

ture resembles coarse meal (the butter should be the size of lentils). Alternate method: Place the above ingredients in a bowl and cut with a pastry cutter until crumbly. Add the milk, and pulse (or whisk with a fork), just until the mixture starts to come together in a sticky mass. Turn onto a floured pastry cloth and gently shape into a ball. With a rolling pin, gently roll the dough into an oval or rectangle large enough to fit the pan. With a sharp knife dipped in flour, cut the dough on the diagonal, starting at the bottom left corner, into roughly 3-inch strips. Repeat, starting at the top left corner, in a crosshatch pattern, to form diamond-shaped wedges. Place the wedges over the fruit, about ⅛ inch apart.

4. Bake in the oven for 20 minutes. Cover loosely with aluminum foil, and reduce the oven heat to 325°F. Bake for 20 minutes more, until the fruit is bubbling up between the biscuit wedges. Let cool for 45 minutes to 1 hour. Serve warm or at room temperature.

Peach Cobbler

With such a large family to feed, my mother always brought fruit in bulk. I remember the weekly trip to DeMartini's, a large roadside fruit and vegetable stand that sold organically grown produce long before the general public became enlightened about such matters. With all that we children nibbled on as we roamed the aisles, Mr. DeMartini used to threaten jokingly to weigh us when we came in and when we went out, and charge my mother for the difference. I learned to select fruit not by size or color, but by smell. And nothing is more fragrant than tree-ripened peaches at the height of the season. My mom would buy a crate, and on the way home our Pontiac station wagon would be steeped in the intoxicating perfume. For supper, she'd make peach cobbler. Serve it warm, with a scoop of vanilla ice cream or simply drizzled with a little cream.

Serves 8 to 10

3 pounds ripe peaches or 2 pounds, 8 ounces (about 8 cups) frozen peach slices

1 tablespoon lemon juice

1¼ cups sugar

1 tablespoon tapioca starch or cornstarch

1½ cups all-purpose flour

1 tablespoon baking powder

¼ teaspoon salt

½ teaspoon lemon zest

¼ cup (½ stick) unsalted butter, chilled and cut into chunks

⅔ cup to ¾ cup buttermilk

1. Preheat the oven to 400°F.

2. Fill a stockpot with water to about two-thirds full, and bring to a boil. Drop the peaches in with a slotted spoon. Parboil 4 or 5 at a time for 2 minutes, then scoop them out and place them in a colander. Rinse under cold water; the skins will slip right off. Pit and slice. Place in an ungreased 9 × 12-inch baking pan or casserole dish. With your fingers, gently toss with lemon juice, then with 1 cup of the sugar and tapioca starch.

3. Cover with aluminum foil and place in the oven until the syrup is bubbling, about 20 minutes (30 minutes if using frozen peaches). Meanwhile, in a medium bowl, mix together the flour, remaining ¼ cup of sugar, baking powder, salt, and zest. Add the butter, and cut with a pastry cutter until the mixture resembles coarse meal. Add ⅔ cup of the buttermilk, whisking with a fork just until it's incorporated. Dribble in more, if need be, just until a soft dough forms. Don't overmix!

4. Spoon in dollops over the hot peaches (it won't cover them all). Bake in the oven for 20 to 25 minutes, until the dough is thoroughly baked (test a chunk with a fork for doneness). Let cool to warm or room temperature before serving.

Persimmon Pudding
with Lemon Sauce

T he persimmon is an oft-misunderstood fruit. Many people I've spoken to have never even tried one; others, who have, wrinkle their noses because they don't know that you have to eat them soft-ripe or they taste, as one friend put it, "like baby aspirin." If you've never had the pleasure of eating a perfectly ripe persimmon, you don't know what you're missing. They're sweet as honey, with a silken flesh that glides over the tongue. The trick is to know when they're ripe: The Hachiya, the larger of the two most common varieties, shaped like a oversize acorn, must be ripened (at room temperature) to the point of appearing almost rotten, or it's completely inedible; the Fuyu, the smaller, flatter cousin to the Hachiya, can be eaten when firm-ripe. Both are equally delicious, though I prefer Hachiyas for this recipe, as they yield more pulp. My mother used to make this at Thanksgiving and Christmas. Drizzled with warm lemon sauce, it's a rare treat. *Serves 10 to 12*

4 to 5 ripe persimmons, to equal 2 cups pulp (see Note)

3 large eggs

1 cup sugar

1½ cups all-purpose flour

1 teaspoon baking powder

1 teaspoon baking soda

½ teaspoon salt

2 teaspoons ground cinnamon

1 teaspoon ground ginger

½ teaspoon ground nutmeg

½ cup unsalted butter, melted

2½ cups whole milk

1 cup chopped walnuts or pecans (optional)

Lemon Sauce (page 201)

1. Preheat the oven to 325°F. Grease a 9 × 12-inch baking pan or casserole dish.

2. Scoop the pulp from the persimmons, discarding the skins. In a blender or food processor, whir until smooth. Place in a large bowl. Add the remaining ingredients, and mix until well blended with an electric mixer on medium speed. Pour into the pan (the batter is quite thin), and bake in the oven for 1 hour, until the edges start to pull away from the sides of the pan. Serve warm, drizzled with Lemon Sauce.

Note: I usually buy the persimmons a week or so in advance to ensure that they'll be properly ripened. Before using, they should be soft-ripe (almost mushy) to the touch, with nearly translucent skins.

Date Pudding with Caramel Sauce

I n England, from whence this derives, pudding is another word for dessert, which is why this is more like a cake than a pudding. Either way, it's light and moist, drenched in a baked-on caramel sauce, with a hint of rum.

Serves 12 to 14

For the pudding

1 cup dates, preferably Medjool

1 teaspoon vanilla extract

1 teaspoon baking soda

2 cups all-purpose flour, sifted

¾ cup sugar

1 teaspoon baking powder

¼ teaspoon salt

5 tablespoons unsalted butter, softened

1 large egg, lightly beaten

For the sauce

7 tablespoons unsalted butter

¾ cup heavy cream

1⅓ cups firmly packed dark brown sugar

2 tablespoons dark rum

1. Bring a 3- to 4-quart saucepan of water to a boil. Add the dates and let simmer on medium-high heat for 5 minutes. Drain, then submerge in a bowl of ice water; remove the skins (they should come off easily underwater) and pits. Return to the saucepan with 1 cup of water, the vanilla, and baking soda. Bring to a boil over medium-high heat and simmer, stirring constantly, for 2 minutes. Set aside to cool to room temperature.

2. Preheat the oven to 350°F and grease a 9 × 12-inch baking pan.

3. Combine the sifted flour, sugar, baking powder, and salt. In a large bowl, cream the softened butter with an electric mixer on medium speed. Add the date mixture and beat on low speed until blended. Stir in the flour mixture and the beaten egg, just until blended (don't overmix!). Scrape into the pan (it's fairly thick), smoothing even with a spatula. Bake in the oven for 25 to 30 minutes, until a toothpick inserted into the center comes out clean. Meanwhile, prepare the sauce.

4. In a small saucepan, place the butter, cream, dark brown sugar, and 3 tablespoons of water. Bring to a boil over medium heat, stirring constantly. Reduce the heat to low and simmer, stirring constantly, for 3 minutes more. Remove from the heat. Stir in the rum. Cover, and set aside in a warm place.

5. Immediately after removing the pudding from the oven, cut it into squares. Spoon the warm sauce over the top, allowing it to seep into the crevices and along the sides of the pan. Return to the oven for 3 minutes more, until the sauce starts to bubble. Let cool in the pan. Serve warm or at room temperature.

Microwave Cranberry Pudding with Butter–Brandy Sauce

*T*his pudding is the perfect thing for last-minute dinner guests, or when your oven is in use: It cooks in minutes in the microwave and looks and tastes like something you slaved over. Make it for a small gathering at Thanksgiving while the turkey is roasting.

Serves 4 to 6

1½ cups finely crushed dry breadcrumbs
1 cup sugar
1 tablespoon all-purpose flour
1½ teaspoons baking powder
¼ teaspoon salt
¼ teaspoon ground cinnamon
¼ teaspoon ground ginger
¼ teaspoon ground allspice
⅓ cup milk
⅓ cup unsalted butter, melted
1 cup coarsely chopped fresh cranberries
1 large egg, lightly beaten
Microwave Butter-Brandy Sauce (recipe follows)

1. Grease the bottom only of a 4-cup Pyrex measuring cup. Cut a parchment round to fit the bottom and grease that, too.

2. Mix together the breadcrumbs, sugar, flour, baking powder, salt, cinnamon, ginger, and allspice. Add the milk, melted butter, cranberries, and egg, and stir vigorously to blend. Scrape the batter into the measuring cup and pack it down so there are no air pockets. Cover tightly with 2 layers of plastic wrap, making sure there are no spaces for the steam to escape.

3. Heat in the microwave on *medium* power (it's important to have it at the correct setting) for 5 minutes. Rotate the measuring cup a half-turn, then microwave on *medium* for 5 to 6 minutes more, until the pudding starts to pull away from the sides of the cup. Carefully peel off the plastic wrap—the escaping steam can easily burn your fingers—and let the pudding sit, uncovered, for 5 minutes. Run a sharp, thin-bladed knife around the edges to loosen it and invert it onto a serving plate. Serve warm, with Microwave Butter-Brandy Sauce (recipe follows) ladled over individual slices.

Microwave Butter-Brandy Sauce

Makes 1 cup

½ cup sugar
1 teaspoon cornstarch
½ cup heavy cream
¼ cup (½ stick) unsalted butter, cut into chunks
1 teaspoon brandy

Combine the sugar and cornstarch in a 4-cup Pyrex measuring cup, and mix well. Add the cream and butter; stir to blend. Microwave, uncovered, on *high* power for 3 minutes, stopping after each minute to stir, making sure all the sugar is dissolved. Stir in the brandy. Let cool slightly before serving.

Chilled Mango Pudding with Pineapple-Rum Sauce

*T*his molded pudding is at once light and rich. Perfect for parties because it looks so pretty at the center of the table.

Makes one 1½-quart pudding

1½ envelopes (about 3½ teaspoons) unflavored gelatin

¾ cup sugar

½ teaspoon salt

1¼ cups mango nectar (it can be found in the fruit juice section of supermarkets)

1 teaspoon lemon zest

1¼ cups chopped firm-ripe mango

2 cups heavy cream

Pineapple-Rum Sauce (recipe follows)

1. Sprinkle the gelatin over ¼ cup of water; set aside to soften.

2. In a small saucepan, combine the sugar and salt. Stir in the mango nectar, and cook over medium heat, stirring constantly, until the sugar is dissolved. Remove from the heat and stir in the softened gelatin.

3. Chill the mixture until thickened; it should form a soft mound when dropped from a spoon. (This takes about 30 to 40 minutes; keep a close watch once it starts to gel, as it hardens quickly at this point.) Fold in the zest and chopped mango.

4. In a medium bowl, whip the cream with an electric mixer on high speed until stiff peaks form. Fold the whipped cream into the gelatin mixture.

5. Scrape into a 1½-quart mold or bowl and chill until firm, at least 6 hours or overnight.

6. Dip the mold into a large bowl (or kitchen sink) partially filled with hot water, for 2 to 3 seconds. Place a serving plate over the top of the mold and invert; gently shake to loosen it. Serve chilled with Pineapple-Rum Sauce.

Pineapple-Rum Sauce

Makes about 1½ cups

One 8-ounce can crushed pineapple, in its own juice
½ cup sugar
1½ tablespoons cornstarch
About ⅔ cup unsweetened pineapple juice
2 teaspoons lemon juice
½ teaspoon lemon zest
1 to 2 tablespoons rum

Drain the pineapple well, reserving the juice; set aside.

In a small saucepan, combine the sugar and cornstarch. Add enough pineapple juice to the reserved juice to equal 1 cup. Stir the juice into the sugar mixture, whisking to keep lumps from forming. Bring to a boil over medium-high heat, then lower the heat and simmer, stirring constantly, until clear and thickened. Remove from the heat; stir in the lemon juice, zest, crushed pineapple, and rum. Chill until ready to serve. Serve cold, ladled over individual servings of pudding.

Chocolate Bread Pudding with Raspberry Sauce

T his is the best of both worlds, in my opinion: It holds it own among the finest of chocolate desserts while retaining its homespun roots. Lighter than most bread puddings, yet at the same time moist and chewy, I describe it as a cross between a brownie and a chocolate soufflé. The raspberry sauce makes the perfect complimentary touch.   *Serves 12 to 14*

16 ounces semisweet chocolate, chopped, or semisweet chocolate morsels
1 cup heavy cream
⅔ cup firmly packed dark brown sugar
5 large eggs, separated
½ cup (1 stick) unsalted butter, cut into chunks
1 teaspoon vanilla extract
4 cups soft white bread cubes, crusts removed (such as challah or another egg bread)
Raspberry Sauce (recipe follows)

1. Preheat the oven to 350°F. Generously grease a 9 × 11-inch baking pan or casserole dish.

2. In a medium saucepan, combine the chopped chocolate and the cream. Cook over the lowest heat, stirring constantly, until the chocolate is melted. Add ⅓ cup of the brown sugar, and stir until dissolved. Remove from the heat. Add the egg yolks, one at a time, stirring after each addition until well blended. Return the pan to the stove and continue cooking over low heat for 2 to 3 more minutes, stirring constantly, until the mixture thickens enough to generously coat a spoon (it will already be somewhat thick, but when it's the proper consistency you should be able to draw a fingertip over the back of the spoon and see a clear path). Remove from the heat. Add the butter and vanilla, stirring until the butter is melted.

3. Place the bread cubes in a large bowl and pour the hot mixture over them. Toss until the mixture is evenly distributed.

4. Beat the egg whites with an electric mixer on high speed until soft peaks form. Gradually add the remaining ⅓ cup of brown sugar, beating until stiff peaks form. Carefully fold the egg whites into the chocolate-bread mixture. Dump into the pan. Nest in a larger pan (such as a roasting pan); pour boiling water into the larger pan to a depth of about an inch. Bake in the oven for 35 to 40 minutes, until set. Serve warm, with Raspberry Sauce.

Raspberry Sauce

Makes 1½ cups

7 tablespoons sugar
4 teaspoons cornstarch
20 ounces (two 10-ounce packages) frozen raspberries, thawed

In a medium saucepan, combine the sugar and cornstarch. Gradually add ⅓ cup of water, whisking to keep lumps from forming. Add the raspberries, and cook over medium heat, stirring constantly, until the mixture is clear and bubbly and thick enough to generously coat a spoon. Remove from the heat. Pour into a fine-mesh sieve placed over a bowl. With the back of a spoon, push through the sieve. Discard the pulp. (Some seeds will pass through; don't worry about it.) Serve warm, ladled over individual servings. Reheat in the microwave just before serving, if necessary.

Banana-Coconut Bread Pudding with Butterscotch Sauce

I love just about anything made with bananas, but until recently I hadn't had much experience with bread puddings. Perhaps because they weren't in my mother's repertoire, or because I didn't think them elegant enough for company. One bite of this pudding and I realized how wrong I'd been to overlook this seemingly humble dessert. ***Serves 12 to 14***

6 cups bread cubes (such as challah or brioche)

3 large firm-ripe bananas, sliced

¾ cup sweetened flaked coconut

¼ cup chopped candied orange peel (optional)

3 large eggs

¾ cup firmly packed light brown sugar

1½ teaspoons ground cinnamon

¼ teaspoon ground nutmeg

¾ teaspoon banana extract (you can substitute vanilla extract)

1½ cups milk

½ cup canned coconut milk

½ cup half-and-half

Butterscotch Sauce (recipe follows)

1. Generously grease a 9 × 12-inch baking pan or casserole dish.

2. Scatter half the bread cubes over the bottom of the baking pan or casserole dish. Arrange the banana slices over the top. Sprinkle with the coconut and the chopped candied peel, if using, and cover with the remaining bread cubes.

3. In a large bowl, whisk the eggs slightly. Add the brown sugar, cinnamon, nutmeg, banana extract, milk, coconut milk, and half-and-half. Whisk until blended. Pour over the bread cube mixture, pressing down with a spatula to make sure all the liquid is absorbed. Cover and chill for 1 hour.

4. Preheat the oven to 350°F.

5. Bake in the oven for 45 to 50 minutes, until the center no longer jiggles when the pan is gently shaken. Serve warm, with Butterscotch Sauce.

Butterscotch Sauce

Makes 1 cup

> 1 egg yolk, lightly beaten
> ¼ cup (½ stick) unsalted butter, cut into chunks
> ⅔ cup dark brown sugar
> ⅓ cup light corn syrup
> 2 teaspoons brandy or dark rum

In the top of a double boiler, combine all the ingredients except the brandy with ¼ cup of cold water. Place *over* boiling water (make sure the bottom of the pan isn't touching the water), and cook, whisking continuously, until the butter is melted and the sauce is thick enough to generously coat a spoon, about 15 minutes. Remove from the heat, and stir in the brandy. Serve warm, ladled over individual servings. Reheat in the microwave, in a Pyrex measuring cup, just before serving, if necessary.

Quick Breads
and Muffins

When the muffin batter was loosely mixed, she divided it into three smaller bowls. Into the first she tossed handfuls of chopped apples and walnuts. In the other two went frozen blueberries and peaches left over from last summer's harvest. By now she knew how many of each kind to bake so that no one went away disappointed. Only the pumpkin-cranberry muffins she made at Thanksgiving and Christmas flew out of here faster than she could keep up with.

Kitty marveled at the popularity of her tea room. Four years ago, armed with little more than a bright idea and the need to augment her kindergarten teacher's salary, she couldn't have foreseen that this place would evolve into a local institution of sorts. A watering hole where neighbors met to strategize about a traffic light they were circulating a petition for . . . and the Ladies' Garden Society gathered to plan their annual begonia festival. Where town councilmen and church deacons and doctors rubbed elbows with minimum-wage workers from the tannery, and children trooped in after school for something to sweeten their walk home.

Here, professors from the university found solace and civilized company away from pierced tongues and purple hair. And young lovers traced their initials in the steamy windows. Kitty knew of several marriage proposals that had been made under this roof. And who could ever forget the Ogilvies' tearful breakup last winter after Everett Ogilvie confessed to his wife of fourteen years that he was in love with their Finnish au pair?

—From *One Last Dance*

219

Banana Bread

*J*udging from the mail I've received over the years, this recipe is the number one favorite of my readers. It's no mystery as to why: The bread is moist and intensely banana flavored; it's also easy to whip up, and makes use of those overripe bananas in every fruit bowl. One year, when my husband and I were staying at one of our favorite resorts, The Horned Dorset, in Puerto Rico, I mentioned to the owner, with whom we'd become friendly, that I thought the banana bread they served at breakfast was a bit bland. I offered to bake him my own recipe, and Wilhelm let me use the kitchen in his house down the road, which was how I came to spend the last day of our vacation baking banana bread for the entire resort—a true busman's holiday! The following morning, Sandy and I got a kick out of watching how quickly it disappeared off the plates on the tables around us. **Makes one 8½ × 4½-inch loaf, or three 3 × 6½-inch loaves**

2 large eggs, at room temperature
½ cup vegetable oil or coconut oil
1 cup Sucanat, turbinado, or Demerara sugar
1 teaspoon vanilla extract
3 *very* ripe bananas (skins should be generously freckled)
1¼ cups all-purpose flour
1 teaspoon baking soda
Pinch of salt
½ cup coarsely chopped walnuts or pecans (optional)

1. Preheat the oven to 350°F. Grease one 8½ × 4½-inch loaf pan, or three 3 × 6½-inch loaf pans.

2. Place the eggs, oil, Sucanat, and vanilla in a large bowl and blend with an electric mixer on low speed for 3 minutes. In a shallow bowl (I use a soup bowl), mash the bananas with a fork. Add to the batter and blend well.

3. Combine the flour, baking soda, and salt. Add to the wet mixture and blend until smooth, about 1 minute. Stir in the nuts, if using.

4. Scrape into the pan(s), and bake in the oven for 45 to 50 minutes (25 to 30 minutes for small loaves), until a toothpick inserted into the center of the loaf comes out clean. If the top is browning too quickly, cover it lightly with aluminum foil the last 10 minutes or so of baking. Let cool for 5 minutes, then remove from the pans and place on a wire rack. Serve warm or at room temperature.

Note: *This bread keeps well refrigerated (it's even better the next day!) for up to a week, tightly wrapped.*

Best-Ever Zucchini Bread

*I*n the days when I had a vegetable garden, I'd swear I could hear the zucchini growing in the night. After weeks of sautéing, baking, stuffing, steaming, and stewing whatever I couldn't give away, my family would be at the point of zucchini boycott. The one thing we never got tired of was this bread: Moist and orange-flavored, studded with flecks of green, it's the answer to zucchini overload.

Makes two 8½ × 4½-inch loaves

2 cups grated zucchini

2 teaspoons orange zest

3¼ cups all-purpose flour

1½ teaspoons baking powder

1½ teaspoons baking soda

1 teaspoon salt

2½ teaspoons ground cinnamon

½ teaspoon ground cloves

4 large eggs, at room temperature

1½ cups sugar

¾ cup vegetable oil or coconut oil

⅔ cup orange juice

⅔ cup coarsely chopped walnuts

1. Preheat the oven to 350°F. Grease the bottoms only of two 8½ × 4½-inch loaf pans.

2. Combine the zucchini and the zest, and set aside.

3. Sift together the flour, baking powder, baking soda, salt, cinnamon, and cloves.

4. In a large bowl, beat the eggs with an electric mixer on low speed. Add the sugar a little at a time, mixing until well blended. Add the oil, juice, and zucchini, beating until blended. Add the flour mixture and nuts, and beat on low speed just until incorporated. Increase the speed to medium and beat just until smooth. Pour into the pans.

5. Bake in the oven for 45 to 50 minutes, until a toothpick inserted into the center of one loaf comes out clean. If the tops are browning too quickly, cover lightly with aluminum foil the last 10 minutes or so of baking. Let cool for 5 minutes, then remove from the pans and place on a wire rack.

Caramel Apple Bread

This unusual, and unusually delicious, bread studded with melted toffee bits and topped with a coconut-flecked glaze is a cross between an applesauce cake and a caramel apple. Serve it toasted for breakfast, or for dessert with a scoop of ice cream.

Makes one 8½ × 4½-inch loaf

1 large egg, at room temperature

1 cup unsweetened applesauce

½ cup (1 stick) unsalted butter, melted

¼ cup firmly packed light brown sugar

1 tablespoon vanilla extract

2 cups all-purpose flour

2 teaspoons baking powder

½ teaspoon baking soda

¼ teaspoon salt

¼ teaspoon ground cinnamon

¾ cup Skor English Toffee Bits

¼ cup unsweetened or sweetened flaked coconut

¼ cup granulated sugar

1. Preheat the oven to 350°F. Grease and flour an 8½ × 4½-inch loaf pan.

2. In a large bowl, blend the egg, applesauce, ¼ cup of the melted butter, the brown sugar, and vanilla with an electric mixer on medium speed. Combine the flour, baking powder, baking soda, salt, and cinnamon. Add to the wet mixture and beat just until incorporated (don't overmix!). Stir in the toffee bits. Scrape into the pan, and bake in the oven for 35 to 40 minutes, until the center of the loaf springs back when lightly pressed.

3. Meanwhile, combine the coconut, granulated sugar, and remaining ¼ cup of melted butter. Spread the mixture over the hot loaf immediately after removing it from the oven, and return it to the oven for 10 to 15 minutes more, until the topping bubbles and starts to brown. (Place a sheet of aluminum foil on the rack below to catch drips.) Immediately after removing it from the oven, run a sharp knife around the edges of the pan to keep the loaf from sticking as it contracts. Let cool for 10 to 15 minutes, then remove from the pan and place on a wire rack. Serve warm or at room temperature.

Cranberry Cornbread

*W*hen my brother and sisters and I were growing up, we loved my mother's cornbread, warm from the oven with maple syrup poured over the top. Here, the cranberries give this sweet cornbread just enough tartness to suit my grownup taste buds. It doesn't even need jam.

Makes one 8 × 8-inch cornbread

1 cup fresh or unthawed frozen cranberries
½ cup confectioners' sugar
1 cup all-purpose flour
¾ cup cornmeal
½ cup granulated sugar
1 tablespoon baking powder
¾ teaspoon salt
1 cup whole milk
1 large egg
2 tablespoons unsalted butter, melted

1. Preheat the oven to 400°F. Grease an 8-inch square baking pan.

2. Slice each cranberry in half and toss with the confectioners' sugar until the cranberries are coated. Add the flour, cornmeal, granulated sugar, baking powder, and salt to the cranberry mixture, and stir to combine.

3. Whisk together the milk, egg, and melted butter. Pour over the cornmeal-cranberry mixture and stir just until the dry ingredients are incorporated (don't overmix!). Pour into the pan. Bake in the oven for 20 minutes, until a toothpick inserted into the center comes out clean. Let cool slightly in the pan before cutting into squares. Serve warm or at room temperature.

Lemon Bread

*T*his is my father-in-law Rob Kenyon's recipe. Its airy texture and lemon glaze make it more of a cake than a bread. It's so moist, it doesn't need butter. Note: You can substitute poppyseeds for nuts, if you like.

Makes one 8½ × 4½-inch loaf

½ cup (1 stick) unsalted butter, softened

1¼ cups sugar

2 large eggs, at room temperature

1 cup plus 3 tablespoons all-purpose flour, sifted

1 teaspoon baking powder

Scant ½ teaspoon salt

½ cup milk

Juice and zest from 1 medium lemon

½ cup chopped walnuts or pecans (or 1½ tablespoons poppyseeds)

1. Preheat the oven to 350°F. Grease an 8½ × 4½-inch loaf pan.

2. In a large bowl, cream the softened butter with an electric mixer on medium speed. Gradually add 1 cup of the sugar, and beat until light and fluffy. Add the eggs one at a time, beating well after each addition. Resift the flour with the baking powder and salt. Add half of the flour mixture to the creamed mixture, and mix on low speed just until blended, scraping the bowl with a spatula as you go along. Add all of the milk, and mix just until blended. Add the remaining flour mixture, zest (reserve the juice for the glaze), and nuts. Mix just until incorporated. Scrape into the pan, and bake in the oven for 55 to 60 minutes, until a toothpick inserted into the center comes out clean.

3. *Meanwhile, prepare the glaze:* Place the lemon juice and remaining ¼ cup of sugar in a small microwave-safe bowl. Cover with plastic wrap and heat in the microwave for 1 minute. Stir to dissolve any sugar that may have settled at the bottom.

4. Immediately after removing the loaf from the oven, poke holes in the top with a toothpick, and drizzle with the glaze. Let cool for 30 minutes before removing from the pan and placing on a wire rack. Serve warm or at room temperature.

Pumpkin-Date Bread

I love our local greenmarket in the fall, when it's a veritable cornucopia of late-harvest vegetables, pears and apples, and heaps of pumpkins. I buy the smaller sugar pumpkins for baking; they yield the most pulp and, true to their name, they're sweeter than the kind used for jack-o'-lanterns. One medium pumpkin will yield enough for two loaves, with plenty left over to freeze for later use. Serve this moist, spicy bread with a cup of hot cider. It's also good made with canned pumpkin.   ***Makes two 9 × 5-inch loaves***

1 cup granulated sugar

1 cup firmly packed dark brown sugar

1 cup vegetable oil or coconut oil

4 large eggs, at room temperature

2 cups pumpkin puree, or one 15-ounce can of pumpkin

3½ cups all-purpose flour

2 teaspoons baking soda

1 teaspoon baking powder

1¼ teaspoons salt

1 teaspoon ground cinnamon

¾ teaspoon ground nutmeg

¾ teaspoon ground allspice

½ teaspoon ground cloves

⅔ cup apple juice

1 cup roughly chopped walnuts or pecans

1 cup chopped dates (see Note)

1. *If using fresh pumpkin, prepare the puree in advance:* Scrub 1 small or medium sugar pumpkin, and cut it in half. Place the halves cut side down on a greased, foil-lined baking sheet. Bake in a 400°F oven for 45 to 60 minutes (depending on the size of the pumpkin) until tender when pricked with a fork. When cool, scrape out and discard the stringy pulp, then scoop out the soft flesh. Puree in a blender or food processor.

2. For the bread, preheat the oven to 350°F. Grease and flour two 9 × 5-inch loaf pans.

3. In a large bowl, blend the granulated sugar, brown sugar, and oil with an electric mixer on medium speed, until smooth. Add the eggs one at a time, beating well after each addition. Add the pumpkin puree, and blend until smooth.

4. Sift together the dry ingredients. To the creamed mixture add in the following order, beating after each addition just until incorporated: a third of the flour mixture; half of the apple juice; half of the remaining flour mixture; the remaining apple juice; then the remaining flour mixture. Stir in the chopped nuts and dates. Pour the batter into the pans. Bake in the oven for 1 hour to 1 hour and 10 minutes, until a toothpick inserted into the center of a loaf comes out clean. If the tops are browning too quickly, cover lightly with aluminum foil the last 10 or 15 minutes of baking. Cool for 5 minutes before removing from the pans and placing on a wire rack. Serve warm or at room temperature.

Note: A quick and efficient way to chop dates is to place them in a food processor with 1 tablespoon of flour for each cup of dates, and pulse until the dates are the size of corn kernels. The flour keeps them from clumping together.

Cherry–Cream Cheese Bread

R eminiscent of a cherry-cheese Danish, this moist bread ribboned with cream cheese is as *festive as it is delicious. It's a standout at bake sales, company picnics, and church socials, so be sure to bake extra for those occasions. You'll need to soak the cherries in advance.*

Makes one 8½ × 4½-inch loaf

1½ cups sugar

1 cup dried sweet or sour cherries

6 ounces cream cheese, softened (not non-fat)

2 large eggs, at room temperature

2 cups all-purpose flour

1½ teaspoons baking powder

½ teaspoon baking soda

½ teaspoon salt

¾ cup whole milk

¼ cup (½ stick) unsalted butter, melted

1 teaspoon almond extract

½ cup roughly chopped walnuts or pecans

1. Several hours or up to a day in advance: In a small saucepan, combine ½ cup of the sugar with 1 cup of water. Cook over medium heat until boiling. Stir in the dried cherries, cover, and set aside.

2. Just before starting the bread, preheat the oven to 350°F. Grease an 8½ × 4½-inch loaf pan.

3. Drain and roughly chop the cherries; set aside.

4. Place the softened cream cheese in a food processor and whir until fluffy. Add 1 of the eggs, and whir until smooth. Scrape into a small bowl, and set aside.

5. Combine the flour, remaining 1 cup of sugar, the baking powder, baking soda, and salt. Make a well in the center of the dry ingredients, and pour in the milk, melted butter, re-maining egg, and the almond extract. Stir with a wooden spoon, or blend with an electric

mixer on low speed, just until the dry ingredients are incorporated (don't overmix!). Fold in the cherries and chopped nuts.

6. Spoon half of the batter into the pan. Spread with the cream cheese mixture, smoothing with the back of a spoon to cover the batter. Spoon in the remaining batter, smoothing the top.

7. Bake in the oven for 1 hour to 1 hour and 10 minutes, until a toothpick inserted into the center comes out clean. If the top is browning too quickly, cover lightly with aluminum foil the last 10 or 15 minutes of baking. Let cool for 5 minutes before removing from the pan and placing on a wire rack. Serve warm or at room temperature. It keeps well in the refrigerator, tightly wrapped.

Eggnog Bread

T his delicately spiced loaf is a great way to use up any eggnog left over from the holidays. Buy whole nutmeg and grate your own, if possible; it's more aromatic than the pre-ground kind.

Makes one 8½ × 4½-inch loaf

1 large egg, at room temperature

1 cup sugar

1 cup eggnog (available in the dairy section of supermarkets around the holidays. If unavailable and you're feeling creative, see the recipe that follows)

½ cup (1 stick) unsalted butter, melted

2 tablespoons dark rum

2¼ cups all-purpose flour

2 teaspoons baking powder

½ teaspoon salt

¾ teaspoon ground nutmeg

1. Preheat the oven to 350°F. Grease an 8½ × 4½-inch loaf pan.

2. In a large bowl, beat the egg with an electric mixer on low speed. Add the sugar, eggnog, melted butter, and rum, and mix until well blended. Sift together the flour, baking powder, salt, and ¼ teaspoon of the nutmeg. Add to the wet mixture all at once, mixing just until the dry ingredients are incorporated. Scrape into the pan. Sprinkle with the remaining ½ teaspoon of nutmeg. Bake in the oven for 50 to 60 minutes, until a toothpick inserted into the center comes out clean. If the top is browning too quickly, lightly cover it with aluminum foil the last 10 minutes or so of baking. Let cool for 5 minutes before removing from the pan and placing on a wire rack. Serve warm or at room temperature.

Eggnog

Makes 1½ quarts

1 cup eggs (about 5 large eggs)
3 cups whole milk
14 ounces sweetened condensed milk
1 tablespoon brandy extract
½ teaspoon vanilla extract
⅛ teaspoon salt
⅛ teaspoon ground nutmeg

1. In a large bowl, beat the eggs until foamy with an electric mixer on low speed. In a separate bowl or large measuring cup, combine the whole milk, sweetened condensed milk, brandy extract, vanilla, salt, and nutmeg. Gradually add to the eggs, beating constantly, until well blended.

2. If serving this as a beverage, add ½ cup brandy or dark rum and omit the brandy extract. Sprinkle with nutmeg just before serving.

Note: You may be uneasy about using raw eggs. I settle the matter by using eggs from free-range hens fed on organic grain, which reportedly have a very low incidence of salmonella. If you want to be one hundred percent safe, use pasteurized eggnog from the supermarket.

Mom's Gingerbread
with Lemon Icing

This is my mother's recipe, and it's the essence of comfort food, its dense molasses flavor off-set by the tart-sweet lemon icing. She made it often when we were growing up, occasion-ally throwing in a handful of raisins. Warm from the oven, there's nothing quite like it.

Makes one 9 × 11-inch sheet cake

1 cup molasses
½ cup (1 stick) unsalted butter, softened
¼ cup sugar
1 large egg, at room temperature
2½ cups all-purpose flour
1 teaspoon baking soda
½ teaspoon salt
1 teaspoon ground ginger
1 teaspoon ground cinnamon
⅔ cup raisins (optional)
Lemon Icing (recipe follows)

1. Preheat the oven to 325°F. Grease and flour a 9 × 11-inch baking pan.

2. An hour or so in advance, place the molasses in a small bowl or Pyrex measuring cup and pour in 1 cup of boiling water; stir to combine. Set aside to cool.

3. Place the softened butter and sugar in a food processor and whir until creamy (see Note). Add the egg, and whir until blended. In a slow, steady stream while the motor is run-ning, add the cooled molasses mixture, whirring until well blended. Combine the flour, baking soda, salt, ginger, and cinnamon. Add the flour mixture to the wet mixture all at once, and pulse a few times, just until smooth. Stir in the raisins, if using. Pour the batter into the pan, and bake in the oven for 40 to 45 minutes, until a toothpick inserted into the

center comes out clean. Let cool slightly in the pan before frosting with Lemon Icing while still warm. Cut into squares. Serve warm or at room temperature.

Note: *You can use an electric mixer, if you like, but this is a thin batter so it's hard to prevent lumps.*

Lemon Icing

Makes enough for one 9 × 11-inch sheet cake

> 3 tablespoons unsalted butter, very soft
> 1 cup confectioners' sugar, sifted
> 1 teaspoon lemon zest
> 2 tablespoon lemon juice

In a small bowl, blend the butter, confectioners' sugar, zest, and lemon juice with an electric mixer on low speed. Beat until spreading consistency (it won't be as thick as regular frosting). Spread over the warm cake.

Granola Bread

*T his hearty loaf is for those days when you're dashing off to work, in too much of a hurry
to sit down to breakfast; make it the night before—it takes only minutes to prepare—
and grab a slice as you're headed out the door the following morning. If you're not in a hurry,
enjoy it toasted with a little honey. It also stores well, tightly wrapped in the refrigerator.*

Makes one 8½ × 4½-inch loaf

1¼ cups all-purpose flour

½ cup whole wheat flour

½ cup firmly packed dark brown sugar

1 teaspoon baking powder

1 teaspoon baking soda

¼ teaspoon salt

2 large eggs

¼ cup vegetable oil or coconut oil

1 cup buttermilk

1¼ cups granola

½ cup raisins, currants, or dried cranberries (optional)

1. Preheat the oven to 350°F. Grease and flour an 8½ × 4½-inch loaf pan.

2. In a large bowl, combine the all-purpose flour, whole wheat flour, dark brown sugar,
baking powder, baking soda, and salt. Whisk the eggs with the oil and buttermilk. Add to
the dry ingredients all at once, along with 1 cup of the granola (and dried fruit, if using).
Stir vigorously with a wooden spoon just until the dry ingredients are incorporated. Pour
into the pan, and sprinkle with the remaining ¼ cup of granola. Bake in the oven for 1 hour
and 15 minutes, until a toothpick inserted into the center comes out clean. Let cool for
5 minutes before removing from the pan and placing on a wire rack. Serve warm or at
room temperature.

Marmalade Bread

*M*y grandmother Mimi, with her satin lounging pajamas and cigarette holder (which she went on using, as a sort of prop, even after she quit smoking), was an Auntie Mame–like figure. In the bathroom she shared with us kids when she came for her annual visit, the towel racks were hung with her lacy underthings, and the counter lined with her cosmetics, including her signature fire-engine red lipstick. Though not particularly domestic, she would devote a couple of days each visit to making two things: doughnuts and orange marmalade. It didn't matter if we still had marmalade left over from her last visit, it was simply what Mimi did—as much a part of her as the white gloves and pillbox hats she wore, and her boxy train case with the tortoise-shell handle that even back then seemed a quaint relic of a bygone era. Dear, departed Mimi: I dedicate this bread to you. *Makes one 8½ × 4½-inch loaf*

1 large egg, at room temperature

⅓ cup honey

½ cup (1 stick) unsalted butter, melted

½ cup fresh orange juice

½ cup orange marmalade

2 tablespoons rum (you can substitute 1 teaspoon rum extract)

1 cup roughly chopped walnuts or pecans

2 cups all-purpose flour

2 teaspoons baking powder

½ teaspoon baking soda

½ teaspoon salt

1. Preheat the oven to 350°F. Grease an 8½ × 4½-inch loaf pan.

2. In a large bowl, beat the egg with an electric mixer on low speed. Add the honey, melted butter, orange juice, marmalade, and rum, mixing until well blended. Blend in the chopped nuts. Combine the flour, baking powder, baking soda, and salt. Add to the wet mixture all at once, and mix just until the dry ingredients are incorporated. Scrape the batter into the pan, and bake in the oven for 50 to 55 minutes, until a toothpick inserted into the center comes out clean. Let cool for 15 minutes before removing from the pan and placing on a wire rack. Serve warm or at room temperature.

Boston Brown Bread

My mother-in-law, Lindy Kenyon, gave me this recipe, which has been around since long before her time. There's a reason it has stood the test of time—it's easy to make and just plain good. Traditionally it's baked in a large coffee can, but if you don't happen to have one on hand, a loaf pan will do.   *Makes one 8½ × 4½-inch loaf*

2 cups whole wheat flour

1 teaspoon salt

1½ teaspoons baking powder

½ teaspoon baking soda

1 large egg, at room temperature

1 cup buttermilk

½ cup molasses

¼ cup (½ stick) unsalted butter, melted

1. Preheat the oven to 350°F. Grease an 8½ × 4½-inch loaf pan (or large coffee can).

2. In a large bowl, combine the flour, salt, baking powder, and baking soda. In a separate bowl, lightly beat the egg, and stir in the buttermilk, molasses, and melted butter. Add to the dry ingredients all at once, whisking with a fork just until incorporated. Pour the batter into the pan, and bake in the oven for 30 minutes, until a toothpick inserted into the center comes out clean. Cool for 5 minutes before removing from the pan and placing on a wire rack. Serve warm or at room temperature.

Apple-Cranberry Bread

This dense, nutty bread, chock-full of apples and cranberries, couldn't be easier to make: Just throw everything into the food processor. I like it on cold winter days, with a mug of tea.

Makes one 8½ × 4½-inch loaf

2¼ cups all-purpose flour

½ cup firmly packed dark brown sugar

1½ teaspoons baking powder

½ teaspoon baking soda

¼ teaspoon salt

¼ cup (½ stick) unsalted butter, chilled and cut into chunks

1 cup fresh or unthawed frozen cranberries

½ medium apple, peeled, cored, and coarsely chopped

⅔ cup apple juice

1 large egg

¼ cup coarsely chopped walnuts

1. Preheat the oven to 350°F. Grease an 8½ × 4½-inch loaf pan.

2. Place the flour, dark brown sugar, baking powder, baking soda, and salt in a food processor, and whir to combine. Add the butter, and pulse until the mixture resembles coarse meal. Add the cranberries and apple, and pulse until the fruit is finely chopped. Add the apple juice and egg, and pulse *just until the mixture is moistened.* Add the nuts, and pulse once or twice to combine. Scrape into the pan, and bake in the oven for 1 hour and 15 minutes, until a toothpick inserted into the center comes out clean. Cool for 5 minutes before removing from the pan and placing on a wire rack. Serve warm or at room temperature.

Lupe's Jalapeño Corn Bread

In my Carson Springs series, family retainer Lupe is renowned for her jalapeño corn bread, which is served at nearly every family occasion. A number of readers wrote requesting the recipe, so here it is. You can adjust the spiciness according to your taste buds. For a milder bread, use just one jalapeño. **Makes one 8 × 8-inch corn bread or 12 muffins**

"The smell of barbecued chicken drifted from the back yard, and Gerry could see past her into the kitchen, where Lupe, her thick black braids wrapped about her head— the only thing about her that hadn't aged—bustled about like the world's oldest general. The table at one end of the cozy living room, an old door propped on saw-horses and covered with an embroidered cloth, was laden with serving bowls and platters and baskets heaped with Lupe's famous jalapeño cornbread . . ."

—From *Taste of Honey*

1½ cups all-purpose flour

¾ cup yellow cornmeal

3 tablespoons sugar

1 tablespoon baking powder

1 teaspoon salt

1 teaspoon ground cumin

1 large egg

2 to 3 jalapeño chiles, minced (see Note)

1 cup milk

¼ cup vegetable oil

1 cup grated cheddar cheese

1. Preheat the oven to 350°F. Grease an 8 × 8-inch square baking pan or a muffin tin.

2. In a large bowl, combine the flour, cornmeal, sugar, baking powder, salt, and cumin. Mix together the egg, minced jalapeños, milk, oil, and grated cheese. Add to the dry mixture all at once, and whisk vigorously with a fork just until moistened. Scrape into the pan (If using a muffin tin, fill each cup about three-quarters full.) Bake in the oven for 20 to 25 minutes (18 to 20 minutes for muffins), until a toothpick inserted into the center comes out clean. Let cool in the pan for several minutes before cutting into squares or removing the muffins from the tin. Serve warm.

Note: *When handling jalapeños, I wear latex gloves, so as to avoid the risk afterward of hand to eye/nose contact, which, though it won't cause any damage, can burn. If you don't have gloves on hand, mince the chiles as follows: Holding the chile vertically, stem side up, slice it open with a thin-bladed sharp knife and, with the tip of the knife, scrape out the seeds and membrane—the hottest part—taking care to handle as little as possible. Wash and drain on paper towels. Place cut side down on a chopping board, and mince.*

All-Purpose Muffins

*T*hink of this basic recipe as a blank canvas on which to unleash your creativity, using whatever fruits, nuts, or berries are at hand. You don't have to be an experienced baker, since the only cardinal rule is to not overmix. This is also a great way to turn children on to baking.

Makes 12 muffins

2 cups all-purpose flour
½ cup sugar
1 tablespoon baking powder
½ teaspoon salt
¾ cup milk
⅓ cup vegetable oil or coconut oil
1 large egg, lightly beaten

1. Preheat the oven to 400°F. Grease a 12-cup muffin tin, or line with baking cups.

2. In a large bowl, combine the flour, sugar, baking powder, and salt. Whisk together the milk, oil, and egg. Add to the dry ingredients all at once, whisking with a fork just until moist (it's okay if there are a few lumps). Stir in the fruits and nuts, in any of the following variations. These are only a few suggestions; don't be afraid to get creative.

> *Apple Streusel:* To the dry ingredients, add 1 cup of finely chopped apple. Substitute apple juice for the milk. For the streusel: Combine ½ cup flour, ¼ cup brown sugar, and ½ teaspoon cinnamon. With your fingers or a pastry cutter, work in ¼ cup (½ stick) of softened butter until the mixture resembles coarse crumbs. Sprinkle over the tops of the muffins before baking.

> *Blueberry:* To the dry ingredients, add 1 cup of fresh or unthawed frozen blueberries, along with 1 teaspoon of orange or lemon zest.

> *Cranberry:* To the dry ingredients, add 1 cup of fresh, unthawed frozen, or dried cranberries, along with 1 teaspoon orange zest.

Orange: To the dry ingredients, add 1 tablespoon of orange zest. Substitute orange juice for the milk.

Whole Wheat: Substitute 1 cup of whole wheat flour for 1 cup of the all-purpose flour. Stir ½ cup chopped walnuts or pecans into the batter.

3. Spoon the batter into the muffin cups to about two-thirds full.

4. Bake in the oven for 15 to 20 minutes, until a toothpick inserted into the center of a muffin comes out clean. Let cool in the tin for 1 to 2 minutes before removing. Serve warm or at room temperature.

Pumpkin-Cranberry Muffins

I used to make these muffins all the time while my kids were growing up. They were so popular that I had to double every batch. They are the essence of autumn—the deep orange of the pumpkin perfectly complemented by the jewel-like nuggets of cranberry. **Makes 12 muffins**

½ cup firmly packed dark brown sugar

2 tablespoons pure maple syrup

½ cup vegetable oil or coconut oil

2 large eggs

1 cup canned pumpkin (*not* pumpkin pie filling) or pumpkin puree (page 226)

1¾ cups all-purpose flour

½ teaspoon baking powder

1 teaspoon baking soda

½ teaspoon salt

½ teaspoon ground cinnamon

½ teaspoon ground nutmeg

½ teaspoon ground allspice

¼ teaspoon ground cloves

⅓ cup apple juice

½ teaspoon orange zest

⅓ cup chopped walnuts or pecans

½ cup fresh, unthawed frozen, or dried cranberries
   (you can substitute raisins or chopped dates)

1. Preheat the oven to 350°F. Grease a 12-cup muffin tin, or line with baking cups.

2. In a large bowl, place the brown sugar, maple syrup, oil, eggs, and pumpkin. Beat with an electric mixer on medium speed until well blended. Sift together the flour, baking powder, baking soda, salt, cinnamon, nutmeg, allspice, and cloves. To the wet mixture, add in the following order, beating after each addition just until blended: half the flour mixture; all of the apple juice; the remaining flour mixture and the zest. Fold in the chopped nuts and cranberries. Spoon into the muffin cups to about two-thirds full. Bake in the oven for 20 to 30 minutes, until a toothpick inserted into the center of a muffin comes out clean. Let cool in the tin for a minute or two before removing. Serve warm or at room temperature.

Apple–Oat Bran Muffins

*A*nother old favorite from my recipe files. Delicately sweet, with a crumbly texture, these make for a healthier muffin than most. Oat bran is reputed to lower cholesterol and the whole wheat flour lends added fiber.

Makes 12 muffins

2 tablespoons dark brown sugar

⅓ cup pure maple syrup (use Grade B, if you can find it)

¼ cup vegetable oil or coconut oil

¾ teaspoon vanilla extract

1 large egg

¾ cup oat bran

1¼ cups whole wheat flour

1½ teaspoons baking powder

¾ teaspoon baking soda

¼ teaspoon salt

¾ cup buttermilk

1¼ cups finely chopped apple (from 1 medium apple)

⅓ cup raisins (optional)

1. Preheat the oven to 375°F. Grease a 12-cup muffin tin, or line with baking cups.

2. Place the dark brown sugar, maple syrup, and oil in a large bowl. Add the vanilla and egg, and beat with an electric mixer on low speed until blended. Combine the oat bran, flour, baking powder, baking soda, and salt. Add half to the wet mixture, blending just until the dry ingredients are incorporated. Blend in the buttermilk. Add the remaining dry ingredients, and blend just until incorporated. Fold in the chopped apples and raisins, if using. Fill the muffin cups to about three-quarters full. Bake in the oven for 18 to 20 minutes, until a toothpick inserted into the center of one muffin comes out clean. Let cool in the tin for 5 minutes before inverting onto a wire rack. Serve warm or at room temperature.

Banana-Nut Muffins

*T*hese muffins are wonderfully bananay. They keep well, too. In fact, they're even better the next day.

Makes 12 muffins

6 tablespoons (¾ stick) unsalted butter

⅓ cup granulated sugar

⅓ cup firmly packed light brown sugar

1½ very ripe medium bananas (skins should be generously spotted)

1 large egg

Rounded ¼ teaspoon ground nutmeg

Rounded ¼ teaspoon ground allspice

¼ cup buttermilk

1½ cups all-purpose flour

1½ teaspoons baking powder

½ teaspoon baking soda

¼ teaspoon salt

⅔ cup roughly chopped walnuts or pecans

Streusel Topping (recipe follows)

1. Preheat the oven to 350°F. Grease a 12-cup muffin tin, or line with baking cups.

2. In a large bowl, cream the softened butter with the granulated and light brown sugars, with an electric mixer at medium speed, scraping the bowl with a spatula as you go along. In a shallow bowl (such as a soup bowl), mash the bananas with a fork. Add to the creamed mixture along with the egg, nutmeg, allspice, and buttermilk. Blend until smooth.

3. Combine the flour, baking powder, baking soda, and salt. Add to the creamed mixture, stirring or beating on low speed just until incorporated. Fold in the nuts. Spoon the batter into the muffin cups to about two-thirds full. Sprinkle with the streusel topping. Bake in the oven for 20 minutes, until a toothpick inserted into the center of one muffin comes out clean. Let cool in the tin for a minute or two before removing. Serve warm or at room temperature.

Streusel Topping

⅓ cup plus 1 tablespoon all-purpose flour

3 tablespoons dark brown sugar

Rounded ¼ teaspoon ground cinnamon

3 tablespoons unsalted butter, softened

Combine the flour, dark brown sugar, and cinnamon. With your fingers, work in the softened butter until the mixture resembles coarse crumbs. Sprinkle over the tops of the muffins before baking.

Pineapple-Coconut Muffins

I adapted this recipe from one given to me by my mother-in-law, Lindy Kenyon. Hers didn't include coconut, but I never met a tropical fruit–flavored baked good that wasn't enhanced by it, so I used it here.   ***Makes 12 muffins***

⅓ cup vegetable oil or coconut oil

⅓ cup granulated sugar

¼ cup honey

1 large egg

2 cups all-purpose flour

¾ teaspoon baking powder

½ teaspoon salt

¾ cup canned coconut milk

½ cup (8 ounces) crushed unsweetened pineapple, well-drained

½ to ⅔ cup sweetened flaked coconut

1. Preheat the oven to 350°F. Grease a 12-cup muffin tin, or line with baking cups.

2. In a large bowl, beat the oil, sugar, honey, and egg with an electric mixer on low speed, until well blended. Combine the flour, baking powder, and salt. To the wet mixture, add in the following order, mixing after each addition just until incorporated: half of the dry ingredients; all of the coconut milk; the remaining dry ingredients. Stir in the well-drained crushed pineapple. Spoon the batter into the cups to about two-thirds full. Sprinkle with the coconut. Bake in the oven for 20 to 25 minutes, until a toothpick inserted into the center of one muffin comes out clean. Let cool in the tin for a minute or so before inverting onto a wire rack. Serve warm or at room temperature.

Maple-Oatmeal Muffins

*O*n a recent trip to Vermont, I was so taken by the vast array of maple products that I bought far too much. (If I had pancakes every Sunday for the rest of my life, I'd still have maple syrup left over!) Which is why I love these muffins: They're sweetened entirely with maple syrup, which not only gives them an intense maple flavor but creates more room in my cupboard.   *Makes 12 muffins*

½ cup milk

1 cup rolled oats

1 cup pure maple syrup (use Grade B, if you can find it)

¼ cup vegetable oil or coconut oil

1 large egg

1½ cups all-purpose flour

2 teaspoons baking powder

Dash of salt

¼ teaspoon ground cinnamon

¾ cup chopped walnuts or pecans

1. Preheat the oven to 375°F. Grease a 12-cup muffin tin, or line with baking cups.

2. Stir the milk into the oats; set aside.

3. Place the maple syrup, oil, and egg in a large bowl. Stir with a wooden spoon, or beat with an electric mixer on low speed, until blended. Add the oatmeal mixture and beat until well blended. Combine the flour, baking powder, salt, and cinnamon. Add to the wet mixture all at once, along with ½ cup of the chopped nuts. Stir just until incorporated. Spoon the batter into the muffin cups to about two-thirds full. Sprinkle the remaining nuts over the tops. Bake in the oven for 20 to 25 minutes, until a toothpick inserted into the center of one muffin comes out clean. Let cool in the tin for a minute or two before inverting onto a wire rack. Serve warm or at room temperature.

Onion-Ricotta Muffins

T*hese are the perfect savory companion to almost any meal—crunchy on the outside and light on the inside, flecked with bits of onion and chopped roasted peppers. A bowl of soup and one or two of these muffins is a meal in itself. The batter also makes great dumplings; drop by spoonfuls over your favorite casserole twenty to thirty minutes before it's ready to come out of the oven.*

Makes 12 muffins

½ cup (1 stick) unsalted butter
1 cup chopped mild sweet onions
1½ cups all-purpose flour
1 tablespoon baking powder
½ teaspoon salt
½ teaspoon dried oregano
2 large eggs
¼ cup drained, chopped roasted red peppers
⅔ cup ricotta
3 tablespoons milk

1. Preheat the oven to 400°F. Generously grease a muffin tin.

2. In a small skillet, melt the butter over low heat. Increase the heat to medium; add the onions, and cook, stirring occasionally, until they're limp and translucent, 3 to 4 minutes. Remove from the heat, and set aside.

3. In a large bowl, combine the flour, baking powder, salt, and oregano. Make a well in the center of the dry ingredients, and add the eggs, chopped peppers, ricotta, milk, and onions (along with any butter in the skillet). Whisk with a fork just until blended (it's okay if there are a few lumps). Spoon the batter into the muffin cups to about three-quarters full. Bake in the oven for 20 to 25 minutes, until golden and a toothpick inserted into the center of one muffin comes out clean. Let cool in the tin for 2 minutes or so before inverting onto a wire rack. Serve warm or at room temperature.

Biscuits and Scones

One of the kettles behind the counter was whistling. While Suzette and her helpers cleared away cups and saucers and plates, Claire made tea the way Kitty had taught her, pouring an inch or so of boiling water into one of the teapots, no two alike, then swirling until the leaves at the bottom were thoroughly soaked before topping it off. She let it steep for a minute before placing it on a tray along with a silver tea strainer, creamer and sugar bowl, and small plate of lemon wedges.

Over the next hour she didn't stop moving. There were more pots of tea to be made, creamers to be refilled, cookies and scones and tarts to be brought in from the kitchen. Yet she never felt tired or harried. Someone had once told her—it might have been Byron—that only the things you didn't like doing made you tired, which would explain why an hour at her desk exhausted her more than five on her feet.

—From *Taste of Honey*

Buttermilk Biscuits

*T*his recipe should be stitched in a sampler and hung on every kitchen wall, though once you've made it a few times you'll know it by heart. The only trick is to handle the dough as little as possible—what's meant by the term "light hand"—since overmixing and/or over-kneading will result in a heavier biscuit. The beauty of these is that you can make them in advance and freeze them unbaked, then on days when you're too busy to fuss in the kitchen, you have only to pop them in the oven. ***Makes 12 biscuits***

2 cups all-purpose flour
1 tablespoon baking powder
¼ teaspoon baking soda
½ teaspoon salt
½ cup lard or butter (you can substitute vegetable shortening), chilled
¾ cup buttermilk

1. Preheat the oven to 400°F. Lightly grease a baking sheet.

2. Place the flour, baking powder, baking soda, and salt in a food processor and whir to combine. Add the lard. Whir for a few seconds, then pulse until the mixture resembles coarse meal. (Be careful not to overprocess, as the little fatty deposits are what make for a lighter biscuit as they melt in the oven). Dump into a bowl. Alternate method: Place the above ingredients in a bowl and cut with a pastry cutter until crumbly. Add ½ cup of the buttermilk, and whisk with a fork, dribbling in more as needed, just until a sticky mass forms.

3. Turn the dough onto a lightly floured surface. Gently, gently, knead it a few times just to bring the dough together. Roll with a floured rolling pin to about ¾-inch thickness, and cut with a floured 2-inch biscuit cutter (don't use anything with a dull edge, like a glass or can; it will smoosh down the edges and the biscuits won't rise as high in the oven).

4. Place the biscuits about 1 inch apart on the baking sheet. Bake in the oven for 12 to 15 minutes, until golden. If freezing, place the unbaked biscuits in a single layer on a baking sheet and place in the freezer until firm, then transfer to a zip-top bag. When ready to bake, place the unthawed frozen biscuits on a greased baking sheet, and bake for 15 to 17 minutes.

Southern-Style Biscuits

*I*n the South, where biscuits are served with nearly every meal, they're typically made with lard or vegetable shortening, which is what makes them so ethereally light. You don't need fancy equipment for these, just a bowl and a wooden spoon, a rolling pin and a biscuit cutter.

Makes 12 biscuits

2 cups all-purpose flour, sifted
4 teaspoons baking powder
1 teaspoon salt
¼ cup (4 tablespoons) lard or vegetable shortening
1 cup milk

1. Preheat the oven to 425°F.

2. Combine the flour, baking powder, and salt. Add the lard, and crumble with your fingers (you can use a pastry cutter, if you like) until the mixture resembles coarse meal. Add the milk and stir vigorously with a wooden spoon until the dough pulls away from the sides of the bowl (this shouldn't take more than 10 or 15 seconds—be careful not to overmix!). Gather into a ball and place on a lightly floured surface. Roll with a floured rolling pin to about ¾-inch thickness. With a floured 2-inch biscuit cutter, cut into rounds. Gather up the scraps; press them together, roll out, and cut.

3. Place the biscuits about 1 inch apart on an ungreased baking sheet. Bake in the oven for 15 minutes, until golden. Serve warm.

Angel Biscuits

These are pretty much foolproof. Leavened with both yeast and baking powder, they live up to their name in that they're so light, they practically levitate. My daughter was fond of baking them when she was growing up. A good introduction to making yeast breads, with a fairly quick payoff (important with children).   ***Makes 16 biscuits***

1 tablespoon dry active yeast

1 tablespoon plus ½ teaspoon sugar

2 cups all-purpose flour

2 teaspoons baking powder

1 teaspoon salt

3 tablespoons unsalted butter, chilled and cut into chunks

½ cup milk

1. Dissolve the yeast in ¼ cup of warm (120°F) water mixed with ½ teaspoon of the sugar. Let sit until bubbly, about 10 minutes.

2. Meanwhile, place the flour, baking powder, remaining 1 tablespoon of sugar, and salt in a food processor. Whir to combine. Add the butter, and whir for a few seconds, then pulse until the mixture resembles coarse meal (don't overprocess!). Dump into a bowl. Alternate method: Place the above ingredients in a bowl and work with your fingers or a pastry cutter until crumbly.

3. Combine the milk with the dissolved yeast; add to the flour mixture. If using a food processor, pulse just until a sticky mass forms. If using alternate method, whisk briskly with a fork just until the dough starts to pull away from the sides of the bowl. Turn onto a lightly floured surface, and knead gently just until the dough holds together. Roll with a floured rolling pin to about ¾-inch thickness and cut into rounds with a floured 2-inch biscuit cutter. Place 1 inch apart on an ungreased baking sheet and cover with a clean dishtowel. Set in a warm place to rise until doubled in bulk, about 1 hour.

4. Preheat the oven to 425°F and lightly grease a baking sheet.

5. Bake in the oven for 10 to 12 minutes, until golden. Serve warm.

Lemon-Ricotta Biscuits

*T*hese give new meaning to that old phrase, melt in your mouth. With my sister Karen's blackberry-apricot jam, made from fruit out of her own backyard, I can think of no better way to start the day.   ***Makes 12 biscuits***

1½ cups all-purpose flour

¾ teaspoon salt

1 tablespoon baking powder

2 teaspoons sugar

1 heaping teaspoon lemon zest

6 tablespoons (¾ stick) unsalted butter, chilled and cut into chunks

2 large eggs

⅔ cup ricotta

1. Preheat the oven to 400°F. Lightly grease a baking sheet.

2. Place the flour, salt, baking powder, sugar, and zest in a food processor and whir to combine. Add the butter and whir for a few seconds, then pulse until the mixture resembles coarse meal (don't overprocess!). Dump into a bowl. Alternate method: Place the above ingredients in a bowl and work with your fingers or a pastry cutter until crumbly.

3. Lightly beat the eggs; add the ricotta, and stir to combine. Add to the flour mixture, and whisk with a fork just until it starts to come together in a sticky mass. Don't overmix!

4. Turn the dough onto a lightly floured surface, and very gently knead just until it holds together (sprinkle with a little flour, if necessary). Roll with a rolling pin to about ¾-inch thickness and cut with a floured 2-inch biscuit cutter into rounds. Place 1 inch apart on the baking sheet and let stand for 10 minutes, lightly covered with a clean dishtowel. You can also store them in the refrigerator, covered with plastic wrap, until ready to bake (up to 1 day). Bake in the oven for 12 to 14 minutes, until lightly golden. Serve warm.

Note: *For savory biscuits, toss a handful of chopped chives or dill into the flour mixture before adding the butter.*

Blueberry Drop Biscuits

W*arm from the oven, there's little that can compare with these biscuits; they're fairly bursting with berries. They don't even need jam.* **Makes 12 generous biscuits**

2 cups all-purpose flour

1 tablespoon baking powder

½ teaspoon salt

½ cup plus 1 tablespoon sugar

1 tablespoon orange zest

½ cup (1 stick) unsalted butter, chilled and cut into chunks

1 large egg

½ cup milk or half-and-half

1 cup fresh or unthawed frozen blueberries

¼ teaspoon ground cinnamon

1. Place the flour, baking powder, salt, ½ cup of the sugar, and zest in a food processor and whir to combine. Add the butter, and whir for a few seconds then pulse until the mixture resembles coarse meal (don't overprocess!). Dump into a bowl. Alternate method: Place the above ingredients in a bowl and work with your fingers or a pastry cutter until crumbly.

2. Whisk together the egg and milk. Add to the flour mixture and whisk briskly with a fork just until moist (it's okay if there are a few lumps). Gently stir in the blueberries. Chill for 10 to 15 minutes.

3. Preheat the oven to 400°F.

4. Combine the remaining 1 tablespoon of sugar and the cinnamon.

5. With a large spoon, drop generous dollops of dough onto an ungreased baking sheet to form 12 biscuits. Sprinkle with the sugar-cinnamon mixture. Bake in the oven for 12 to 15 minutes, until golden. Serve warm.

Pesto Biscuits

In summer, when basil grows like topsy, I buy it in big bunches at the farmers' market and make pesto for the freezer. If you don't make your own pesto, you can buy it in almost any delicatessen or upscale supermarket. Serve these savory biscuits with spaghetti and meatballs.

Makes 12 biscuits

2 cups all-purpose flour
1 tablespoon baking powder
¼ teaspoon salt
½ cup (1 stick) unsalted butter (6 tablespoons chilled and cut
    into chunks, 2 tablespoons melted)
½ cup milk
¼ cup pesto
2 tablespoons grated Parmesan cheese

1. Preheat the oven to 400°F.

2. Place the flour, baking powder, and salt in a food processor, and whir to combine. Add 6 tablespoons of the chilled butter. Whir for a few seconds, then pulse just until crumbly. Dump into a bowl. Alternate method: Place the above ingredients in a bowl and work with your fingers or with a pastry cutter until crumbly.

3. Whisk together the milk and pesto. Add to the flour mixture, and whisk with a fork *just until it's moistened.* Dribble in more milk, if the dough is too stiff.

4. Turn onto a lightly floured surface. Knead a couple of times to bring the dough together, taking care not to handle it too much (that's the secret to a "light hand"). Roll with a floured rolling pin to about ¾-inch thickness, and cut with a floured 2-inch biscuit cutter (don't use anything with a dull edge, like a glass or a can; it will smoosh the edges and the biscuits won't rise as high in the oven). Brush with the remaining 2 tablespoons melted butter. Sprinkle with the grated Parmesan.

5. Bake in the oven for 10 to 12 minutes, until golden. Serve warm.

Old-Fashioned Cream Scones

Years ago, on my first trip to London, I stayed at the Savoy Hotel, where they serve a high tea right out of Masterpiece Theatre, complete with harpist. From my first bite of a real English scone slathered with clotted cream and strawberry jam, I was a goner. Now I make them regularly for Sunday breakfast, so my husband and I can eat like royalty without leaving home.

Makes 8 generous scones

2 cups all-purpose flour

1 tablespoon baking powder

½ teaspoon salt

6 tablespoons (¾ stick) unsalted butter, chilled and cut into chunks

3 large eggs

2 tablespoons honey

½ cup plus 1 tablespoon heavy cream

1. Preheat the oven to 400°F.

2. Place the flour, baking powder, and salt in a food processor, and whir to combine. Add the butter and whir for a few seconds, then pulse until the mixture is crumbly, but not pulverized. Dump into a bowl. Alternate method: Place the above ingredients in a bowl and work with your fingers or with a pastry cutter until crumbly.

3. Lightly beat 2 of the eggs. Add the honey and ½ cup of the cream, and whisk to combine. Add to the flour mixture and whisk with a fork just until a sticky mass forms. Turn onto a lightly floured surface and with floured fingers gently pat into a ball, then into about a 1-inch-thick round. With a floured spatula, transfer to an ungreased baking sheet. Using a *very* sharp knife dipped in flour, and taking care not to smoosh down the edges, cut the dough into 8 equal wedges. Don't pull them apart.

4. Whisk together the remaining egg and 1 tablespoon of cream. Brush over the tops of the scones. Bake in the oven for 12 to 15 minutes, until golden. Serve warm or at room temperature.

Maple–Oat Bran Scones

This is a variation on the Scottish scone, which is traditionally made with oatmeal. The oat bran gives it a finer crumb that, flavored with maple syrup, puts it in a class all its own.

Makes 16 scones

2¼ cups all-purpose flour
½ cup oat bran (you can substitute quick-cooking oats)
1 tablespoon baking powder
¾ teaspoon salt
1 tablespoon sugar, plus more for sprinkling (optional)
¾ cup (1½ sticks) cold unsalted butter or lard, chilled and cut into chunks
3 large eggs
¼ cup pure maple syrup
5 tablespoons heavy cream

1. Preheat the oven to 400°F.

2. Place the flour, oat bran, baking powder, salt, and sugar in a food processor and whir to combine. Add the butter and whir for a few seconds, then pulse until the mixture is crumbly but not pulverized (don't overprocess!). Dump into a bowl. Alternate method: Place the above ingredients in a bowl and work with your fingers or with a pastry cutter until crumbly.

3. Lightly beat two of the eggs with a fork. Add the maple syrup and 4 tablespoons of the cream; whisk to combine. Add to the flour-butter mixture and whisk just until a sticky mass forms.

4. Turn onto a lightly floured surface and knead gently a few times. Roll with a floured rolling pin to about ¾-inch thickness. With a floured 2-inch biscuit cutter, cut the dough into rounds and place them on an ungreased baking sheet. Gather up the scraps, roll out, and cut.

5. Whisk together the remaining egg and remaining 1 tablespoon of cream. Brush over the rounds. Sprinkle with sugar, if desired. Bake in the oven for 12 to 14 minutes, until lightly golden. Serve warm or at room temperature.

Coconut Scones

These are every bit as light and flaky as the traditional English scone, subtly enhanced by the coconut. When I'm baking for just my husband and me, I freeze half the dough for later use. When I'm ready to use it, I just thaw it in the refrigerator overnight and pop it in the oven the next morning.   *Makes 8 generous scones*

2¼ cups all-purpose flour
½ cup sweetened flaked coconut
1 tablespoon baking powder
¼ teaspoon salt
5 tablespoons sugar
6 tablespoons (¾ stick) unsalted butter or lard, chilled and cut into chunks
3 large eggs
½ cup canned coconut milk
1 tablespoon milk

1. Preheat the oven to 400°F.

2. Place the flour, flaked coconut, baking powder, salt, and sugar in a food processor, and whir to combine. Add the butter and whir for a few seconds, then pulse until the mixture is crumbly but not pulverized (don't overprocess!). Dump into a bowl. Alternate method: Place the above ingredients in a bowl and work with your fingers or with a pastry cutter until crumbly.

3. Lightly beat 2 of the eggs. Add the coconut milk, and whisk to combine. Add to the flour mixture, and whisk with a fork just until a sticky mass forms. Turn onto a lightly floured surface and with floured fingers knead gently a few times. Lightly press the dough with your hand to about a 2-inch thickness, and transfer to an ungreased baking sheet. Using a sharp knife dipped in flour, cut the dough into 8 equal wedges, taking care not to smoosh down the edges. Don't pull apart.

4. Whisk together the remaining egg and the milk. Brush over the tops of the unbaked scones. Bake in the oven for 12 to 15 minutes, until golden. Serve warm or at room temperature.

Oatmeal–Marmalade Scones

*A*nother variation of the Scottish scone, this one made with rolled oats and marmalade. Heartier and a bit moister than the English variety, they're almost as good toasted the next day.

Makes 11 scones

1⅔ cups all-purpose flour
½ cup quick-cooking oats
2 teaspoons baking powder
2 tablespoons sugar
½ teaspoon salt
½ teaspoon ground cinnamon
½ cup (1 stick) unsalted butter or lard, chilled and cut into chunks
3 large eggs
¼ cup orange marmalade
3 tablespoons plus 1 teaspoon milk

1. Preheat the oven to 375°F.

2. Place the flour, oats, baking powder, sugar, salt, and cinnamon in a food processor, and whir to combine. Add the butter and whir for a few seconds, then pulse until the mixture is crumbly but not pulverized (don't overprocess!). Dump into a bowl. Alternate method: Place the above ingredients in a bowl and work with your fingers or with a pastry cutter until crumbly.

3. Lightly beat 2 of the eggs. Add the marmalade and 3 tablespoons of the milk; whisk to combine. Add to the flour-butter mixture and whisk with a fork just until it starts to come together in a sticky mass. Turn onto a lightly floured surface and knead gently (as if it were made of moonbeams) a few times. Roll with a floured rolling pin to about 1-inch thickness. With a 2-inch biscuit cutter dipped in flour, cut the dough into rounds and transfer them to an ungreased baking sheet.

4. Whisk together the remaining egg with the remaining 1 teaspoon of milk; brush over the tops of the unbaked scones. Bake in the oven for 15 to 20 minutes, until golden. Serve warm or at room temperature.

Sweet Potato Scones

A wonderful use for any leftover puree from the Sweet Potato Pie (page 172). If you don't happen to have any puree on hand, it's easy enough to make: Just bake two medium to large sweet potatoes in a 375°F oven for 45 minutes to an hour until tender when pricked with a fork. When they're cool enough to handle, scoop out the insides, discarding the skins, and whir in a blender or food processor until smooth.   ***Makes 8 generous scones***

2½ cups all-purpose flour

⅓ cup firmly packed dark brown sugar

1 tablespoon baking powder

½ teaspoon salt

¾ teaspoon ground cinnamon

½ cup (1 stick) unsalted butter or lard, chilled and cut into chunks

¾ cup sweet potato puree (you can substitute canned pumpkin)

½ cup plus 1 tablespoon half-and-half

1 large egg

1 tablespoon granulated sugar

1. Preheat the oven to 375°F.

2. Place the flour, brown sugar, baking powder, salt, and ½ teaspoon of the cinnamon in a food processor, and whir to combine. Add the butter and whir for a few seconds, then pulse until crumbly but not pulverized (don't overprocess!). Dump into a bowl. Alternate method: Place the above ingredients in a bowl and work with your fingers or with a pastry cutter until crumbly.

3. Whisk together the sweet potato puree and ½ cup of the half-and-half. Add to the flour mixture, and whisk with a fork just until it comes together in a sticky mass. Turn the dough onto a lightly floured surface, and knead gently a few times, just until it holds together. Pat it into a round about 2 inches thick, and with a floured spatula transfer it to an ungreased baking sheet. With a sharp knife dipped in flour, carefully cut it into 8 wedges, taking care not to smoosh down the edges. Don't pull apart.

4. Whisk together the egg and remaining 1 tablespoon of half-and-half. Brush over the tops of the unbaked scones. Combine the remaining ¼ teaspoon of cinnamon and the granulated sugar. Sprinkle over the tops of the scones. Bake in the oven for 25 to 30 minutes, until golden. Serve warm or at room temperature.

Yeast Breads and Rolls

But there was no secret to Kitty's baking. Had she been pressed to name a magic ingredient, she'd have said simply: patience. Taking the time to nurture each batch of dough and letting it rise in a quiet, warm place. Knowing it was a form of respect and, yes, affection even, toward those who would savor the end result. Another word for it, she supposed, was love . . .

—From *One Last Dance*

About Yeast Breads . . .

Yeast breads are like orchids: They don't require a lot of skill; just give them what they need and the rest will take care of itself. Temperature is the main thing to keep in mind. The water in which you dissolve the yeast must be warm, but not hot (120°F for dry yeast). I recommend testing it with a thermometer the first couple of times, until you can gauge the temperature with your finger. Stir in the yeast and give it ten minutes or so to expand and bubble. Note: A teaspoon of sugar or honey mixed into the water will cause the yeast to expand faster.

Temperature comes into play as well when the dough is rising. The dough must be in a warm place (75 to 80 degrees) free of drafts. I put mine in a preheated 350°F oven with the heat turned off; it rises perfectly with no risk of drafts. (Leave the door propped open if the oven is too warm). If your oven is in use, place the bowl of dough on a rack set over a large saucepan or roasting pan filled with hot water. Keep in mind that dough rises more quickly at higher altitudes. Also, white flour rises more quickly than other flours, such as wheat and rye. The dough is properly risen, unless otherwise called for in the recipe, when it has doubled in bulk. If you let it rise more than that, the dough will start to collapse. If this happens, punch it down and let it rise again.

Many recipes call for scalded milk, a holdover from before the days of pasteurization when it was necessary to kill the bacteria. These days, it's useful mainly in melting any solid fats called for in the recipe. I generally heat the milk just enough to melt the solids, then let it cool to lukewarm.

Most bread dough requires kneading, which isn't brain surgery, though it takes a bit of patience. I grew up watching my mother do it, so it's second nature to me. Basically it's just a matter of folding and refolding the dough, pressing down hard with the heels of your hands and/or pounding with your fists, sprinkling a little flour over it as it becomes too sticky to handle, until it becomes smooth and elastic, anywhere from six to ten minutes. If you have a standing mixer with a dough hook, you don't have to go to the trouble of kneading by hand, though you may find, as I have, that it can be therapeutic.

Once the dough is kneaded, place it in a large bowl (large enough to accommodate it when it's doubled in bulk) greased with oil or butter. Turn the dough once to ensure that all sides are greased. Cover the bowl with a clean dishtowel that's been soaked in warm water and wrung out.

When the dough has doubled in bulk, punch it down and turn it onto a lightly floured surface. Generally the second kneading is just a matter of getting rid of the air bubbles that have formed. When you've kneaded out all the bubbles, divide the dough as called for in the recipe. To shape into loaves for 9 × 5-inch or 8½ × 4½-inch loaf pans, flatten or pound each ball of dough into roughly an 8 × 12-inch rectangle. Starting at the shorter end, roll tightly, tucking in the edges as you go along, until you have a smooth loaf. Pinch together the seams to seal them. Place in greased loaf pans, seam side down. Cover with a damp dishtowel and set in a warm place to rise until doubled in bulk (this should only take about 45 minutes).

For a browner, crunchier crust, brush the dough with a little milk or melted butter before it goes into the oven. If it's browning too quickly, cover lightly with aluminum foil the last five to ten minutes of baking.

The loaf is done when you rap on it with a knife handle and it sounds hollow.

Oatmeal Bread

*T*his is my mother's recipe, which she made often when we were growing up. I distinctly recall coming home from school to the sight of dough rising in her brown ceramic bread
bowl, big enough to bathe an infant, the kitchen fragrant with its yeasty aroma. It's sweeter and
moister than white bread, with a faint nuttiness from the oats, and so addictive I once ate an
entire loaf in one day (back when I was a skinny kid, and could eat anything I wanted without
gaining weight—sigh). It's equally delicious warm from the oven or toasted the next day.

Makes two 8½ × 4½-inch loaves

1 cup quick-cooking oats, plus more for the tops of the loaves
½ cup (1 stick) plus 2 tablespoons unsalted butter
½ cup plus 1 teaspoon honey
1 tablespoon salt
2 envelopes (4 teaspoons) active dry yeast
2 large eggs, lightly beaten
5½ to 6 cups all-purpose flour

1. Bring 2 cups of water to a boil. Meanwhile, place the oats, ½ cup of the butter, ½ cup of
the honey, and salt in a large bowl. Add 1½ cups of the boiling water, setting aside the remaining ½ cup. Stir to combine; let sit until lukewarm. When the reserved water has
cooled enough to comfortably immerse a finger (120°F), stir in the remaining 1 teaspoon
of honey, then the yeast; let sit until bubbly, about 10 minutes. Add to the oat mixture, and
beat with an electric mixer on low speed until smooth. Add the eggs and 1 cup of the flour,
blending until smooth. Add the remaining flour a cup at a time, mixing with your hands
when the dough becomes too stiff to beat. (Use only enough flour to make a soft dough that
pulls away from the side of the bowl.) Turn onto a floured surface and knead until smooth,
6 to 8 minutes. Place in a large greased bowl; turn once and cover with a damp dishtowel.
Place in the refrigerator for 2 hours (it will rise a little).

2. Grease two 8½ × 4½-inch loaf pans.

3. Punch down the dough, and turn it onto a floured surface. Knead until it's smooth. Cut it in half, shape it into 2 loaves, and place in the pans. Cover with a damp dishtowel and set in a warm place to rise, until doubled in bulk, about 2 hours.

4. Preheat the oven to 375°F.

5. Melt the remaining 2 tablespoons of butter, and brush it over the risen loaves. Sprinkle the tops with oats. Bake in the oven for 45 minutes to 1 hour, until a loaf sounds hollow when tapped with a knife handle. Let cool in the pans for 5 minutes before inverting onto a wire rack. Serve warm or at room temperature.

Alabama Light Bread

A throwback to my Southern heritage, this bread lives up to its name: It truly is light as a feather. I made it often when my kids were little; they loved it toasted with cinnamon butter.

Makes two 9 × 5-inch or 8½ × 4½-inch loaves

1 cup milk

½ cup (1 stick) unsalted butter, cut into chunks

2 teaspoons salt

½ cup plus 1 teaspoon sugar

2 envelopes (4 teaspoons) active dry yeast

2 large eggs, lightly beaten

6½ to 7 cups all-purpose flour

Cinnamon Butter (recipe follows)

1. Place the milk and butter in a small saucepan. Cook over low heat, stirring constantly just until the butter melts. Pour the mixture into a large bowl. Stir in the salt and ½ cup of the sugar. Let cool to lukewarm.

2. Meanwhile, dissolve the remaining 1 teaspoon of sugar in 1 cup of warm (120°F) water; stir in the yeast, and let sit until bubbly, about 10 minutes. Add to the cooled milk mixture along with the eggs and beat with an electric mixer on low speed just until blended. Add 4 cups of the flour and blend on low speed until incorporated; increase the speed to medium and beat until smooth. Stir in the remaining flour a cup at a time (reserve ½ cup for kneading), until the dough pulls away from the side of the bowl.

3. Turn the dough onto a floured surface, and knead until smooth and elastic, 6 to 8 minutes. Place in a large greased bowl; turn once and cover with a damp dishtowel. Set in a warm place to rise until doubled in bulk, about 1¼ hours.

4. Grease two 9 × 5-inch or 8½ × 4½-inch loaf pans.

5. Punch down the dough, and turn it onto a floured surface. Cover it and let it rest for 10 minutes. Divide it in half and knead each half until there are no more air bubbles. Shape into loaves, and place in the pans. Cover with a damp dishtowel, and set in a warm place to rise until doubled in bulk, 45 to 60 minutes.

6. Preheat the oven to 400°F.

7. Bake in the oven for 25 to 30 minutes, until a loaf sounds hollow when tapped with a knife handle. Let cool in the pans for a minute or two before inverting onto a wire rack. Serve warm or at room temperature.

Cinnamon Butter

Makes about 1 cup

> ½ cup (1 stick) salted or unsalted butter, softened
> 1 cup dark brown sugar
> 2 teaspoons ground cinnamon

Cream the softened butter. Add the brown sugar and cinnamon, and blend until smooth. Scrape into a serving dish and serve at room temperature, with toast or bread warm from the oven.

Graham Bread

*A*nother old favorite from my mother's recipe files. This brick-shaped loaf isn't much to look at, but let your taste buds be the judge. With its nutty flavor and crunchy crust combined with a chewy inside, it's one of the best breads I know. Better yet, it requires no kneading.

Makes two 8½ × 4½-inch loaves

2 tablespoons plus 1 teaspoon sugar

2 envelopes (4 teaspoons) active dry yeast

2 cups milk

2 teaspoons salt

2¼ cups all-purpose flour

About 3¼ cups graham flour (available in health food stores;
    the brand I use is Bob's Red Mill—see Sources)

1. Dissolve 1 teaspoon of the sugar in ½ cup of warm (120°F) water; stir in the yeast, and let sit until bubbly, about 10 minutes.

2. Meanwhile, combine the milk, remaining 2 tablespoons of sugar, and the salt in a small saucepan. Heat just until lukewarm. Pour into a large bowl. Stir in the yeast mixture and all-purpose flour, mixing until well blended. Add the graham flour a cup at a time, mixing with your hands when the mixture become too stiff to stir, until it forms a soft dough that pulls away from the side of the bowl. Cover with a damp dishtowel and set in a warm place to rise until doubled in bulk, 1½ to 2 hours.

3. Grease two 8½ × 4½-inch loaf pans.

4. Punch down the dough to remove the air bubbles. Divide it in half and place in the pans. Cover with a damp dishtowel and set in a warm place to rise until doubled in bulk, 45 to 60 minutes.

5. Preheat the oven to 400°F.

6. Bake in the oven for 10 minutes. Reduce the oven temperature to 375°F and bake for 30 to 40 minutes more, until a loaf sounds hollow when tapped with a knife handle. If the loaves are browning too quickly, cover them loosely with aluminum foil. Let cool in the pans for a minute or two before inverting onto a wire rack. Serve warm or at room temperature.

Old World Potato Bread

T he stained, dog-eared card in my recipe file speaks for itself. This bread requires a bit of extra effort, but the results—light, smooth-textured loaves—are worth it. It's perfect for dinner parties, as most of the work is done in advance; the dough rises in the refrigerator overnight.   *Makes two 9-inch round loaves*

½ cup sugar
1 tablespoon salt
2 envelopes (4 teaspoons) active dry yeast
1 cup unseasoned mashed potatoes (see Notes)
½ cup (1 stick) plus 3 tablespoons unsalted butter, softened
2 large eggs, lightly beaten
About 7½ cups all-purpose flour

1. In a large bowl, combine 2 cups of warm (120°F) water with the sugar and salt; stir in the yeast. Let sit until bubbly, about 10 minutes.

2. Add the mashed potatoes, ½ cup of the softened butter, the eggs, and 3½ cups of the flour. Beat with an electric mixer on low speed until incorporated; increase the speed to medium and beat for 2 minutes more. Add the remaining flour a cup at a time, mixing with your hands when the mixture becomes too stiff to beat, until it forms a soft dough that pulls away from the side of the bowl. Melt 1 tablespoon of the remaining butter, and brush it over the top. Cover with a double thickness of aluminum foil, and place in the refrigerator to rise until doubled in bulk, 2 to 3 hours. Punch down, cover, and refrigerate overnight.

3. The following morning, grease two 9-inch round cake pans.

4. Turn the dough onto a floured surface, and knead until smooth and elastic, about 10 minutes. Divide in half, and shape each half into a smooth ball. Place in the pans. Melt the remaining 1 tablespoon of butter, and brush it over the tops. Cover with a damp dishtowel, and set in a warm place to rise until doubled in bulk, 1½ to 2 hours.

5. Preheat the oven to 400°F.

6. With a sharp knife, make 3 lengthwise cuts on the surface of each loaf. Bake in the oven for 40 minutes, until a loaf sounds hollow when tapped with a knife handle. Dust with flour. Serve warm or at room temperature.

Notes: *If you don't happen to have any leftover mashed potatoes on hand, they're easy enough to make. Just place a large peeled and quartered potato in a medium saucepan; cover with water and bring to a boil over high heat; reduce the heat to medium and cook until tender when pierced with a fork (15 to 20 minutes). Whir in a food processor, or beat with an electric mixer, with a few tablespoons of milk, until smooth.*

If you're using leftover mashed potatoes stored in the refrigerator, warm them in the microwave first.

Nanny's Swedish Rye Bread

My dear friend Jon Giswold was kind enough to share this recipe with me. It comes wrapped up in memories of his Swedish grandmother, Alice Lysdahl, who would bake it for the grandchildren on Sunday mornings, in Arco coffee cans. The loaves, Jon recalls, resembled large mushrooms. He says he can still smell the aroma of that bread. If you don't happen to have any coffee cans lying around, you can bake it in round cake pans.   **Makes two loaves**

1½ tablespoons active dry yeast
3½ to 4 cups all-purpose flour
2 cups milk
¼ cup granulated sugar
½ cup molasses
2 teaspoons salt
2 tablespoons lard (you can substitute butter or vegetable shortening)
2 cups rye flour

1. Combine the yeast and 2 cups of the all-purpose flour in a large bowl. Place the milk, sugar, molasses, salt, and lard in a medium saucepan. Cook over low heat, stirring constantly until the lard is melted. The mixture should be warm—120°F—but not hot; let it cool a bit, if it gets too hot. Add it to the flour mixture. Beat with an electric mixer on low speed for 30 seconds, pausing once or twice to scrape the side of the bowl. Increase the speed to medium, and beat for 3 minutes more. Add the rye flour and 1 cup of the remaining all-purpose flour (set aside the remaining ½ cup for kneading). Stir with a wooden spoon until it forms a soft dough that pulls away from the side of the bowl.

2. Turn the dough onto a lightly floured surface. Knead until smooth and elastic, 6 to 8 minutes. Place in a greased bowl; turn once and cover with a damp dishtowel. Set in a warm place to rise until double in bulk, 1½ to 2 hours.

3. Grease two 8½ × 4½-inch loaf pans or 8-inch round cake pans.

4. Punch down the dough. Turn it onto a lightly floured surface, and knead to release the bubbles. Cover and let it rest for 10 minutes. Divide in half, and shape each half into a loaf or a smooth ball. Place in the pans. Cover with a damp dishtowel, and set in a warm place to rise until nearly doubled in bulk, about 1 hour.

5. Preheat the oven to 350°F.

6. Bake in the oven for 40 to 45 minutes, until a loaf sounds hollow when tapped with a knife handle. Let cool in the pans for a minute or two before transferring onto wire racks. Serve warm or at room temperature.

Focaccia with Garlic and Rosemary

*F*ocaccia is a flat bread that lends itself to a variety of toppings. In this version, drizzled with garlic-infused olive oil and sprinkled with rosemary, it's a marvel of simplicity that transcends its humble origins.

Makes one 12 × 15-inch focaccia

For the bread

½ teaspoon honey

1 envelope (2 teaspoons) active dry yeast

4½ to 5 cups all-purpose flour

1½ teaspoons salt

⅓ cup olive oil

For the topping

3 or 4 cloves minced garlic

¼ cup olive oil

2 tablespoons fresh or dried rosemary

About 1 teaspoon kosher salt

1. Stir the honey into 1⅓ cups of warm (120°F) water. Stir in the yeast, and let sit until bubbly, about 10 minutes.

2. Meanwhile, combine 1 cup of the flour and the salt in a large bowl. Add the yeast and olive oil. Beat with an electric mixer on medium speed, adding the remaining flour a little at a time (reserve ¼ cup for kneading), until a soft dough forms that pulls away from the side of the bowl.

3. Turn the dough onto a lightly floured surface and knead until smooth but still soft and stretchable, sprinkling with the reserved flour when it becomes too sticky, 2 to 3 minutes.

4. Place it in a large greased bowl; turn once and cover with a damp dishtowel. Let rise until tripled in bulk, about 1½ hours.

5. Grease a baking sheet with olive oil and sprinkle lightly with cornmeal.

6. Punch down the dough and turn it onto a lightly floured surface. Knead to remove the air bubbles. Cover and let it sit for 5 minutes. Roll it with a floured rolling pin roughly to fit the size of the pan. Cover with plastic wrap and let it rise until doubled in bulk, 45 minutes to 1 hour. Meanwhile, prepare the topping:

7. In a small skillet over medium heat sauté the minced garlic in the oil until just beginning to brown. Remove from the heat and pour into a measuring cup.

8. Preheat the oven to 400°F.

9. Prick the surface of the dough all over with a fork. Drizzle it with the garlic–olive oil and sprinkle with the rosemary and kosher salt. Bake in the oven for 25 to 30 minutes, until golden brown. Serve warm.

Cinnamon Bread

E very year my mother would make a dozen or more of these loaves to give away at Christmastime to people like our mailman and our teachers at school. I can still recall the pleasure of carrying a freshly-baked loaf, drizzled with icing and decorated with candied fruit, to my teacher. Nowadays the smell of cinnamon bread baking in the oven always evokes memories of the holiday season, though it's wonderful any time of the year.

Makes two 8½ × 4½-inch loaves

2 cups milk
3 tablespoons unsalted butter
2 tablespoons granulated sugar
1 envelope (2 teaspoons) active dry yeast
1¾ teaspoons salt
6½ cups all-purpose flour
½ cup dark brown sugar
2 tablespoons ground cinnamon

1. Place the milk and 2 tablespoons of the butter in a medium saucepan. Cook over low heat, stirring constantly, until the butter is melted. Let cool to lukewarm.

2. In a large bowl, combine ¼ cup of warm (120°F) water and 1 teaspoon of the granulated sugar. Stir in the yeast and let sit until bubbly, about 10 minutes. Add the milk mixture, salt, 1 cup of the flour, and the remaining granulated sugar. Beat with an electric mixer on low speed until blended.

3. Stir in the remaining flour, a cup at a time (reserve ½ cup for kneading), until it forms a soft dough that pulls away from the side of the bowl. Turn onto a floured surface and knead, working in the reserved flour as needed, until smooth and elastic, 8 to 10 minutes. Place in a greased bowl; turn once and cover with a damp dishtowel. Set in a warm place to rise until doubled in bulk, about 1½ hours.

4. While the dough is rising, combine the dark brown sugar and the cinnamon.

5. Grease two 8½ × 4½-inch loaf pans.

6. Punch down the dough and turn it onto a floured surface. Knead to remove the air bubbles. Divide in half and shape each half into a smooth ball. With a rolling pin dusted with flour, roll one ball into roughly a 9 × 14-inch rectangle. Melt the remaining tablespoon of butter, and brush half of it over the dough. Sprinkle with half of the cinnamon-sugar mixture. Roll it up tightly, starting at the shorter end, tucking in the edges as you go along; pinch the seams together to seal. Repeat with the remaining ball of dough.

7. Place in the pans, seam side down. Cover with a damp dishtowel, and set in a warm place to rise until doubled in bulk, about 45 minutes.

8. Preheat the oven to 375°F.

9. Bake in the oven for 40 to 45 minutes, until nicely browned and just starting to pull away from the sides of the pans. Let cool in the pans for several minutes before turning onto a wire rack.

10. When the loaves are cool, you can drizzle them with a glaze made from 1 cup of confectioners' sugar and 4 to 5 tablespoons of milk (dribble in more milk, if need be). Decorate each loaf with bits of candied fruit (my mother made candied flowers using half a candied cherry and a green citron cut into eighths for the petals).

Braided Cardamom Bread

*T*his is a slightly sweet and wonderfully aromatic bread, studded with bits of candied orange peel. It's gorgeous to look at, too, which makes it perfect for holiday tables and buffets.

Makes 1 large braided loaf

½ cup sugar

1 envelope (2 teaspoons) active dry yeast

1½ teaspoons whole cardamom seeds

¾ teaspoon salt

¾ cup chopped candied orange peel

1 cup milk

⅓ cup unsalted butter, melted

1 large egg plus 2 yolks

5 cups all-purpose flour

1. In a large bowl, combine ½ cup of warm (120°F) water and 1 teaspoon of the sugar. Stir in the yeast, and let sit until bubbly, about 10 minutes.

2. Meanwhile, seal the cardamom seeds in a small plastic zip-top bag and bash them with a wooden mallet or rolling pin until roughly ground (or use a spice grinder). Add to the yeast mixture along with the salt, remaining sugar, chopped candied orange peel, milk, melted butter, 1 cup of the flour, and the 2 egg yolks. Beat with an electric mixer on low speed until blended. Add the remaining flour a cup at a time, and mix, using your hands if the mixture becomes too stiff to stir, until it forms a soft dough that pulls away from the side of the bowl.

3. Turn the dough onto a floured surface, and knead until it's smooth and elastic, about 10 minutes. Let it rest for a minute or two while you wash and grease the bowl. Return the dough to the bowl, and turn once. Cover it with a damp dishtowel, and set it in a warm place to rise until doubled in bulk, 2 to 3 hours.

4. Grease a baking sheet.

5. Turn the dough onto a floured surface, and knead to release the bubbles. Divide into thirds, and roll each third into a 16-inch rope. Place the ropes vertically alongside one another, and pinch them together at one end. Braid the ropes as tightly as possible without stretching the dough, starting at the pinched end; when you've gone as far as you can go, pinch together and fold under the remaining ends. Place the loaf on the baking sheet, and cover it with a damp dishtowel. Set it in a warm place to rise until doubled in bulk, about 45 minutes.

6. Preheat the oven to 325°F.

7. Whisk the egg with 1 teaspoon of water, and brush over the loaf (you won't need it all). Bake in the oven for 45 to 50 minutes, until the loaf sounds hollow when tapped with a knife handle. Place it on a wire rack to cool. Serve warm or at room temperature.

Orange Rolls

I make these light and lovely rolls at Thanksgiving. If they aren't all gobbled up, they're always among the first leftovers to go the next day. Recently a fan e-mailed me to let me know they were a hit they when she made them for her coworkers. For variety's sake, make them with the sweet butter or cream cheese filling. ***Makes 24 rolls***

1 envelope (2 teaspoons) active dry yeast
¼ cup sugar
2 large eggs, lightly beaten
½ cup (1 stick) unsalted butter, melted
½ cup (4 ounces) sour cream
1 tablespoon orange zest
1 teaspoon salt
3½ to 4 cups all-purpose flour

1. In a large bowl, combine ¼ cup of warm (120°F) water and 1 teaspoon of the sugar. Stir in the yeast, and let sit until bubbly, about 10 minutes. Add the remaining sugar, eggs, 6 tablespoons of the melted butter, sour cream, zest, and salt. Beat with an electric mixer on low speed until well blended. Add the flour a cup at a time, mixing with your hands when the mixture becomes too stiff to beat, until a soft dough forms that pulls away from the side of the bowl. Cover with a damp dishtowel, and set in a warm place to rise until doubled in bulk, about 2 hours.

2. Grease a baking sheet.

3. Punch down the dough, and turn it onto a floured surface. Knead until it's smooth and elastic, 8 to 10 minutes. Divide in half, and shape each half into a ball (see Note). With a sharp knife, cut each ball into 12 wedges. Shape each wedge into a ball, and place 1 inch apart on the baking sheet. Cover with a damp dishtowel, and set in a warm place to rise until doubled in bulk, about 1 hour.

4. Preheat the oven to 350°F.

5. Brush the rolls with the remaining 2 tablespoons of melted butter. Bake in the oven for 20 minutes, until golden brown. Serve warm or at room temperature.

*Note: As a variation, for sweeter rolls, roll out each of the larger balls into rounds about ¼-inch thick. Combine ¾ **cup of sugar** and **1 tablespoon orange zest**. Melt **3 tablespoons of unsalted butter**. Brush each round of dough with 1 tablespoon of the melted butter (or spread with **2 ounces of softened cream cheese**), and sprinkle with half of the sugar-zest mixture. Cut each round into 12 equal-size wedges (as if cutting a pie). Roll up each wedge, starting with the wide end, and mold it to form a crescent. Place on the baking sheet, point side down, about 1 inch apart. Brush with the remaining butter. Bake as directed for the unfilled rolls.*

Pumpkin Rolls

I discovered this recipe years ago when combing through my cookbooks looking for a way to use up some pumpkin puree left over from making soup. I've made these rolls many times since, even when I don't happen to have any puree on hand. Canned pumpkin works just as well and it's a whole lot easier.

Makes 24 rolls

1 cup milk

6 tablespoons (¾ stick) unsalted butter

¼ cup pure maple syrup

1½ teaspoons salt

1 cup canned pumpkin or pumpkin puree

½ teaspoon sugar

1 envelope (2 teaspoons) active dry yeast

2 large eggs

1 teaspoon orange zest

6½ cups all-purpose flour

1. Place the milk and 4 tablespoons of the butter in a medium saucepan. Cook over low heat, stirring constantly, until the butter is melted. Remove from the heat, and add the maple syrup, salt, and pumpkin. Set aside to cool until lukewarm.

2. Place ¼ cup of warm (120°F) water in a large bowl. Stir in the sugar, then the yeast. Let sit until bubbly, about 10 minutes. Add the cooled pumpkin mixture, eggs, zest, and 2½ cups of the flour. Beat with an electric mixer on medium speed until well blended, about 3 minutes. Add the remaining flour a cup at a time (reserve ½ cup for kneading), mixing with your hands when the dough becomes too stiff to beat. Turn it onto a floured surface and knead until it's smooth and elastic, 6 to 8 minutes. Place it in a large greased bowl; turn once and cover with a damp dishtowel. Set in a warm place to rise until doubled in bulk, about 2 hours.

3. Grease two 9 × 12-inch baking pans.

4. Punch down the dough and turn onto a floured surface, kneading to remove the air bubbles. Divide in half and shape each half into about a 12-inch rope. Cut each rope into twelve 1-inch slices. Cover and let rest for 10 minutes. Roll each slice into a ball and place 1 inch apart in the pans. Melt the remaining 2 tablespoons of butter and brush over the tops. Cover with a damp dishtowel and set in a warm place to rise until almost doubled in bulk, about 45 minutes.

5. Preheat the oven to 375°F.

6. Bake in the oven for 20 to 25 minutes, until lightly golden. Break open one roll to test for doneness. Serve warm or at room temperature.

Easy Almond Wreaths

T he very first Pillsbury Bake-Off winner, in 1949, was a lucky lady by the name of Theadora Smafield, from Wisconsin, who impressed the judges with her No-Knead Water-Rising Twists. (As a note of interest, the $50,000 prize was bestowed by then First Lady Eleanor Roosevelt.) I've adapted this simple classic by substituting almond extract for vanilla and adding almond paste to the sugar-nut coating. The results, with all due respect to Mrs. Smafield, are out of this world.

Makes 12 wreaths

3½ to 4 cups all purpose flour
¾ cup sugar
1 teaspoon salt
1 package (2 teaspoons) active dry yeast
¾ cup whole milk
½ cup (1 stick) unsalted butter
1 teaspoon almond extract
2 large eggs
⅓ cup whole almonds
3 ounces almond paste, chilled and broken into chunks

1. In a large bowl, combine 1 cup of the flour, ½ cup of the sugar, salt, and yeast. In a small saucepan, heat the milk and butter over low heat just until the butter is melted—the mixture should be warm (120°F), but not hot. Add to the flour mixture along with the almond extract and eggs. Beat with an electric mixer on low speed until the dry ingredients are incorporated. Increase the speed to medium and beat for 2 minutes more. Stir in the remaining flour, mixing with your hands if the dough becomes too stiff to beat. Cover the bowl with plastic wrap, then with a towel, and set it in a warm place to rise for 30 to 40 minutes, until double in bulk.

2. Grease 2 baking sheets.

3. Meanwhile, prepare the coating: Place the remaining ¼ cup of sugar, almonds, and almond paste in a food processor. Pulse until the nuts are ground medium-fine. (The almond paste is in fine crumbs at this point.) Place the mixture in a shallow bowl, such as a soup bowl.

4. One by one, tear off handfuls of dough (about ¼ cup) and shape and stretch each one into about a 6-inch rope. Roll each rope in the sugar-nut coating. Twist, and bring the two ends together, overlapping them slightly, to form a wreath; pinch to seal. Place 1 inch apart on the baking sheets. Cover, and let rise in a warm place for 15 minutes.

5. Preheat the oven to 375°F.

6. Bake in the oven for 20 to 25 minutes, until golden brown. Serve warm.

Kitty's Cinnamon Sticky Buns

I n One Last Dance, *Kitty Seagrave, proprietress of the Tea & Sympathy tea room, couldn't keep these buns in stock. No sooner would she pull a batch from the oven than it would be snatched up while still warm. No life crisis, including her mother's being jailed for murdering Kitty's father, wasn't eased by one of her cinnamon sticky buns. The best thing about this tried and true recipe is that you can make it a day in advance and leave the unbaked buns in the fridge overnight. Allow several hours at room temperature for them to rise before going into the oven.*

Makes 12 buns

For the dough

About 2¼ cups all-purpose flour

3 tablespoons sugar

¾ teaspoon salt

1 package (2 teaspoons) active dry yeast

⅓ cup milk

3 tablespoons unsalted butter, cut into chunks

1 large egg yolk

For the filling

3 tablespoons sugar

½ teaspoon ground cinnamon

2 tablespoons unsalted butter, softened

For the topping

3 tablespoons firmly packed dark brown sugar

3 tablespoons unsalted butter, softened

2 teaspoons light corn syrup

¼ cup chopped walnuts or pecans

1. *For the dough:* In a large bowl, combine 1 cup of the flour with the sugar, salt, and yeast. In a small saucepan, place ⅓ cup of water and the milk and butter. Cook over low heat, stirring constantly, until the butter is melted—the mixture should be warm (120°F), but not hot. Add to the flour mixture along with the egg yolk. Beat with an electric mixer on low speed until well blended, about 3 minutes. Stir in the remaining flour (set aside a few tablespoons for kneading), ½ cup at a time, until the mixture forms a soft dough that pulls away from the side of the bowl. Turn onto a floured surface and knead until the dough is smooth and elastic, 6 to 8 minutes. Place in a large greased bowl; turn once and cover with a damp dishtowel. Set in a warm place to rise until doubled in bulk, about 1 hour. Meanwhile, prepare the filling and topping.

2. *For the filling:* Combine the sugar and cinnamon. Have the softened butter ready at spreading consistency.

3. Generously grease a muffin tin.

4. *For the topping:* Combine the brown sugar, butter, and corn syrup. Beat with an electric mixer on medium speed until smooth. Drop the mixture by heaping teaspoons into the muffin tin. Place about 1 teaspoon of chopped nuts into each cup.

5. Punch down the dough and turn it onto a floured surface, kneading to remove the air bubbles. Shape the dough into a ball. Roll with a floured rolling pin into roughly an 18 × 12-inch baking pan. Spread with the softened butter. Sprinkle with the sugar-cinnamon mixture. Starting with the longer side, roll the dough tightly to form a log, pinching the ends to seal. Cut into 12 slices and place cut side down in the topping-filled muffin tin.

6. Cover with a damp dishtowel and set in a warm place to rise until doubled in bulk, 35 to 40 minutes. Or cover with plastic wrap and place in the refrigerator overnight (if using this method, allow several hours to rise at room temperature before baking).

7. Preheat the oven to 375°F.

8. Bake in the oven for 20 minutes, until golden. If browning too quickly, cover the buns loosely with aluminum foil the last 5 to 10 minutes of baking. Cool for 1 minute in the tin before inverting onto a wire rack. Serve warm or at room temperature.

Sources

Entering the ***New York Cake & Baking Supplies*** shop in New York City is like tumbling down a hole into a baker's wonderland. They stock every kind of baking tool imaginable, and some you didn't know existed, along with pans in every size and shape and a mind-boggling array of cookie cutters. Chocolate comes in brick-sized blocks, in a range of flavors, from Valrhona bittersweet guanaja to Callebaut white chocolate. You'll find a veritable garden of sugar flowers and a rainbow array of decorating icing and gels, sprinkles and glitter. When I shop there, I wander the aisles in a kind of daze. On those occasions when my husband is good enough to accompany me (knowing he will soon reap the benefits), he always brings something to read. The good news is that you don't have to live in New York City to shop there. Check out their Web site, and order by phone or fax:

➤ ***New York Cake & Baking Supplies***
   56 West 22nd Street, New York, NY 10010
   Phone: (212) 675-CAKE
   Fax: (212) 675-7099
   www.nycake.com

One of my favorite cooking supply stores is ***Sur La Table.*** It has everything, and I do mean *everything,* you can think of along those lines. On a recent trip to Seattle, I spent more than an hour wandering the aisles of the store near Pike Place Market, returning home with a shopping list of things to order on-line. You can contact them at:

➤ ***Sur La Table***
   P.O. Box 34707, Seattle, WA 98124-1707
   (800) 243-0852
   www.surlatable.com

Two on-line sources I use often are **Cooking.com** and **Williams-Sonoma.** Both offer a wide variety of cookware and baking supplies, as well as condiments, herbs and spices, and interesting things in jars. If you don't have access to a computer, you can call or write to them and request a catalogue:

> ➤ *Cooking.com*
> 2850 Ocean Park Blvd., Suite 310, Santa Monica, CA 90405
> (800) 663-8810
> www.cooking.com

> ➤ *Williams-Sonoma*
> 100 North Point Street, San Francisco, CA 94133
> (800) 541-2233
> www.williams-sonoma.com

Another good source for baking equipment and ingredients like flour, grains, nuts, dried fruit, and chocolate is **King Arthur Flour.** You can request their catalogue or order on-line:

> ➤ *The Baker's Catalogue*
> P.O. Box 876, Norwich, VT 05055-0876
> (800) 827-6836
> www.kingarthurflour.com

I love anything with maple. Luckily, the small, family-owned purveyor I buy from at our local greenmarket has an address and a Web site, so you can order by catalogue or on-line:

> ➤ *Deep Mountain Maple*
> P.O. Box 68, West Glover, VT 05875
> (802) 525-4162
> www.deepmountainmaple.com

I'm fortunate enough to live only a few blocks from **Kalustyan's,** one of the country's great spice emporiums, in the district colloquially known as Curry Hill, due to the large number of Indian and Pakistani shops and restaurants. I've seen people swoon with joy upon entering this hallowed space, which is perfumed with aromatic herbs and spices and stocked with a wide variety of exotic staples and prepared foods. Who knew there were so many different kinds of basmati rice? Or that there was such a thing as green chile chutney?

In addition to every herb and spice imaginable, they sell various oils and vinegars, dried fruits and nuts, condiments, coffee, and tea. If you can't get there, you can order on-line:

➤ *Kalustyan's*
123 Lexington Avenue, New York, NY 10016
(212) 685-3451
www.kalustyans.com

A good source for whole-grain flours and grains, nuts, natural sweeteners, and yeast is *Bob's Red Mill.* Well-stocked health food stores carry many of their products, but you can also order from them on-line or by mail:

➤ *Bob's Red Mill Natural Foods*
5209 S.E. International Way, Milwaukie, OR 97222
www.bobsredmill.com

Every year at Christmas, my in-laws, who live in Georgia, send us several pounds of shelled pecans from *The Mascot Pecan Company.* They're meatier and sweeter than any pecans I've tasted. Whatever we don't eat, I store in the freezer for baking. You can order on-line or by calling their toll-free number:

➤ *The Mascot Pecan Company*
P.O. Box 760, Glennville, GA 30427
(800) 841-3985
www.mascotpecan.com

A good source for organically grown nuts and dried fruits, such as dates, cranberries, blueberries, and cherries, is the on-line cooperative *Local Harvest*, at:

➤ *Local Harvest*
www.localharvest.org

Lard has gotten a bit of a bad rap in recent years. Once a staple in the home cook's kitchen, it's since been demonized by those who see it as the enemy of good health. In actual fact, it's lower in saturated fat than butter and the non-hydrogenated kind contains none of the bad trans-fatty acids of margarine and vegetable shortening. Indeed, it contains the same mononounsaturated fats found in olive oil, which are known to lower cholesterol. It also makes the lightest biscuits and pie crusts known to mankind. The only downside, as I see it, is that naturally processed lard, not the hydrogenated stuff sold in supermarkets, can be hard to obtain, depending on where you live. Your butcher might carry it—ask for leaf lard, as opposed to fat back. You'll have to render it yourself, but doing so takes very little time or effort: Cut it into chunks and process in the food processor until it's creamy, then heat it in a pan over the stove until it's liquefied, and strain it through a fine-mesh sieve into a jar. If you have a hard time finding it, buy it on-line from *Niman Ranch,* a purveyor of naturally produced meats from animals than are fed no antibiotics or hormones; they sell non-hydrogenated leaf lard:

> *Niman Ranch*
  (510) 808-0340
  www.nimanranch.com

Another food that's gotten an undeservedly bad reputation is coconut oil. Is it just coincidence that its demonization, and subsequent banishment from packaged products like cookies and snack foods, resulted in a rise in revenues for domestic seed oils? Draw your own conclusions. All I know for sure is that it's trans-fat free, with short and medium-chain fatty acids that make it healthful, according to the nutritional experts I consulted; in fact, in the countries where coconut oil is used primarily, the populations have consistently lower cholesterol levels than in the United States! Better yet, it makes for a light, flaky texture when used in baking, and it doesn't go rancid when stored at room temperature.

The brand I use is *Spectrum,* which you'll find in most well-stocked health food stores and in high-end supermarkets like Whole Foods and Strawberry Fields. They make an entire line of oils, many of them certified organic. The thing to keep in mind with coconut oil is that it hardens at room temperature in all but very warm climates. I just pop the jar in the microwave for a minute to liquefy it.

> *Spectrum Organic Products*
  (800) 995-2705
  www.spectrumorganics.com

Another good source is Tropical Traditions, which sells unrefined, wet-milled coconut oil from small farms in the Philippines:

> *Tropical Traditions*
  (866) 311-2626
  www.tropicaltraditions.com

For those times when you want the smell and taste of bread just out of the oven but don't have time to make it yourself, you can cheat (I promise I won't tell) by ordering partially baked loaves from one of my favorite grocery store/bakeries, in the tiny town of Pescadero, California. They arrive in a timely fashion and include flavorful varieties like garlic herb, cheesey cheddar artichoke, and roasted garlic. I keep several loaves in my freezer so I always have "homemade" bread for any last-minute dinner guests. Just pop one in the oven and, fifteen minutes later, you have a crusty, hot loaf.

➤ *Arcangeli Grocery Co. / Norm's Market*
287 Stage Road, P.O. Box 350, Pescadero, CA 94060
Phone: (650) 879-0147
Fax: (650) 879-1825
www.arcangeligrocery.com

Index

tutti-frutti meringue frosting, Lady Baltimore cake with, 50–51

ultimate lemon squares, 123
upside-down cake, pineapple, 34

vanilla wafers:
    in raspberry marzipan cheesecake, 80–81
    in seedless grape chiffon pie, 150–51
    in white chocolate–raspberry pie, 154–55
velvet Bundt cake, 16–17
vodka, in homemade Kahlúa, 130

walnut(s):
    in apple-cranberry bread, 237
    in applesauce cake with maple–cream cheese frosting, 38–39
    in apple-spice cupcakes with caramel frosting, 42–43
    in banana bread, 220–21
    -banana caramel torte, 70–72
    in banana-nut muffins, 244–45
    in banana streusel coffee cake, 20–21

in best-ever zucchini bread, 222
in caramel banana-walnut torte, 70–71
in carrot cake, 31
in Cayou Cove coffee cake, 26–27
in cherry–cream cheese bread, 228–29
in cherry winks, 96–97
in chocolate-cherry cake with easy fudge frosting, 35–37
in Corn Flake macaroons, 94
in French silk pie, 170–71
in fudge meltaways, 126
in Kahlúa brownies with homemade Kahlúa, 129–30
in Kitty's cinnamon sticky buns, 288–89
in lemon bread, 225
in maple chiffon cake with maple–cream cheese frosting, 62–63
in maple-oatmeal muffins, 247
in marmalade bread, 235
in mocha buttercrunch pie, 168–69
in oatmeal cake, 32–33
in oatmeal–chocolate chip cookies, 90–91

in orange-cranberry cake, 40–41
in persimmon pudding with lemon sauce, 206–7
in pineapple upside-down cake, 34
in pumpkin-cranberry muffins, 242
in pumpkin-date bread, 226
in rainforest bars, 121
shortbread cookies, 104
in tutti-frutti meringue frosting, 51
in white Russian pie, 166–67
white chocolate:
    –cream cheese frosting, blue-ribbon chocolate cake with, 55–57
    in creamy lemon pie, 162–63
    –raspberry pie, 154–55
white Russian pie, 166–67
whole wheat muffins, 241
winks, cherry, 96–97
wreaths, easy almond, 286–87

yeast breads and rolls, see breads, yeast; rolls, yeast

zucchini bread, best-ever, 222
Zwieback toast, in creamy lemon pie, 162–63